Technogenarians

Sociology of Health and Illness Monograph Series

Edited by Hannah Bradby
Department of Sociology
University of Warwick
Coventry
CV4 7AL
UK

Current titles

Technogenarians
Studying Health and Illness Through an Ageing, Science, and Technology Lens

Edited by

Kelly Joyce and Meika Loe

WILEY-BLACKWELL

A John Wiley & Sons, Ltd., Publication

Contents

Notes on Contributors

Katie Brittain is a Lecturer in Social Gerontology within the Institute of Health and Society at Newcastle University. She is an experienced health services researcher with an academic background in sociology; she uses both quantitative and qualitative research methods to examine the social impact that illness can have on the lives of older people. Her recent work has focused around the wellbeing of older people and their lived experiences, particularly around how technology might support older people to 'age in place'.

Abigail Brooks teaches in the Women's and Gender Studies Program at Boston College. Her current book project investigates the meanings everyday women ascribe to ageng in an increasingly normalized culture of cosmetic surgery in the United States.

Denise A. Copelton is Assistant Professor of Sociology at The College at Brockport, State University of New York. Her prior publications examine the lived experience of pregnancy, breastfeeding, and abortion. Her current research explores the social experience illness, with a focus on celiac disease and social aspects of following a gluten-free diet.

Jennifer Fishman is Assistant Professor in the Biomedical Ethics Unit and the Department of the Social Studies of Medicine at McGill University. Her work examines the social and ethical dimensions of new biomedical technologies as they travel from the laboratory to the clinic. Her newest project examines the emergence of personalized genomic medicine.

Kelly Joyce is an Associate Professor of Sociology at the College of William and Mary. Dr. Joyce's publications include *Magnetic Appeal: MRI and the Myth of Transparency* (Cornell University Press, 2008) as well as peer reviewed articles in *Science as Culture*, *Social Studies of Science*, and *Sociology of Health and Illness*. Her main research areas are: (1) visualization in science and medicine; (2) medical knowledge and practice; and (3) ageing, science, and technology.

Sharon R. Kaufman is Professor of Medical Anthropology at University of California, San Francisco. Her current research explores technologies of life extension, risk awareness and time management in an aging society. She is the author, most recently, of … *And a Time to Die: How American Hospitals Shape the End of Life* (University of Chicago 2006).

Meika Loe is Associate Professor of Sociology and Women's Studies at Colgate University in New York, USA. She is the author of *The Rise of Viagra: How the Little Blue Pill Changed Sex in America* (NYU Press, 2004). She is currently writing a book on the oldest old in America.

Taina Kinnunen is an acting professor of Cultural Anthropology at the University of Oulu, Finland. She examines the relationship between body and culture including fieldwork on cosmetic surgery and extreme body building. Her recent projects include research on the new working body and embodiment of ubiquitous technologies.

Barbara L. Marshall is Professor of Sociology at Trent University in Peterborough, Canada. She has published widely in the areas of gender, sexuality and theory.

Her current research focuses on the re-sexing of ageing bodies and the graying of 'sexual health' as these are related to the pharmaceutical reconstruction of sexual lifecourses.

Courtney Everts Mykytyn earned her doctorate in Cultural Anthropology from the University of Southern California in 2007. She is currently working on a book that draws from a decade of research in anti-ageing science and medicine.

Louis Neven is interested in the design of technologies for elders and the way such technologies shape and are shaped in everyday life (care) practices. Louis works for the Science Technology and Policy Studies group at the University of Twente (NL) and is a visiting PhD student at the Centre for Science Studies at Lancaster University (UK). He is currently finalising his PhD thesis on user representations of elders in the design of Ambient Intelligent technologies, which is due to appear early 2011.

Johanna M. Wigg, PhD, is a social gerontologist committed to advancing the field of dementia research. She engages in daily, direct care of elders living with dementing illnesses, while simultaneously conducting research that seeks to increase knowledge concerning the social care of individuals living with dementia. Dr. Wigg is an independent consultant on dementia care who lectures, teaches, and is currently writing a book examining the 'myths' of dementia.

1

Theorising technogenarians: a sociological approach to ageing, technology and health
Kelly Joyce and Meika Loe

Science and technology are central to the lived experiences and normative definitions of health and illness for ageing people. From pharmaceuticals, to walking aids, to cell phones, old people interact with technologies and science on a daily basis. Everyday technologies as well as biomedical interventions can be part of the way older adults pursue, maintain, and negotiate life. In this way, old people are cyborgs in contemporary life, blending machine and biology in both their personal identities and their relations to the external world.

This monograph builds on sociology of health and illness scholarship and expands the analytical lens to include the myriad ways old people interact with science and technology to negotiate health and illness. For elders, perceptions of health and illness may not be limited to acute illness experiences, but may include an everyday understanding of a changing state of health and wellbeing that is managed and made more tenable through the use of multiple, assistive technologies and environmental design modifications. Old individuals may rely on a range of everyday technologies such as stairway railings, phones, adjusted toilet seats, and walking aids to create safer spaces and maintain health and mobility. Elders may also manage an array of drugs and supplements to treat chronic conditions such as high cholesterol, hypertension, diabetes, and vitamin deficiencies. But, old people are not passive consumers of technologies such as walking aids and drugs. Elders creatively utilise technological artifacts to make them more suitable for their needs even in the face of technological design and availability constraints. In this way they are technogenarians; individuals who create, use, and adapt technologies to negotiate health and illness in daily life. Combining science and technology studies and medical sociology frameworks together provides a framework to examine technogenarians in action.

Science and technology studies[1] (also called STS, science studies and science, medicine and technology studies) puts science and technology in the centre of analyses. It is a multi-disciplinary approach that draws from fields such as history, sociology, political science, and anthropology. Genealogies of STS scholarship highlight works by Thomas Kuhn (1962), Ludwik Fleck (1972 [1935]), and Robert Merton (1973) as early exemplars of the field, but a sustained effort to study the relations between society, science, and technology took off in the 1970s in North America and Europe. International professional societies such as the Society for Social Studies of Science (4S) were formed in 1975. The European Association for the Study of Science and Technology (EASST) was officially created shortly after in 1981.

This is the first publication to highlight ageing, health and technology and to bring science and technology studies and sociology of health and ageing approaches together in a sustained manner. Although there is overlap between sociologists of health and illness and science and technology studies scholars, we make the connections explicit in this collection.

As sociologists of medicine, technology, and ageing, we track some of the stakeholders (*e.g.* physicians, assisted living homes, elders, and caregivers) involved in the ageing, health, and technology matrix as well as use qualitative methods to explore how elders actively use (or do not use) technologies to maintain health. This move simultaneously puts health technologies and medical science under the analytical lens and theorises elders as actors who creatively negotiate health and illness in particular contexts. Studies often evaluate the effectiveness of old people's use of technologies (*e.g.* Cutler *et al.* 2003, Dickerson *et al.* 2007, Selwyn 2004), but few put elders' meaning making, creativity, and bodies at the centre of analysis of technology, science, and health.[2]

Ageing populations, health, and ageism

Current debates about changes in retirement age, the increasing cost of medical care, and demographic changes regarding the aged population in the United States, Canada, United Kingdom, Japan, and many other countries make studying the ageing, health, technology, and science junction necessary and timely. Referred to as the 'graying' of America, the US Census Bureau predicts that the percentage of people over the age of 65 in the US will grow from 13 per cent of the total population in 2008 to 20 per cent shortly after the year 2030 (Kinsella and He 2009). Canada is also predicted to 'gray', moving from having 13.7 per cent of its population over 65 in 2006 to approximately 20 per cent of its population being over 65 by 2024 (Martel and Caron Malenfant 2007). Some countries (*e.g.* Italy, Germany, and Japan) already report that approximately 20 per cent of their populations are over 65 and many European countries are close behind with percentages ranging from 15 per cent to 19 per cent. In 2008, with the exception of Japan and Georgia, the top 25 countries with the largest percentage of people over 65 were all in Europe (Kinsella and He 2009). Within these nations, the number of the oldest old (people over 80 years) are increasing as well.

The rise of an ageing population takes place in a broader context of ageism and age relations. US gerontologist Robert Butler (1969) created the term ageism to describe discrimination against older people and the changes associated with ageing. Building on the language of the social movements of the 1960s and 1970s that challenged discrimination against people of colour (racism) and women (sexism), Butler offered the term ageism to describe the dimensions of US society that are biased against old people and ageing. Ageism can be present, for example, in the realms of ideas and beliefs, interpersonal interactions, and institutional practices and policies. How ageism takes place varies by local and national contexts. There is no one way ageism takes place; its prevalence, forms, and intensity can differ by class, profession, gender, sexuality, and ethnicity and by local and national contexts (Bergling 2004, Cruikshank 2003, Gullette 2004).

An age relations approach (Calasanti 2003) builds on the concept of structural ageism, exposing a system of inequality based on age that privileges the not-old at the expense of the old. Such an approach makes explicit how ageist policies and institutional practices as well as ageist attitudes can be insidious, pervading everything from an individual's sense of self and others, to biomedical practices. Thus, this collection not only exposes macro-level age-based stratification, but also micro-level ageism including that which may be internalised by the old themselves.

To challenge ageism, we intentionally use language in this book that positions people as both agentic *and* old. We use 'old' to defy social stigma, to naturalise and neutralise ageing, and to emphasise social stratification related to age. We also use the terms elders, technogenarians, and 'graying the cyborg'. Language emphasising 'elderhood' comes from gerontologist Bill Thomas's (2004) influential research emphasising three key developmental stages in life: childhood, adulthood, and elderhood. The phrase 'graying the cyborg' comes from a call for scholarship by sociologists Joyce and Mamo (2006) that reclaims old men and women as knowledgeable technoscientific users, rather than as victims of technology and design. Science writer Cynthia Fox (2001) initially used the term technogenarians to describe the economically privileged baby boomers for whom technologies are in development. We expand this term to include any old person who uses technologies in daily life to create or maintain health. Tools can be simple, established ones such as can openers or slow cookers, or complex new technologies such as surveillance tags or companion robots. In using technogenarians and other terms listed above, we join advocacy groups and academics situated internationally who aim to reposition ageing individuals as experienced and active instead of doddering and feeble. This framing calls attention to the way old people approach technology, science, and health in creative ways.

Finally, we remain cautious about buzzwords such as 'productive ageing' and 'successful ageing' that respectively emphasise activity and busyness, and youthful looks and able-bodiedness, as well as individual responsibility and control. Such ideologies are unevenly present in various regions and nations and are not necessarily shared in all cultures. Nonetheless, as we point out, these cultural ideals remain central to the biomedicalisation of ageing, an increasingly global project (Calasanti and Slevin 2001, Katzko et al. 1998).

Theorising science, technology, ageing, and health

Putting science, technology, and ageing at the centre of analysis opens up discussion of two trends that mark the contemporary health and illness landscape. In the first trend, ageing bodies, minds, and emotions are increasingly classified and understood as illnesses through biomedicalisation processes. Biomedicalisation refers to the tendency to define any emotional, mental, and physical processes as medical problems (Clarke et al. 2004, Conrad 2007). Irving Zola (1972), Eliot Friedson (1970), and Jesse Pitts (1968) initially described this phenomenon, which has remained a focus of sociological analysis ever since.[3] In his ground-breaking essay 'Medicine as an Institution of Social Control', Zola noted how sleeplessness, alcoholism, pregnancy, and other behaviours and bodily processes once defined as socially unacceptable or normal became redefined as illnesses by the 1970s. As additional aspects of being were redefined as medical problems, physicians and other health-care professionals gained more control over the management and treatment of life.

Medicalisation affects all ages, but it has particular implications in an ageist society. In societies that position youthful bodies as the norm, the changes associated with ageing are ripe for being labelled pathological. Sociologists, anthropologists, and gerontologists have carefully documented the transformation of the emotional, mental, and physical changes associated with ageing into 'illnesses' (Cruikshank 2002, Estes and Binney 1989, Gubrium 1986, Kaufman 1994, and Lock 1993). For example, the biomedical construction of Alzheimer's disease redefined memory loss as an illness category during the 1960s and 1970s (Gubrium 1986). What had been a normal component of ageing was reconfigured into disease through the creation and delineation of medical diagnostic categories.

Although the desire for the fountain of youth has a long history, anti-ageing medicine grew significantly in the 1990s. The mix of private and public health insurance in combination with consumer-driven healthcare in the United States provided fertile ground for its expansion. The American Academy of Anti-Aging Medicine (A4M) was founded in 1993, and reports approximately 20,000 members worldwide in 2009. Although the American

Board of Medical Specialties, the American Osteopathic Association Bureau of Osteopathic Specialists, and the American Medical Association do not recognise the field of anti-ageing medicine, anti-ageing physicians tap into cultural concerns about ageing and are establishing a foothold in clinical practice. Anti-ageing medicine represents one possible extension of biomedicalisation processes. Instead of *particular* mental, physical, or emotional processes being turned into a disease, now the ageing process itself is understood as pathology.

At the same time that the claim is made that the ageing body can and should be restored into a youthful one, there are a growing number of companies, professionals, and institutions that recognise the varied physical, mental, and emotional changes that can be associated with ageing. In this second trend, individuals, academic centres, and businesses aim to create assisted living technologies and inclusive design projects so that older people can age at home. The focus in this market-based framework is on transforming technologies and architectural design to accommodate potential changes in hearing, memory, balance, sight, or other physical and cognitive abilities as well as creating technologies (*e.g.* robots, phones for the hearing impaired) to help meet emotional needs. The ageing body is still enabled and constrained, but it is not targeted for transformation from the inside out as it is in anti-ageing medicine.

Academic research centres were formed throughout the 1990s to focus on innovation for ageing populations. For example, Cornell University's Environmental Geriatrics program emphasises how modifications to homes can help older people prevent bone fractures and other injuries that can have a severe impact on their health. Increasing technology use (*e.g.* of motorised stair lifts, handheld showerheads, and cognitive enhancement technologies in automobiles) is believed to help ageing individuals experience a wider range of mobility. The MIT AgeLab aims to invent new technologies that help people stay active and mobile across the lifespan. Other universities have also created programmes that evaluate and develop assisted living and inclusive design projects (*e.g.* University of Rochester Center for Future Health, Georgia Institute of Technology's Center for Research and Education on Aging and Technology Enhancement). Such centres get financial support from universities, businesses, and government agencies.

Beyond centres located at universities, private companies are designing and creating living spaces with the varied abilities of old people in mind. Oatfield Estates, a retirement community in Oregon, United States, is a high-end example of this residence type. In Oatfield Estates, residents wear badges that signal to the dozens of infrared and radio-frequency sensors inside the facility and outside on the grounds. Healthcare and administrative workers as well as family members use the badges to keep track of residents' location. Monitors in beds and chairs track residents' sleep patterns, weight, and movement (Kornblum 2006, Scharnberg 2006).[4] Similarly, the National Green House Project across the US has transformed elder health, housing, and care, by replacing high-rise nursing homes with small-houses featuring private rooms and shared common space and kitchen (Kane *et al.* 2007).

Both university and private industry responses to ageing raise issues of race, class, sexuality, and gender inequalities and access. Unequal economic, social, and political relations will have an impact on how individuals use or do not use biomedical and environmental applications. Environmental geriatric or gerontechnological innovations and assisted living communities also require us to grapple with concerns about surveillance, privacy, and freedom. For example, projects in development include a smart floor designed to send an emergency help alert when it senses a person has fallen, a driving sensor that switches off distractions like the radio if the driver's blood pressure suddenly rises, as well as an electronic pill dispenser that is programmed to give readouts to clinicians on how many pills an individual has taken and at what time. These innovations raise important questions about power, inequality and elder-focused surveillance technologies.

Collection overview

This collection of chapters adds theoretical and empirical depth to our understanding of two concurrent trends: (1) the biomedicalisation of ageing bodies, minds, and emotions – a process exemplified by the rise of anti-ageing or longevity medicine, and (2) the rise of gerontechnology industries and professions – fields that largely take ageing processes as a given. These trends might be considered contemporary manifestations of what Carol Estes (1979) dubbed 'the ageing enterprise'; that is, both highlight individual consumption as a solution to changes associated with ageing. A growing body of social science scholarship examines the historical emergence, practice of, and perceptions of anti-ageing medicine, and we include several innovative contributions in this collection. However, despite the growing investment by universities, governments, and companies in elder-based technology, critical and empirical analysis of the networks, values, and inequalities embedded in gerontechnology is still needed.

This book sociologically investigates how and where biomedicalisation, anti-ageing medicine practices, and the design and use of gerontechnologies overlap and diverge in relation to ageism, health, and illness.

The first part of the book examines the biomedicalisation of ageing – an approach to health and illness that includes anti-ageing medicine or longevity medicine with its emphasis on 'optimal health' or the prevention of any aspect of ageing (mental, physical, or emotional). Courtney Mykytyn draws on ethnographic methods and discourse analysis to provide a socio-historical explanation of the transformation and expansion of anti-ageing medicine from the 1990s to today. Mykytyn exposes the complex knowledge production and contestation surrounding anti-ageing, as it shifted in perception from a 'backwater science', to a fully-fledged arena of inquiry and practice. This emergence and solidification was aided by the internet, scientific claims, public and private funding, and legitimising institutions. Jennifer Fishman, Richard Settersten Jr. and Michael Flatt explore how anti-ageing physicians in the US make sense of what they do. Building on data gathered from in-depth interviews with practitioners, the authors analyse how anti-ageing doctors' rhetoric emphasises a return to 'the art of medicine', which includes more time with patients, off-label use of pharmaceuticals, repeated laboratory tests, and the use of nutrition and other low-tech techniques in treatment plans. Despite the commitment to delivering personalised and holistic care, Fishman and colleagues demonstrate how these same physicians also embrace a form of surveillance medicine that involves both patient and practitioner in the medical management of ageing avoidance.

The next four chapters consider how (changing) views about ageing shape the practice of medicine more broadly. Barbara Marshall examines how contemporary sexual medicine and biogerontology have joined forces at the present time. The social ramifications of this include virility surveillance and medical attention to late-life sexuality in the name of healthy ageing. Marshall pays particular attention to what she calls the pharmaceutical imagination, and how, through direct-to-consumer advertisements, ideas about elder sexualities (which are simultaneously gendered and racialised) are created and circulated. Sharon Kaufman takes us into an American medical clinic to analyse physicians' and patients' approaches to longevity and end of life technologies. Kaufman's research shows how the imagined appropriate age for surgeries such as heart surgery has expanded to include people in their nineties in the United States. Using ethnographic methods, she introduces the theoretical concept 'time left' to show how patients and their intimate circle make decisions about whether to pursue a particular treatment option over others.

Abigail Brooks and Taina Kinnunen explore perceptions of cosmetic surgery in the US and Finland, respectively. Brooks' chapter explores how American women's attitudes about femininity and ageing are shaped in the context of deciding whether to use anti-ageing medicine and technology. Drawing from in-depth interviews with women between the ages of 47 and 76, Brooks shows how a successful ageing paradigm (which allows for some signs of ageing) is being replaced by what she calls 'the ideal of a feminised agelessness'. Within this ideal, women are expected to continually work to reverse, minimise, and prevent signs of ageing and maintain appearances (*e.g.* perky breasts, flat stomachs) associated with a particular version of femininity. Even women who choose *not* to use anti-ageing techniques are well aware of this new standard and evaluate themselves in relation to it. Turning the analytical lens to Finland, Kinnunen's chapter demonstrates how arguments for cosmetic surgery and anxieties about one's appearance are shaped by ageist discrimination, national contexts, and globalisation. Kinnunen utilises in-depth interview data to shows how ageism and pressure to be more like Americans (who are understood as happy and outgoing) create a context in which Finnish people 'choose' cosmetic surgery to alter both their appearance and emotional selves. By transforming physical characteristics understood as Finnish (*e.g.* heavy foreheads, sagging eyelids and potato noses), Kinnunen's respondents also aim to make themselves more 'white' and thus higher up a perceived racial hierarchy within Europe.

The second part of the collection explores the rise of gerontechnology. Two pieces analyse gerontechnology use in the context of dementia and wandering. Katie Brittain, Lynne Corner, John Bond and Louise Robinson utilise interviews and focus groups conducted in the UK with people with dementia, to analyse how outside places and landscapes can be viewed as both 'therapeutic' and frightening in the context of memory loss. Specifically, Brittain and colleagues argue that technologies of place can be used for support and assistance, to maximise the independence of people living with dementia. Johanna Wigg uses ethnographic methods to examine health and wellbeing outcomes in the context of two different technological approaches for controlling wandering at dementia care facilities in the US: locked doors and motion detectors. Wigg argues that important distinctions exist between surveillance technologies that chiefly engage in social control, and surveillance technologies that encourage greater independence in wandering.

Three chapters analyse elder technology users and put sociology of health and illness into dialogue with STS work on studies of users of science and technology. In analysing technology use as well as non-use, each chapter offers important critiques of gerontechnology in terms of design, use, and definition. Denise Copelton draws on participant observation and interviews with members of a hospital-sponsored walking club in the US to explore the social construction of pedometers by fitness researchers, group leaders, and walkers themselves. Copelton demonstrates that while pedometers may be praised by health experts as tools for assisting in the achievement of fitness goals, walkers may value sociability over technologies that create distinctions and hierarchies when it comes to health motivation and maintenance. Meika Loe examines everyday technology use among women nonagenarians ageing at home in the US. Her chapter draws on in-depth interviews to expose how lifelong care work repertoires are utilised by the oldest old to identify, adjust, use and reject familiar and new technologies such as computers, slow cookers, and automobiles for their everyday mobility, communication, and physiological health. Louis Neven examines elder test users and their approaches to robots in the Netherlands. Taking up a new trend in healthcare,

Neven documents the rise of robot companions worldwide, and tracks 'iRo', a robot in the making. This work contributes to theories of users and innovation by illuminating when and how elder test users and ageism contribute to health robot design and adoption.

Moving from medical to elder-centred definitions of health

While biomedicine seeks to promote an ideal of healthy ageing in our contemporary life, scholarship in this collection suggests that such an equation may be overly simplistic and not representative of elders' lives. A focus on elders makes it clear that (a) doctors and medicine are not at the centre of people's own definitions of health and wellbeing, and (b) health includes mental, physical and emotional wellbeing in combination with social capital. This is true regardless of whether elders embrace anti-ageing medicine, biomedicine more generally, gerontechnologies, or aspects of all three as they negotiate daily life and wellness in North America and Europe.

Elders who pursue cosmetic surgery, anti-ageing medicine, and/or gerontechnologies embrace an idea of health that includes emotional, intellectual, and physical wellbeing. Part of the appeal of anti-ageing medicine is that it promises health in mental, emotional, and physical dimensions of life. A key insight of the contributors to this volume is that old people use medical techniques to achieve physical, mental, and emotional transformations. As the chapters by Brooks, Kinnunen, and Fishman *et al.* demonstrate, ageing people pursue cosmetic surgery and anti-ageing therapies to feel better, cultivate better treatment by others, and (ideally) achieve happiness.

But, medicine is just one strategy elders use to cultivate wellbeing in mind, emotion, and body. Exercise, robots, communication technologies, and mobility devices are all part of the toolkit old people assemble to stay healthy and connected to their communities. Copelton's analysis of pedometers (an innovation that failed to be adopted), for example, illustrates how people desired companionship over measurements that fostered competition and hierarchies. Neven's analysis of robot innovation further demonstrates how both designers and test users understand health to be a function of emotional, cognitive, and physical dimensions of one's life. Loe's discussion of nonagenarians illuminates how women rely on communication technologies, transportation technologies, domestic technologies, *and* medical treatments to maintain wellness and independence. In these examples, the aim of technology use is not 'optimal health' with its implied anti-ageing, cultivation of youth definition of optimal, but rather support for the body and mind as each changes across the lifespan. This work reveals how technologies can be used to support elders' lives and wellbeing, including participation in communities, mobility, intellectual growth, emotional connections, and physical care.

Elders featured in this volume actively confront and complicate the biomedicalisation of ageing, pushing us to look beyond medicine to understand how health and wellbeing can be maintained and achieved. Contributors to this volume posit that biomedicine, technologies, and policies aimed at old people can enable as well as constrain and hinder elders in their own self-care. When elders rely on medical expertise and technological tools, it is the combination of these tools and associated social, emotional, and psychological contexts surrounding this use that can offer value, meaning, and enhanced health. When successful, gerontechnology can enable elders to create social safety nets, 'link lives', and manage self-care routines, all of which can empower elders to age at home comfortably. Whether striving to look forever youthful with products and surgeries, creatively utilising mobility devices and medications, or critiquing robot companions and pedometers, elders are technogenarians – creatively negotiating technology and science to maintain independence and health across the lifecourse.

Acknowledgements

We thank Toni Calasanti for her careful reading of and comments on this piece, Hannah Bradby for her support, and Liz Ackroyd for shepherding the monograph through the review, copyedit, and publishing process.

Notes

1   For overviews of science and technology studies, see Hess (1997), Hackett *et al.* (2007), Harding (2008), or Sismondo (2010).
2   Exceptions to this include but are not limited to Loe (2004) and Twigg (1997).
3   Conrad (1992) and Rosenfeld and Faircloth (2006) provide thorough overviews of the medicalisation thesis.
4   In 2008 Oatfield Estates residents were charged $4,300 per month; Oatfield Estates did not accept Medicaid because the organisation thought that reimbursement rates were too low.

References

Bergling, T. (2004) *Reeling in the Years: Gay Men's Perspectives on Age and Ageism*. New York, NY: Southern Tier Editions, Harrington Park Press.
Butler, R. (1969) Age-ism: another form of bigotry, *The Gerontologist*, 9, 243–46.
Butler, R. (1975) *Why Survive? Being Old in America*. New York: Harper and Row.
Calasanti, T. (2003) Theorising age relations. In Biggs, S, Lowenstein, A. and Hendricks, J. (eds) *The Need for Theory: Critical Approaches to Social Gerontology*. Amityville, New York: Baywood Publishing Company.
Calasanti, T. and Slevin, K. (2001) *Gender, Social Inequalities, and Aging*. New York: AltaMira Press.
Calasanti, T.M. and Slevin, K.F. (2006) *Age Matters: Realigning Feminist Thinking*. New York, NY: Routledge.
Clarke, A., Shim, J., Mamo, L., Fosket, J. and Fishman, J. (2004) Biomedicalization: technoscientific transformations of health, illness, and U.S. biomedicine, *American Sociological Review*, 68, 161–94.
Conrad, P. (1992) Medicalisation and social control, *Annual Review of Sociology*, 18, 209–32.
Conrad, P. (2007) *The Medicalization of Society: On the Transformation of Human Conditions into Treatable Conditions*. Baltimore, MD: Johns Hopkins University Press.
Cruikshank, M. (2002) *Learning to be Old: Gender, Culture, and Aging*. Lanham, MD: Rowman and Littlefield Publishers.
Cutler, S., Hendricks, J. and Guyer, A. (2003) Age differences in home computer availability and use, *Journal of Gerontology*, 58B, 5, S271–S280.
Dickerson, A., Molnar, L., Eby, D., Adler, G., Bedard, M., Berg-Weger, M., Classen, S., Foley, D., Horowitz, A., Kerschner, H., Page, O., Silverstein, N., Staplin, L. and Trujillo, L. (2007) Transportation and aging: a research agenda for advancing safe mobility, *The Gerontologist*, 47, 5, 578–90.
Estes, C. (1979) *Aging Enterprise: a Critical Examination of Social Policies and Services for the Aged*. Chichester, UK: Wiley, John and Sons, Inc.
Estes, C. and Binney, E. (1989) The biomedicalization of aging, *Gerontologist*, 29, 5, 587–96.
Fleck, L. (1972 [1935]) *Development and Genesis of a Scientific Fact*. Chicago, IL: University of Chicago Press. Translated by Fred Bradley and Thaddeus Trenn.

Fox, C. (2001) Technogenarians: the pioneers of pervasive computing aren't getting any younger, *Wired*, (Issue 9.11, November). Retrieved 5 October, 2009 http://www.wired.com/wired/archive/9.11/aging_pr.html.

Gubrium, J. (1986) *Old-timers and Alzheimers: the Descriptive Organization of Senility*. Greenwick, CJ, Jai Press Inc.

Gullette, M.M. (2004) *Aged by Culture*. Chicago, IL: University of Chicago Press.

Hackett, E., Amsterdamska, O., Lynch, M. and Wajcman, J. (eds) (2007) *The Handbook of Science and Technology Studies*, 3rd Edition. Cambridge, MA: MIT Press.

Harding, S. (2008) *Sciences from Below: Feminisms, Postcolonialities, and Modernities*. Durham, NC: Duke University Press.

Hess, D. (1997) *Science Studies: an Advanced Introduction*. New York: New York University Press.

Joyce, K. and Mamo, L. (2006) Graying the cyborg: new directions of feminist analyses of aging, science, and technology. In Calasanti, T. and Slevin, K. (eds), *Age Matters: Realigning Feminist Thinking*. New York: Routledge.

Kane, R., Lum, T., Cutler, L., Degenholtz, H. and Tzy-Chyi, Y. (2007) Resident outcomes in small-house nursing homes: a longitudinal evaluation of the initial Green House Program. *Journal of the American Geriatrics Society*, 55, 6, 832–9.

Katzko, M.W., Steverink, N., Dittmann-Kohli, F. and Herrera, F. (1998) The self-concept of the elderly: a cross-cultural comparison, *Availa International Journal of Aging and Human Development*, 46, 3, 171.

Kinsella, K. and He, W. (2009) *U.S. Census Bureau, International Population Reports, P95/09-1, An Ageing World: 2008*. Washington, DC: US Government Printing Office.

Kornblum, J. (2006) Assisted living facility gets technology assist, *USA Today*. Retrieved 16 October, 2009: http://www.usatoday.com/tech/news/techinnovations/2006-07-05-elder-tech_x.htm

Kuhn, T. (1962) *The Structure of Scientific Revolutions*. Chicago, IL: University of Chicago Press.

Lock, M. (1993) *Encounters with aging: Mythologies of menopause in Japan and North America*. Berkeley, CA: University of California Press.

Loe, M. (2004) *The Rise of Viagra: How the Little Blue Pill Changed Sex in America*. New York: New York University Press.

Martel, L. and Caron Malenfant É. (2007) *Portrait of the Canadian Population in 2006, by Age and Sex*. Census Analysis Series, Census 2006. Ottawa, Ontario: Statistics Canada Catalogue No. 97-551-XWE2006-001.

Merton, R. (1973) *The Sociology of Science: Theoretical and Empirical Investigations*. Chicago, IL: University of Chicago Press.

Nelson, T.D. (2002) *Ageism: Stereotyping and Prejudice against Older Persons*. Cambridge, MA: MIT Press.

Pitts, J. (1968) Social control; the concept. In Sills, D. (ed.) *International Encyclopedia of the Social Sciences*, Volume 14. New York: Macmillan.

Quadagno, J. (2008) The field of social gerontology. In Barrosse, E. (ed.) *Aging and the Life Course: an Introduction to Social Gerontology*. New York: McGraw-Hill.

Rosenfeld, D. and Faircloth, M. (2006) Medicalized masculinities: the missing link? In Rosenfeld, D. and Faircloth, C. (eds) *Medicalized Masculinites*. Philadelphia, PA: Temple University Press.

Scharnberg, K. (2006) Keeping track of Dad: technology allows aging Americans to enjoy more independence while families monitor them from miles away, *Chicago Tribune*. Retrieved 18 October, 2009: http://www.elitecare.com/keeping_track_dad.

Sismondo, S. (2010) *An Introduction to Science and Technology Studies*, Second Edition. Malden, MA: Wiley-Blackwell.

Selwyn, N. (2004) The information aged: a qualitative study of older adults' use of information and communications technology, *Journal of Aging Studies*, 18, 4, 369–84.

Thomas, W.H. (2004) *What are Old People For?* MA: VanderWyck and Burnham.

Twigg, J. (1997) Deconstructing the social bath: help with bathing at home for older and disabled people, *Journal of Social Policy*, 26, 2, 211–32.

Zola, I. (1972) Medicine as an institution of social control, *American Sociological Review*, 20, 487–504.

2

A history of the future: the emergence of contemporary anti-ageing medicine

Courtney Everts Mykytyn

Introduction

In July of 1990, the *New England Journal of Medicine* published an article by Daniel Rudman stating that 'the effects of six months of human growth hormone (hGH) on lean body mass and adipose tissue were equivalent in magnitude to the changes incurred during 10 to 20 years of ageing' (Rudman *et al.* 1990). 'In many respects,' writes Natalie Angier of the *New York Times*, 'the treatment cut almost 20 years from their bodies' (Angier 1990). Four years earlier, pharmaceutical giant Eli Lilly synthesised the amino acid chain for human growth hormone; the difficult process of drawing hGH from human cadavers was circumvented and Humatrope® was born. Funded in part by Eli Lilly, the Rudman study declared that science *can* intervene on ageing. Arousing researchers and clinicians, this seemingly successful intervention and the study's publicity marked a beginning for anti-ageing medicine. By grounding the pursuit to forestall ageing within the arena of 'scientific evidence', anti-ageing proponents had found a 'legitimate' hook on which to hang their hopes.

Central to anti-ageing (AA) is the belief that ageing is a painful, biological decline, eventually knowable and fixable. This 'eventually', the predictions AA poses, have provided the scaffold for its scientific and cultural traction (Mykytyn 2006a, 2008). While many believe that 'no [interventions] available today have been demonstrated to influence the processes of ageing' (Olshansky 2002, Olshansky *et al.* 2002), the belief that we are close to its discovery is palpable. Predictions that efficacious therapies are feasible in the near future drive the emergence of this field of knowledge and practice that has, thus far, provided zero to few viable interventions, depending upon whom one asks and how 'intervention' is defined.

Predictions, as recent scholarship shows (Borup 2006, Brown and Michael 2003, Cooper 2006, Fujimura 2003, Rose 2006), are themselves cultural objects. They marshal intellectual, social, and economic resources and guide activities towards their fulfilment or deterrence. Predictions are important players in 'subject formation' (Fortun and Fortun 2005) and the building of legitimacy in emerging fields like AA. However, while compelling predictions are critical to a field's beginnings, its sustenance depends upon a convergence from predictions to expectations. This seemingly fuzzy, often subtle, and very intriguing line is critical. Where predictions involve possibilities, expectations involve certainties. While predictions reveal a temporally-set cultural imagination, expectations yield the contours of a cultural common sense.

AA rhetoric has increasingly moved from a question of 'if' to questions of 'when' and 'how'. Malcolm Gladwell (2000) argues that trends can be understood, at least in part, through the idea of the 'tipping point', the 'levels at which the momentum for change becomes unstoppable'. In the case of scientific interventions in ageing, a number of watersheds have rendered its pursuit a fact of contemporary biotechnology, a fact that brings a future into present practice. This, in effect, exposes a kind of tipping point between predictions and expectations for these endeavours. The Rudman study, certainly not the first attempt to intervene directly in the process of ageing, provides one such point. The internet boom of the middle 1990s, and the genetic hopes of the early 2000s have set in motion a rhetorical shift from AA predictions to expectations in certain arenas.

Here, I briefly outline the history of AA science and medicine in the US from 1990 to 2008. This is a story of emergence, of on-going efforts to legitimise AA in the face of great resistance, and of battles to protect the 'good name' of gerontology (Mykytyn 2007). This history of the cultural production of ageing is entwined with emerging biotechnological advancements that render seemingly fantastical futures possible. It is a history of the generation of certain kinds of futures, of expectation-building, and the production of a cultural logic around ageing. I do not make any claims to evaluate efficacies here but, instead, explore the ways AA development has called into play both the future and the past, the everyday politics and grand machinations of rhetoric and work regarding interventions in ageing. I examine the history and the role of history in the shift from hopes to predictions to expectations as one aspect of professionalisation and subject formation. By way of AA being a contemporary field of tomorrow, this is a history of that future.

Background

The biomedico-scientific domains of AA have grown tremendously since the early 1990s, emerging from a kind of 'backwater'[1] into a fully fledged arena of inquiry and practice. There are now thousands of AA medical clinics, organisations devoted to the promulgation of AA ideas, researchers working on interventions in universities and biotech firms, companies marketing products, and scholars examining the ethical and social consequences of AA goals. While the bulk of research, practice, and consumption takes place in the US, its presence as legitimate science is hardly American. Clinics operate on every continent, with a concentration in North America, Europe (Robert 2004), Australia (Cardona 2007, Underwood et al. 2007) and in the Pacific Rim. Their locations tend to mirror greater national wealth, a higher concentration of older individuals, an embrace of science, as well as an openness towards 'holistic' medicine. Just as AA is nebulous in the US, so we certainly find great differences in approach, meaning, and context around the world (Robert 2004). A comparative study of these would be a welcome addition to this scholarship.

Though loosely organised and highly controversial as a scientific subject or medical 'specialty', AA proponents position ageing as a process that can and should be ameliorated. The term 'anti-ageing medicine' is, however, highly contentious (Arking et al. 2003, Butler 2001, de Grey et al. 2002a,b, Gavrilov 2002, Mykytyn 2006b) in part because so many people and groups are doing such different things. Some researchers and practitioners have embraced other terms such as 'longevity medicine', 'age management', and 'engineered negligible senescence' to distance themselves from what they see as profit-mongering or quackery. I acknowledge these positions and have chosen to use the term 'anti-ageing' as it encompasses the greatest swathe of proponents and is the term most in circulation.

AA proponents mark ageing as a therapeutic entrypoint, though, for a majority of proponents I have interviewed, it matters little whether ageing is natural or caused by disease; ageing is painful and biomedicine ought to do something about it (Mykytyn 2007). For some, the goal of avoiding death is paramount. These 'immortalists' are perhaps the noisiest but not the majority of proponents (Mykytyn forthcoming). A preponderance of published writings and my interviews centre AA around ameliorating the decline and extending life,[2] which are actually different from avoiding death (see Dumas and Turner 2007, Moreira and Palladino 2008, Vincent 2006 for discussion of death and AA, see Blackburn and Rowley 2004, PCBE 2002 for discussion of AA not in relation to immortality). The scourge of ageing that has echoed throughout my research, lies not in its final culmination but rather in the torture of its journey. While death is clearly an end result of a physical decline and an interloper in the quest for more time, it is pain not death, a sense of loss of self in life not loss of life in death, that so offends many AA advocates.

Methods

This chapter draws from multi-sited, anthropological research conducted in the US from 1999 through 2007. First, I have conducted 23 open-ended, ethnographic interviews with practitioners in their clinics and researchers in their offices in two major US cities, as well as over beer and pancakes (though rarely at the same sitting) in conference hotel lobbies with people from the US, England, and Germany. These tape-recorded, formal interviews ranged from two to five hours in length and in four instances led to follow-up interviews. Additionally, at conferences and seminars, I engaged in many 'informal' discussions that I detailed in fieldnotes produced the same day.

Participant observation serves as the second prong of this work. I have observed in AA clinics, arriving for interviews an average of 1.5 hours early to observe in waiting rooms. One physician allowed me to be present in two patient examinations and took me through a 'mock' exam myself, interviewing me as an initial patient and conducting the full battery of tests save the costly bloodwork. I also attended three national AA conferences, four monthly meetings of an AA science group, a public seminar held by a local AA clinic, and numerous sessions held at the Gerontology Society of America annual meetings three separate years. I tape-recorded sessions wherever possible and also produced detailed fieldnotes.

Writings on AA are abundant and provide the third pillar of this research. Many groups and individuals have established internet listserves/blogs from which I read voluminous daily posts regarding the philosophy, politics, and science of AA. Along with the plethora of academic and popular writing in journals, magazines, books, newspapers, pamphlets, and on websites, the texts dealing with AA provide a rich body of data from which this analysis arises.

Using a 'grounded theory' approach (Russell and Ryan 1998), I code transcripts and texts and identify themes as they emerge. Repeatedly analysing the various data thematically is a process through which the phenomena of AA become increasingly illuminated through multiple vantage points, allowing for comparisons across data with respect to the ways in which themes manifest themselves with each informant/text and the contexts in which they arose. Using a self-constructed database to track repeated coding sessions, I am able to collate and analyse many 'types' of information simultaneously. Having conducted research on AA since 1999, I have not only amassed a huge amount of longitudinal data; I have also had the opportunity to witness the recent development of AA.

1990–1995: Hopes and anti-ageing beginnings

The 1990 Rudman article fertilised scientific ground for AA. The A4M (American Academy of Anti-Aging Medicine) notes that this study is an 'important milestone in the history of clinical anti-ageing' (A4M 2002a). According to the *New England Journal of Medicine*, the '1990 article by Rudman and colleagues receives as many "hits" in a week as other 1990 articles do in a year' (Drazen 2003), even 13 years later. In light of this inordinate 'hit' frequency and the continuing controversy surrounding hGH administration, the *New England Journal of Medicine* attaches all downloads of the Rudman article to two far more cautionary articles on hGH. The adoption of his work without the benefit of additional research vexed Rudman until his death in 1994 (Alexander 2006); however, his admonitions were nearly inaudible in the din of hope and excitement his research ignited.

Rudman and his group were neither the first nor only people interested in AA in recent times. Throughout history and across cultures, the desire to not-age has been documented (Gruman 1966 [2003], Roughly 2000). For example. since the 1930s, US gerontologists have worked on Caloric Restriction, a means by which lifespan can be extended by drastically reducing the amount of calories consumed. Michael Rose proposed the evolutionary theory of ageing in 1986 (Rose 2005) and has been an outspoken proponent of the viability of developing AA interventions in the near future (Rose 2004). Outside academia, health advocates were publishing books on ageing and life extension, focusing primarily upon what are now categorised as 'lifestyle choices' (Pearson and Shaw 1982, Walford 1986). Imagining an intervention to ageing is not unique to Rudman. However, while Rudman offered a 'hard science' approach that seemed to work without the drudgery of halving one's daily calories, his research also came at a particularly auspicious time.

During the late 1980s and early 1990s, concerns were mounting over population ageing, more specifically, the onslaught of baby-boomers[3] approaching middle and later ages. A huge demographic, the boomers are also expected to live longer than ever before (USDHHS 1991). Social implications of expected longer lifespans spurred a flurry of worry both academically and publicly. US news articles on boomers rose 1294 per cent between 1980 and 1990[4] and by 1995, that number increased another 121 per cent. Especially in 1992, with the first boomer White House of Clinton/Gore, the topic of the ageing boom became part of a national dialogue. During this time, boomers were given a new public face, less youthful than their Woodstock poster-child, and marred by a frightening doom of looming social security shortfalls and rising health care costs.

The baby-boomers did not come only in great numbers, they also brought significant challenges to the 'traditional' ways of doing medicine. Complementary and alternative medical practices were steadily gaining popularity during this time (and have continued (Baer 2003)) and boomers were increasingly willing to challenge their physicians and the healthcare system (see also Mykytyn 2006c and Robert 2004), especially as direct-to-consumer pharmaceutical advertisements 'empowered' patients to request specific drugs from their physicians (Loe 2006). By the early 1990s, the notion of categorical medical authority had been severely eroded (Starr 1982) and a consumer-driven medical system was emerging (Conrad 2007, Moreira and Palladino 2008, Stevens 1971[1998]). With the potential for boomers as some scholars suggest, to 'change the basic concepts of health in old age' (Blanchette 1998: 76), how is it that AA medicine became one option?

This generation has been steeped in an ethic of liberation (Binstock 2004): the civil rights movement, the second wave of feminism, and self-help are all aspects of 'emancipation' from the status quo that have come of age along with the boomers (Alexander 2003). Self-help, which is built upon the notion that individuals have the ability to greatly affect their own lives with proper guidance (McGee 2005), is of particular importance. If humans can shed the weight of social force by empowering the self with regard to finances and relationships, then perhaps we can also break from undesirable biologies, especially in a time of dramatic talk of genetic engineering and biotechnological 'breakthroughs' (Kiernan 2006,

Smart 2003). The enormous consumption of self-help products in the 1990s and beyond reflect the enticement of liberation.

Prevalent discourses around the 'culture of perfectibility (Taussig *et al.* 2003, Mykytyn 2008) also midwived the production of a host of interventions such as drug therapies, lifestyle 'choices' and cosmetic surgeries aimed at surmounting objectionable biologies. The consumption of drugs such as Prozac that 'frees' the self from undesirable neurochemical reactions so that people can 'feel like themselves' (Elliot 2003) made liberation from the body a problem of consuming appropriate goods. 'Medicalising discontent' by structuring intricate problems into medical situations (Loe 2006), as exemplified by the marketing of Viagra, marks the body as fallible but ultimately fixable. What Marshall describes as the 'culture of virility' (Marshall 2006), I argue is endemic to liberation ideologies. With late capitalism's dependence upon corporate ideas of flexible production, imagery of the 'innovative agile body' (Martin 1994: 245) propagates a more fluid construction of the body. Thus, the marketing of drugs like Viagra and Prozac directly to consumers, the proliferation of the notion of 'personal health responsibility' that came packaged with 'good' 'lifestyle choices' (Goldstein 2000), the almost required use of AA cosmetic surgeries among ageing celebrities and consumers, and the construction of ageing as both an individual and social problem (Friedan 1993, Gullette 2004, Vincent 2006 among many), seeds the possibility of biological emancipation.

Not only the boomers, but entire disciplines are embedded in notions of liberation (Bailey 2005). The sciences in the 20th century are 'concerned with our growing capacities to control, manage, engineer, reshape, and modulate the very vital capacities of human beings as living creatures' (Rose 2006: 3). The 20th century 'new biology' has reconfigured the universal longevity quest, in part because researchers have grown up with the futurology of science fiction literature, giving the quest a new 'significance and urgency' (Adams 2004). The field of biogerontology is itself moored to the 'possibility of overcoming limits' (Cooper 2006) and is a discipline that has long been motivated by ideas of 'continuous and endless transformation' (Moreira and Palladino 2008). Only certain kinds of transformations are, however, sought after; the vision of the future may change but science is always the means to its realisation.

The notion of liberation requires a future unlike what a current trajectory implies. Our tomorrow could be different from the tomorrow our parents experienced. Thus, liberation is part and parcel of resisting the expected future and predicting an alternative. In many ways, liberation ideologies depend upon histories of potential while eschewing histories of the common/universal as emblematic of time-honoured traditions whose time may have come.

While Rudman's work seemed readily applicable to patients, and many physicians prescribed hGH as an AA therapy despite the fact that it is not approved by the US Food and Drug Administration, scientists began AA research with some fairly astounding success. Cynthia Kenyon (1996), for example, doubled the lifespan of nematode worms in 1993 through a single gene mutation. In 1999, she and Leonard Guarente, a biologist whose work with sirtuin proteins showed slowed ageing in yeast, founded Elixir Pharmaceuticals. With scientific research yielding laboratory as well as clinical promise, the notion of an intervention in ageing began to generate a host of institutional/cultural practices.

The early 1990s birthed some nascent structures of an AA field. Biotech firms and companies selling hGH and nutraceuticals saw great profit potential (Hall 2003, Solomon 2005, West 2003). While many of these companies folded or failed to hand down quick results, they drew attention to the scientific basis of AA and helped to place it within the framework of 'real' (and profitable) science. The International Longevity Center and Gerontology Research Group, organisations devoted to the study and dissemination of the implications of social ageing and the biology of ageing/anti-ageing respectively were formed around this time.

A significant development of this period was the founding of the American Academy of Anti-Aging Medicine (A4M). In 1993, Ronald Klatz and Robert Goldman launched the A4M which would play an enormous role in placing AA on the national scene despite the huge controversies they would encounter. The A4M defines AA medicine (a term it claims coinage of) as a 'medical specialty', which attempts to mark its practice as both legitimate and unique, different from what other physicians are doing, and grounded in biomedicine. Labelling their work as a specialty demands a set of professionalising practices. This included a body of standard practices taught and 'credentialed', with at least the appearance of 'expertise' grounded in both clinical skill and the continuing production of knowledge (Stevens 1971[1998], Weisz 2006). Towards that end, the A4M hosted its first of many conferences on the 'science' of AA in 1994 and established a 'credentialing' board for physicians in 1997.

While momentum began to build, the field remained relatively marginal; AA optimism was not widespread. In an effort to protect consumers from seemingly dodgy claims, the US government issued a warning against 'anti-aging remedies' that consumers had spent over two billion dollars annually to acquire (Napier 1994, see also NIA 1994, King 1996). These worries would become even more contentious in the years to come as the biogerontological establishment launched a 'war' on AA 'entrepreneurs' (Binstock 2003). Bioethical concerns also emerged; for example, the eminent gerontologist Leonard Hayflick argued that no efficacious intervention will be developed in our lifetime and questioned the morality of the goal (1994, 2000, see also Callahan 1994, Singer 1991). Calls to 'resist the siren song of the conquest of ageing and death' (Kass 2004) continue to this day often under the mantle of human rights (Dumas and Turner 2007, Fukuyama 2002) and gender and class inequity (Holstein 2001) (see also Post and Binstock 2004, Stock and Callahan 2004).

Nonetheless, by 1995, the drudgery of ageing became infused with the hope of scientific triumph. Within gerontology, debates were beginning to address not only the feasibility of this scientific goal but also its morality. Consumers were spending millions per year at AA clinics and on AA products. Popular media were fascinated by AA; biotech firms and pharma/nutraceutical companies were lured by its potential for profits. However, AA ideas were just beginning to ferment and still retained a science-fiction texture. During these early years, AA interventions could be characterised as hopes – not quite compelling enough to be fully fledged predictions as they still circulated around the periphery of the mainstream discourse, but still tantalising enough to engender conversation and tempt the more adventurous.

1996–1999: Predicting a new framework for ageing

The late 1990s ushered in a phase of expansion, marking the transition in AA discourse from the hopes of a relative few to compelling predictions from a growing minority. Increasing scientific attention took the form of popular science books, scholarly articles, and conferences. The media devoted more stories to the radical topic of not ageing. In 1996 membership in the A4M vaulted to 2,600 – a 217 per cent increase over the previous year. Klatz attributes this jump[5] to the 1996 launching of the hugely successful A4M website (Mykytyn 2001) which, by 1999, boasted upwards of two million hits per month.

Perhaps the greatest driving force for the proliferation of AA ideas during this time was the internet boom. Cyberspace provided a relatively inexpensive forum well suited to talk of frontiers and promise (Fischer 2004: 23–4); the internet created space for charging the biomedical complex with myopic conservatism. The alternative, offered by the A4M and others, became the cutting-edge of innovation that could both point to scientific research for legitimacy and market products that 'your doctor doesn't know about'. These voices, circulating freely online, outlined possibilities for a new future of ageing.

This story of pioneers-versus-mainstream had become a significant narrative for constructing legitimacy. While opponents (particularly of the A4M) locate AA medicine within a history of quackery and predatory commerce (Butler 2001), the A4M and many clinicians framed theirs as a history of revolution (Mykytyn 2006c). In a similar vein, though different vantage point, some within the academy place biogerontology within a history of 'catatonia' (de Grey 2004), structurally held to dogmatic, unproductive mainstream approaches (Miller 2004).

Throughout the late 1990s, popular interest in AA grew tremendously. The A4M continued to professionalise the 'specialty' by publishing the first medical textbook and numerous popular books on AA, establishing 'credentialing' boards and, creating the Consumer Education and Research Council in an attempt to set the organisation apart from 'fraudulent' activities (A4M n.d.). Over 139 books were published during this time; many were 'how-to' manuals with such rousing titles as *Outlive Your Enemies* (Sanford 1996), geared to individuals wanting to take responsibility for their own health (see Goldstein 2000). Yet, a few of these books were written by researchers interested in and largely optimistic for the prospects of an efficacious intervention (Austad 1997, Fossel 1996).

The sanguine exuberance paraded by the A4M was not unique: AA science also began to move from a 'backwater' (SENS n.d.). In 1999 a 'small group of eminent academic scientists who had their reputations to think of' (Kolata 1999) convened a roundtable to devise a list of research milestones, the Strategies for Negligible Senescence (SENS) (de Grey *et al.* 2002a,b).

Vying for an increase in funding, a call that would ring more loudly in subsequent years, and despite the taint of pseudoscience that had marked such quests through the history of the discipline (Binstock 2003), these academics positioned the predictions for this science as compelling enough to warrant public discussion.

'They were in good company both within a general excitement around scientific possibility surrounding the cloning of Dolly the sheep in 1996 and within the field of AA. The *Journal of Anti-Aging Medicine* was founded in 1998 under the editorship of Michael Fossel as a peer-reviewed journal, a marker of scientific legitimacy. Additionally, the1990s witnessed a growth of biotech interest with the formation of numerous companies dedicated to various AA efforts: Elixir (co-founded by Kenyon), Advanced Cell Technology, Eukarion, Geron, and Genentech among them (Hall 2003, Solomon 2005). The promise of huge profit, like the financial gold mine that Pfizer discovered with the marketing of Viagra in 1998.

While important groundwork towards mobilising physician and public support was laid during the early 1990s, the second phase (1996–1999) gave rise to increasing gerontological interest alongside an entrenched AA activism. Institutions critical of the process of professionalisation (Stevens 1971[1998]) are emerging in material form with conferences, journals, and organisations and in symbolic form with an increasing vocabulary through which to discuss AA. The future of ageing in AA constructions had effectively marshalled enough contemporary support to warrant these institutions. Both by challenging the sluggishness of scientific innovation and by heralding AA ideas produced by science, AA researchers and clinicians alike were using science to kindle science. By the end of 1999, it seemed to be working. With AA ideas rooted in public consciousness and with some measure of gerontological optimism, the new millennium would usher in a fresh chapter in the emergence of AA. No longer would the gerontological community be so apt to dismiss the predictions of AA; the wrangling for authority would be fiery.

2000–2008: From predictions to expectations

The new millennium, invigorated by the sequencing of the human genome, was a time of both exhilaration and apprehension over emerging biotechnologies. Predictions and 'hype' thundered through popular media and it seemed as if all were possible (Brown 2003), providing AA development good company. The trope of historical scientific triumph has been so powerful that its future triumph seems inevitable. Within this narrative of 'progress,' and building upon the momentum of the late 1990s, the rhetoric of AA became one that largely had built within it an expectation that AA would prevail.

The power of biotechnology's promise for the future is read vividly in how AA proponents construct the past. For example, the A4M argues that because of medical advancements the average life expectancy in industrialised nations has risen dramatically over the century and that there is no reason to think that such progress could not continue. Others contend that the major longevity work has already been done; simply extending the historical trajectory yields a faulty basis for predicting success. The 'biotech factor', however, continues to be a stalwart narrative. Countering arguments that the 'nearly universal engineering pattern is one of diminishing returns' (Weinstein 2006), is the notion that technological progress is accelerating (de Grey and Sprott 2004) and will provide the 'quantum leap, accelerating the extent and achievement of scientific discovery' (A4M 2000b: 8). Ray Kurzweil, noted futurist with whom a luncheon was auctioned off on the internet site ebay to benefit the Methuselah Foundation (MMP 2005), argues that the tempo of technical progress is 'doubling every decade' and that with 'aggressive application' of our scientific knowledge, life extension therapies will emerge over the next couple of decades (Kurzweil and Grossman 2004). Thus, for many, biotechnological progress should not only be included in thinking about any historical trajectory, it must be thought of within the context of its own staggering growth.

As the prospect of success became a topic for increased consideration, including deliberation in the President's Council on Bioethics (PCBE 2003, see also Mykytyn forthcoming), the excitement became palpable with hopeful stories on National Public Radio, in *Science Magazine*, *Newsweek* and *Scientific American* (2000) among many others. Academic publications skyrocketed in the mid-2000s with numerous books and journal issues devoted to questions of AA. For example, *Science* published a special edition on ageing stating that 'scientific research on biological mechanisms of aging may be at the end of the beginning' (Martin *et al.* 2003: 1341). This 'end of the beginning', reveals a shift away from the dismissal of AA goals and towards a potent discussion of means and ethics.

With this mounting enthusiasm, many gerontologists felt it necessary to protect the public from those, like the A4M, seen as trying to sell quackery as science. In a rare move on the part of the magazine, *Scientific American* issued a position statement, signed by 51 gerontologists, stating that no 'anti-aging' therapy currently exists (Olshansky *et al.* 2002) though they maintained optimism for future research. Similarly, some of the same authors bestowed a 'Silver Fleece' award upon A4M's Klatz and Goldman's nutraceuticals company for 'the most ridiculous, outrageous, scientifically unsupported or exaggerated assertions about intervening in aging or age-related diseases' (University of Illinois 2004). Moreover, the uproar begun by Rudman intensified in 2005 when Perls and colleagues (2005) published an article in *JAMA* critiquing the distribution of hGH for AA means, and warning that the data were too preliminary to warrant treatment.

Responses to these denunciations were vigorous. The American Association of Retired Persons discussion board, for example, was riddled with comments suggesting that the *Scientific American* authors were themselves 'selling fear to support drug companies' bottom lines'. The A4M responded to the position with a paper positing that 'the death cult of gerontology desperately labors to sustain an arcane, outmoded stance that aging is natural and inevitable' (A4M 2002a). Further, Klatz and Goldman filed a defamation lawsuit (ultimately not settled in their favour) against Olshansky and Perls following the Silver Fleece 'ceremony' in Australia (Manier 2005). The *JAMA* article sparked a flurry of letters to the Editor, generally in support of hGH use, or, at least, citing other data that complicate the pat 'no' issued by the article. The A4M reiterated its stance that the authors cherry-picked studies that conflated all 'pseudo' products with prescription hGH in an 'attempt to damage the Anti-Aging medical profession' (A4M 2005). The A4M, an organisation that struggles to acquire/maintain legitimacy in the gerontological community but nevertheless boasts booming membership (20,000 by 2009 [A4M 2009]), tenders these attempts to marginalise their practice by strategically locating gerontology as entrenched bullies of conservatism.

Aubrey de Grey and his SENS (Strategies for Negligible Senescence) program have provoked even more tempests both within and without academe. Founding the Methuselah Mouse Prize in 2003 to award researchers who demonstrate viable interventions in mice, de Grey believes that the prize will foster interest and cannibalise research monies.[6] By the end of 2008, contributions had reached $4.5 million with another $7 million directed specifically at SENS research (MMP 2008). De Grey's energetic promotion of SENS has earned him a great deal of publicity, not all of it laudatory.

In 2005, *MIT Technology Review* Editor Jason Pontin solicited a 'New Yorker'-like piece on de Grey (Pontin 2005). Nuland's lengthy profile describes de Grey as a 'beneficent man of goodwill' yet argues that efforts of de Grey that could 'surely destroy us in attempting to preserve us' (Nuland 2005). Becoming the most widely read article for *TR* in 2005, this piece provoked great discussion – 'in many cases, very angry indeed' (Pontin 2005). Pontin responded by offering a $10,000 prize (another $10,000 was added to the prize by De Grey's Methuselah Foundation) to any molecular biologist who submits an 'intellectually serious argument that SENS is so wrong that it is unworthy of learned debate' (Pontin 2005). In July of 2006, the judges conceded that that none of the submissions 'met the criterion of the challenge and disproved SENS' though the Estep *et al.* (2006) submission was 'the most eloquent' (Pontin 2006).

While more certainly deserves to be said here, the denigration of SENS as 'pseudoscience' is particularly salient. The judges felt that Estep was 'too quick … in labelling ideas as 'pseudo-scientific' (Pontin 2006, see also Garreau 2007). Estep directly challenged de Grey's personal expertise, arguing that de Grey 'uses emotionally charged propaganda' and that his plan is 'hypothetical and untested' (Estep *et al.* 2006). The legitimacy of SENS and de Grey as an academic are repeatedly called into question (see in addition Warner *et al.* 2005) all the while the ideas and the man continue to capture attention in both academic circles and the media (such as de Grey's February 2008 appearance on the comedy news show 'The Cobert Report'). For his part, de Grey welcomes challenges to his ideas, as they are 'good' for keeping the discussion going.[7]

In what has been dubbed a revision of the *Scientific American* paper four years later and a veritable 'sea change in public opinion' (fightaging 2006), the 'Longevity Dividend' was written to place the 'concerted effort to slow aging' on the national agenda (Olshansky *et al.* 2006). Lead author Jay Olshansky had been the driving force behind the *Scientific American* paper and had arguably led the battle against the A4M and other AA 'entrepreneurs'. In the debut of the Longevity Dividend venture on Capitol Hill, Olshansky argued that ageing was poised to undergo a revolution. This public initiative, notably not embracing the terminology of 'AA', makes the case that science has the potential to intervene upon ageing. The Longevity Dividend discusses the science behind such interventions, situating this as a rational, objective, and real project vetted by sober scientists, but focuses primarily upon the benefits that AA interventions would engender. The authors 'envision a goal that is realistically achievable: a modest deceleration in the rate of aging sufficient to delay all aging-related diseases and disorders by about seven years'. This 'gift to humanity' (Olshansky in Immortality Institutes 2006) depends not upon the success of science, as that is presumed to be inherent, but rather upon the financial investment in its pursuit.

This was well received by many who welcome increased publicity for AA but was also roundly criticised for not being ambitious enough (fightaging 2006). One commenter referred to it as 'striving for the booby prize. If humanity had developed using this kind of approach I sincerely doubt we would be where we are today.[8] Despite its modest goals, the Longevity Dividend found a kind of middle ground between the 'catatonic' biogerontologists (de Grey 2004) and those who believe that extreme life-extension is imminent. In a way, 'mainstream science' had co-opted the notion of intervening into ageing that had only a few years earlier been relegated to the sidelines of irrelevance and fantasy.

The 2000s dispensed a whirlwind of AA activity, much of it fluttering around the ethical considerations of whether we should pursue AA, which professionals are legitimate, and which scientific means to achieve a successful intervention should be sought. Appearing less frequently are discussions of feasibility, of whether or not interventions in ageing could even happen. This reflects a discourse shift from the previous decade. Provided the requisite funding is made available, science is expected to prevail and the question has become not whether AA is possible, but whether it is worthwhile.

Conclusion

Anti-ageing merges histories of the development of hGH and companies seeking interventions, ageing baby-boomers, the arguably human universal desire to halt ageing, the internet, the belief in biotechnological progress, and a trend towards biological perfectibility and 'better-than-well' medical practices. The protagonist in this unfolding story is ageing, and more specifically, the relationship between ageing and biomedicoscience (Mykytyn 2008, 2007). While AA research challenged mainstream frameworks of ageing and made possible swelling discussions of AA objectives and methods, AA medicine made relevant its desirability, and the appeal of AA possibilities made it attractive to popular media; the emergence of AA concepts and practices in these various arenas reveals the complex and reciprocal relationships that give rise to scientific imagination, innovation, and practice. Emerging from the 'backwater,' the appeal and promise of intervening in ageing in both scientific and clinical practice has found footing in the very science that it had so vehemently critiqued. As the drive to intervene in ageing evolved, comparisons with failed quests subsided. While a growing group of biogerontologists and practitioners declare potential, bioethicists on the PCBE (President's Council on Bioethics) and elsewhere warn of detrimental social consequences, though often soberly recognise such interventions as inevitable.

Since the Rudman study was published in 1990, the idea that biomedicine can indeed intervene in the processes of ageing has become far more tenable. This idea has been built upon a cluster of practices and institutions that serve to support the legitimacy of AA as a scientific and clinical specialty that attends to emerging forms of life and their interlocutors. In the early part of the 1990s, AA emerged with breathless hopes and often situated itself against mainstream scientific practice while simultaneously drawing upon scientific research to bolster its claims. By the latter half of the decade, the notion of intervening in ageing had become a topic of academic discussion, limited perhaps, but open nonetheless. AA had emerged from a kind of distant, crossed-fingers hope to a set of predictions compelling enough to marshal significant cultural, intellectual, and economic resources. By the turn of the century, AA predictions built upon the unremitting framing of AA within the realm of science, had substantiated itself within some scientific, clinical, and activist circles. The general shift in rhetoric from issues of feasibility to scientific means, timelines, social consequences, and moral positionings reveals a movement towards expecting AA to succeed. The conversion from hope to predictions to expectations oversimplifies the messiness of the development of AA as it is still far from a fact of life for the vast majority of people. Nonetheless I offer it as a way of understanding the history of subject formation and the production of knowledge around ageing and biomedicine.

In this chapter, I have outlined a history of AA medicine, an assuredly abridged history, riddled with omissions and biased by personal interests and the limits of journal space. I have sought to suggest that predictions require history for their authority and perhaps more obviously, that the past, present, and future are indivisible. AA is a story of prediction which is itself a story of histories, of continuing reinforcement for some and dismantling of others. Predictions are critical in this field that has had arguably little to go on, especially in its early development. In many regards, though I do not believe it has escaped its relatively modest enclave of proponents and practitioners yet, certain goals of AA medicine have crossed over into the realm of expectation.

Evolutionary biologist Michael Rose asks:

> how will the treatment of our aging achieve its tipping point? How will it go from fervent hope to medical practice? (2005: 120).

I would argue that, at least in the case of AA, there are numerous tipping points, beginning with the Rudman study of 1990 and the employ of the internet to disseminate, sell, distort and discuss ideas. It seems that by the new millennium, the cat was out of the proverbial bag in terms of the belief that AA, in some form or another, was probable with enough funding. There is much work to be done for any intervention to make it to the marketplace if it ever will, and I believe that, as the history of technology also shows that there will be far more failures than successes. Nonetheless, as my history suggests, the science and experience of ageing may indeed be crossing the threshold into an anti-ageing era.

Acknowledgements

Part of this research has been made possible by a generous grant from the WennerGren Foundation and through a fellowship at the Institute for Advanced Study of Science, Technology and Society in Graz, Austria. I would also like to thank the many people who helped with this research and analysis: Cheryl Mattingly, Lanita Jacobs-Huey, Vern Bengtson, Sadie Moore, Roman Mykytyn, Ian Everts, and, of course, Meika Loe and Kelly Joyce for editing such an interesting collection of chapters.

Notes

1   Interview: de Grey, 29 June 2008.
2   Interview: de Grey, 29 June 2008.
3   The cohort of people born between 1946 and 1964.
4   Per a news article search on the Google News engine for 'baby boomers' 9 September 2008.

5   Interview: Ronald Klatz, 27 February 2004.
6   Personal communication: 30 March 2001.
7   Interview: de Grey, 29 June 2008
8   Email sent over the GRG listserve, 6 August, 2006.

References

Adams, M. (2004) The Quest for Immortality. In Post, S. and Binstock, R. (eds) *The Fountain of Youth*. Oxford: Oxford University Press.
*Alexander, B. (2003) *Rapture: How Biotech Became the New Religion*. New York: Basic Books.
Alexander, B. (2006) A drug's promise (or not) of youth, *Los Angeles Times*, WEST Magazine, 9 July.
American Academy of Anti-Aging Medicine (n.d.) Available from: http://www.worldhealth.not/p/140,3319.html, [accessed 20 March 2004].
American Academy of Anti-Aging Medicine (A4M) (2002a) Official position statement on the truth about human aging intervention, Available from: http://www.worldhealth.net/p/96,333.html, [accessed 11 June 2003].
American Academy of Anti-Aging Medicine (A4M) (2002b) World Health Organization's ageing and health, *MCARE*, 1.
American Academy of Anti-Aging Medicine (A4M) (2005) Official A4M response to JAMA commentary on growth hormone, email newsletter, newsletter@a4m.com, 14 November 2005.
American Academy of Anti-Aging Medicine (A4M) (2008) A4M Newsletter, 7 May.
American Academy of Anti-Aging medicine (A4M) (2009) About the A4M, Available from: http://www.worldhealth.net/pages/about, [accessed 19 January 2009].
Angier, N. (1990) Growth hormone and the drive for a more youthful state, *New York Times*, 6 July.
Arking, R., Butler, R., Chiko, B., Fossel, M., Gavrilov, L., Morley, J.E., Olshansky, S.J., Perls, T. and Walker, R.F. (2003) What is anti-aging medicine? *Journal of Anti-Aging Medicine*, 6, 91–106.
Austad, S. (1997) *Why We Age*. New York: J. Wiley and Sons.
Baer, H. (2003) The work of Andrew Weil and Deepok Chopra, *Medical Anthropology Quarterly*, 17, 2, 233–50.
Bailey, R. (2005) *Liberation Biology*. Amherst, NY: Prometheus Books.
Binstock, R. (2003) The war on 'Anti-Aging Medicine': maintaining legitimacy, *The Gerontologist*, 43, 4–14.
Binstock, R. (2004) Anti-Aging Medicine and research, *Journal of Gerontology: Biological Sciences*, 59A, 6, B523–B33.
Blanchette, P and Valcour, V. (1998) Health and aging among baby boomers, *Generations*, 22, 76–80.
Blackburn, E. and Rowley, J. (2004) Reason as our guide, *PLOS Biology*, 2, 4, e116.
Borup, M., Brown, N., Konrad, K. and van Lente, H. (2006) The sociology of expectations in science and technology, *Technology Analysis and Strategic Management*, 18, 3–4, 285–98.
Brown, N. (2001) Hope against hype – accountability in biopast presents and futures, *Science Studies*, 16, 2, 3–21.
Brown, N. and Michael, M. (2003) A sociology of expectations, *Technology Analysis and Strategic Management*, 15, 1, 3–18.
Butler, R. (2001) Is there an 'Anti-Aging' medicine? *Generations*, XXV, 4, 63–65.
Callahan, D. (1994) Manipulating human life. In Blank, R. and Bonnicksen, A. (eds) *Medicine Unbound*. New York: Columbia University Press.
Caplan, A. and Moody, H. (2004) Is aging a disease? Available from: http://www.sagecrossroads.com, 22 January 2004, [accessed 10 December 2004].
Cardona, B. (2007) 'Anti-aging medicine' and the cultural context of aging in Australia, *Annals of the New York Academy of Sciences*, 1114, 216–29.
Conrad, P. (2007) *The Medicalization of Society*. Baltimore: Johns Hopkins University Press. Cooper, M. (2006) Resuscitations, *Body and Society*, 12, 1, 1–23.

de Grey, A. (2004) The curious case of the catatonic biogerontologists, Available from: http://www.longevitymeme.org/articles/viewarticle.cfm?page=2&article_id=19, [accessed 25 August 2005].

de Grey, A., Ames, B., Anderson, J., Bartke, A., Campisi, J., Heward, C.B., McCarter, R.J.M. and Stock, G. (2002a) Time to talk SENS: critiquing the immutability of human aging, *Annals of the New York Academy of Science*, 959, 452–62.

de Grey, A., Gavrilov, L., Olshansky, S.J., Coles, L.S., Cutler, R.G., Fossel, M. and Harman, S.M. (2002b) Antiaging technology and pseudoscience, *Science*, 296, 656a.

de Grey, A. and Sprott, R. (2004) How soon until we control aging, electronic document http://www.sagecrossroads.com, 5 November 2004, [accessed 10 December 2004].

Drazen, J. (2003) Inappropriate advertising of dietary Supplements, *New England Journal of Medicine*, 348, 9, 777–8.

Dumas, A. and Turner, B. (2007) The life extension project, *Health Sociology Review*, 16, 1, 5–17.

Elliot, C. (2003) *Better than Well: American Medicine Meets the American Dream*, New York: W.W. Norton and Company.

Estep, P. III, Kaeberlein, M., Kapahi, P., Kennedy, B., Lithgow, G., Martin, G., Melov, S., Powers, R.W. III and Tissenbaum, H. (2006) Life-extension pseudoscience and the SENS plan, *MIT Technology Review*, Available from: http://www.technologyreview.com/sens/docs/estepetal.pdf, 109(3), 80–84, [accessed 12 March 2007].

Fischer, M. (2004) *Emergent Forms of Life and the Anthropological Voice*. Durham, NC: Duke University Press.

Fightaging (2006) Pitching healthy life extension as the 'Longevity Dividend', Available from: http://www.fightaging.org/archives/000779.php, March 7, [accessed 7 August 2006].

Fortun, K. and Fortun, M. (2005) Scientific imaginaries and ethical plateaus in contemporary US toxicology, *American Anthropologist*, 107, 1, 43–54.

Fossel, M. (1996) *Reversing Human Aging*, New York: William Morrow.

Friedan, B. (1993) *The Fountain of Age*. New York: Simon and Schuster.

Fujimura, J. (2003) Future imaginaries. In Goodman, A., Heath, D. and Lindee, M.S. (eds) *Genetic Nature/Culture*. Berkeley: University of California Press.

Fukuyama, F. (2002) *Our Posthuman Future*. New York: Picador.

Garreau, J. (2007) The invincible man; Aubrey de Grey, 44 Going on 1,000, wants out of old age, *The Washington Post*, October 31, C1.

Gavrilov, L. (2002) Scientific legitimacy of the term 'anti-aging', *Journal of Anti-Aging Medicine*, 5, 129–50.

Gladwell, M. (2000) *The Tipping Point: How Little Things Can Make a Big Difference*. New York: Little, Brown and Company.

Goldstein, M. (2000) The culture of fitness and the growth of CAM. In Kelner, M. and Wellman, B. (eds) *Complementary and Alternative Medicine*. Amsterdam: Harwood Academic.

Gruman, G.J. (1966 [2003]) *A History of Ideas about the Prolongation of Life*. Philadelphia: American Philosophical Society.

Gullette, M.M. (2004) *Aged by Culture*. Chicago: University of Chicago Press.

Haber, C. (2004) Life extension and history, *Journal of Gerontology: Biological Sciences*, 59A.6, B515–B522.

Hall, S. (2003) *Merchants of Immortality*. New York: Houghton Mifflin Company.

Hayflick, L. (1994) *How and Why We Age*. New York: Random House.

Haylick, L. (2000) The future of ageing, *Nature*, 408, 37–38.

Holstein, M.B. (2001) A feminist perspective on anti-aging medicine, *Generations*, XXV, 4, 38–43.

Immortality Institute (2006) forum, Available from: http://www.imminst.org/forum/index.php?s=&act=ST&f=69&t=8913&st=80#entry96573, March 2 [accessed 7 August 2006].

Kass, L. (2004) L'Chaim and its limits. In Post, S. and Binstock, R. (eds) *The Fountain of Youth*, Oxford: Oxford University Press.

Kenyon, C. (1996) Ponce d'elegans, *Cell*, 84, 4, 501–4.

Kiernan, V. (2006) *Embargoed Science*. Chicago: University of Illinois Press.

King, R.T. Jr (1996) The elderly obtain 'rejuvenation' drug via network of doctors, *Townsend Letters for Doctors and Patients*, 31 July.

Kolata, G. (1999) Pushing limits of the human life span, *New York Times*, 9 March.

Kurzweil, R. and Grossman, T. (2004) *Fantastic Voyage*. USA: Rodale Inc.

Loe, M. (2006) *The Rise of Viagra: How the Little Blue Pill Changed Sex in America*. New York: New York University Press.

Manier, J. (2005) Professor sued over anti-aging comments, *The Chicago Tribune*, 19 June.

Marshall, B. (2006) The new virility: viagra, male aging and sexual function, *Sexualities*, 9, 3, 345–62.

Martin, E. (1994) *Flexible Bodies*. Boston: Beacon Press.

Martin, G., LaMarco, K., Strauss, E. and Kelner, K. (2003) The end of the beginning, *Science*, 299, 1339–41.

McGee, M. (2005) *Self-help, Inc.* New York: Oxford University Press.

Methuselah Mouse Prize (2005) Charity auction in support of the M prize for longevity research a success, Available from: http://www.mprize.org/, [accessed 29 July 2005].

Methusalah Mouse Prize (2008) Available from: http://www.mprize.org/index.php?pagename=mj_donations_funding [accessed 4 January 2009].

Miller, R. (2004) Extending life: scientific prospects and political obstacles. In Post, S. and Binstock, R. (eds) *The Fountain of Youth*, Oxford: Oxford University Press.

Moreira, T. and Palladino, P. (2008) Squaring the curve, *Body and Society*, 14, 3, 21 47.

Mykytyn, C.E. (2001) Anti-aging online, presented at the Committee for the Anthropology of Science and Technology, and Computers Conference, 22 – 23 July, Los Angeles.

Mykytyn, C.E. (2006a) Anti-aging medicine predictions, moral obligations, and biomedical intervention, *Anthropology Quarterly*, 79, 1, 5–32.

Mykytyn, C.E. (2006b) Contentious terminology and complicated cartography of anti-aging medicine, *Biogerontology*, 7, 4, 279–85.

Mykytyn, C.E. (2006c) Anti-aging medicine: a patient/practitioner movement to redefine aging. *Social Science and Medicine*, 62, 3, 643–53.

Mykytyn, C.E. (2007) *Executing Aging: An Ethnography of Process and Event in Anti-Aging Medicine*. PhD dissertation, University of Southern California.

Mykytyn, C.E. (2008) Medicalizing the optimal, *Journal of Aging Studies*, 22, 4, 313–21.

Mykytyn, C.E. (forthcoming), Anti-aging is not necessarily anti-death: bioethics and the front lines of practice, *Medicine Studies*.

Napier, K. (1994) Unproven medical treatments lure elderly, *FDA-Consumer*, 28, 2, 33–37.

National Institute on Aging (1994) Age page, Available from: http://www.nia.nih.gov/health/agepages/lifeext.html, [accessed 17 June 2002].

Nuland, S. (2005) Do you want to live forever? *MIT Technology Review*, Available from: http://www.technologyreview.com/articles/05/02/issue/feature_aging.asp, February [accessed 2 March 2005].

Olshansky, S.J. (2002) Exclusive: the truth about human aging, Available from: http://www.scieam.com/explorations/2002/051302 aging, [accessed 17 June 2002].

Olshansky, S.J., Hayflick, L. and Carnes, B. (2002) No truth to the fountain of youth, *Scientific American*, 286, 6, 92–95.

Olshansky, S.J., Perry, D., Miller, R.A. and Butler, R. (2006) In pursuit of the longevity dividend, *The Scientist*, March, 28–36.

Pearson, D. and Shaw, S. (1982) *Life Extension*. New York: Warner Books.

Perls, T., Reisman, N. and Olshansky, S.J. (2005) Provision or distribution of growth hormone for 'anti-aging', *Journal of the American Medical Association*, 294, 16, 2086–90.

Pontin, J. (2005a) The SENS challenge, *MIT Technology Review*, Available from: http://pontin.trblogs.com/archives/2005/07/the_sens_challe.html, 28 July, [accessed 25 August 2005).

Pontin, J. (2006b) Is defeating aging only a dream?: No one has won our $20,000 challenge to disprove Aubrey de Grey's anti-aging proposals, *MIT Technology Review*, Available from: technologyreview.com, July 11, [accessed 2 August 2006).

Post, S. and Binstock, R. (eds) (2004) *The Fountain of Youth: Scientific, Ethical and Policy Perspectives on a Biomedical Goal*. Oxford: Oxford University Press.

President's Council on Bioethics (PCBE) (2002) Adding years to life (transcripts), Available from: http://www.bioethics.gov/transcripts/dec02/session1.html, December 12, [Accessed 15 September 2003].

President's Council on Bioethics (PCBE) (2003) *Beyond Therapy: Biotechnology and the Pursuit of Happiness*. New York: Dana Press.

Robert, L. (2004) The three avenues of gerontology, *Journal of Gerontology: Biological Sciences*, 59A, 6, B540–2.

Roughly, N. (2000) *Human Universals and their Implications*. New York: Walter de Gruyter.

Rose, M. (2004) The metabiology of life extension. In Post, S. and Binstock, R. (eds) *The Fountain of Youth*. Oxford: Oxford University Press.

Rose, M. (2005) *The Long Tomorrow*. New York: Oxford University Press.

Rose, N. (2006) *The Politics of Life Itself*. Princeton, NJ: Princeton University Press.

Rudman, D., Feller, A.G., Nagraj, H.S., Gergans, G.A., Lalitha, P.Y., Goldberg, A.F., Schlenker, R.A., Cohn, L., Rudman, I.W. and Mattson, D.E. (1990) Effects of human growth hormone in men over 60 years old, *The New England Journal of Medicine*, 323, 1, 1–6.

Russell, B. and Ryan, G. (1998) Text analysis: qualitative and quantitative methods. In. Bernard, H.R (ed.) *Handbook of Methods in Cultural Anthropology*. Walnut Creek, CA: AltaMira Press.

Sanford, T. (1996) *Outlive Your Enemies*. Hauppauge, NY: Nova Kroshka Books.

Scientific American (2000) The Quest to Beat ageing, Summer Quarterly.

SENS (n.d.) Available from: http://research.mednet.ucla.edu/pmts/aging.htm, [accessed 25 June 2003].

Singer, P. (1991) Research into aging. In. Ludwig, F. (ed.) *Life Span Extension*. New York: Springer Publishing Company.

Smart, A. (2003) Reporting the dawn of the post-genomic era, *Sociology of Health and Illness*, 25, 1, 24–49.

Solomon, L.D. (2005) *The Quest for Human Longevity*. New Brunswick, NJ: Transaction Publishers.

Starr, P. (1982) *The Social Transformation of American Medicine*. New York: Basic Books.

Stevens, R. (1971 [1998]) *American Medicine and the Public Interest*. Berkeley: University of California Press.

Stock, G. and Callahan, D. (2004) Would doubling the human life span be a net positive or negative for us either as individuals or as a society? *Journal of Gerontology: Biological Sciences*, 59A, 6, B554–9.

Underwood, M., Bartlett, H. and Hall, W. (2007) Community attitudes to the regulation of life extension, *Annals of the New York Academy of Sciences*, 1114, 288–99.

University of Illinois at Chicago Press Release (2004) 'Silver Fleece' awards warn consumers of anti-aging misinformation, Available from: http://www.newswise.com/articles/view/503478/, [accessed 10 October 2004].

U.S. Department of Health and Human Services (1994) Vital statistics of the United States, 1990, Life Tables, 11, 6, DHHS Publication No. (PHS) 94-1104.

Vincent, J. (2006) Ageing contested, *Sociology*, 40, 4, 681–98.

Walford, R. (1986) *The 120 Year Diet*. New York: Simon and Schuster.

Warner, H., Anderson, J., Austad, S., Bergamini, E., Bredesen, D., Butler, R., Carnes, B.A., Clark, B.F.C., Cristofalo, V., Faulkner, J., Guarente, L, Harrison, D.E., Kirkwood, T., Lithgow, G., Martin, G., Masoro, E., Melov, S., Miller, R.A., Olshansky, S.J., Partridge, L., Pereira-Smith, O., Perls, T., Richardson, A., Smith, J., von Zglinicki, T., Wang, E., Wei, J.Y. and Williams, T.F. (2005) Science fact and the SENS agenda, *EMBO reports*, 6, 1006–8.

Weinstein, B. (2006) Stop making SENS, *MIT Technology Review*, 109, 3, Available from http://www.technologyreview.com/sens/docs/estepetal.pdf, [accessed 1 March 2007].

Weisz, G. (2006) *Divide and Conquer: a Comparative History of Medical Specialization*. Oxford: Oxford University Press.

West, M. (2003) *The Immortal Cell*. New York: Doubleday.

3

In the vanguard of biomedicine? The curious and contradictory case of anti-ageing medicine
Jennifer R. Fishman, Richard A. Settersten Jr and Michael A. Flatt

Introduction

Anti-ageing medicine, a specialty in which healthcare providers typically see patients in stand-alone clinics, has grown exponentially over the last five years. Anti-ageing medicine is difficult to characterise in uniform terms, but its essential mission, as expressed by the American Academy of Anti-Aging Medicine (A4M), is 'to detect, prevent, and treat aging-related disease and to promote research into methods to retard and optimise the human aging process. ... [D]isabilities associated with normal aging are caused by physiological dysfunction which in many cases are open to medical treatment, such that the human lifespan can be increased, and the quality of one's life enhanced as one grows chronologically older' (American Academy for Anti-Aging Medicine 2008). In this chapter, we argue that the rise of anti-ageing medicine, as an early indicator of an emerging model of healthcare, is emblematic of the current condition of American biomedicine. Anti-ageing medicine has developed as a response to the perceived problems of biomedicine while at the same time retaining many of biomedicine's underlying ideologies.

The still largely ideological concepts of consumer-directed healthcare, personalised medicine and preventive health have found strong footing in the specialty of anti-ageing medicine. Through interviews with 31 US-based anti-ageing practitioners, we examine how practitioners incorporate a personalised, individualised approach to their work as an attempt to move away from what they see as the 'assembly line' insurance-managed healthcare industry in the United States. They are more reluctant than conventional practitioners to use mass-market pharmaceutical drugs and more likely to rely on seemingly 'old-school' medical techniques, such as in-depth interviewing and repeated laboratory tests. However, their motivation is not merely a reaction to conventional medicine, but it is also derived from philosophical beliefs about the role of the physician, the nature of the physician-patient relationship, and the function of biomedicine to create an optimal self, not just a self free of illness. Our analyses examine how this supposedly new area of biomedicine fits into contemporary practice and discourse in the field.

In one of the first published articles to use the term 'biomedicalization', Estes and Binney (1989) describe how ageing has come to be seen as a biomedical problem – that is, as a problem of individual physiological pathologies – and how the growing biomedical ageing industry has been manufactured to treat these problems. In the 20 years that followed, ageing became fully biomedicalised and biomedicine itself changed dramatically. Besides turning 'normal' processes of ageing into pathological ones, all aspects of life are now heavily affected by biomedicalisation (Clarke *et al.* 2003). For example, improving one's quality of life is considered a perfectly worthwhile motivation for seeking biomedical attention. Relatedly, Nikolas Rose describes 'the politics of life itself' as neither delimited by the poles of illness and health, nor focused on eliminating pathology to protect the destiny of the nation. Rather it is concerned with our growing capacities to control, manage, engineer, reshape, and modulate the very vital capacities of human beings as living creatures (2006: 3).

These concepts form the ideological backdrop of biomedicine that anti-ageing medicine both replicates and to which it responds. Ultimately, anti-ageing providers embrace the notion of the 'vital self' and address it through discourse about optimisation and balance. Yet, they simultaneously wish to reject other aspects of 'vital politics' that look like more traditional 'surveillance medicine' (Armstrong 1995), such as efficiency and evidence-based medicine and a one-size-fits-all form of care. Anti-ageing providers see themselves as the antithesis of the impersonal, routinised, insurance-managed care offered by other physicians. Above all, anti-ageing medicine is construed as something drastically different from what is now the 'conventional' practice of medicine. These providers hope to deliver personalised care that is tailor-made for each patient. This is marked by in-depth appointments, careful monitoring of a wide range of biomarkers, concern with the patient's broader quality of life, and a specialised programme of health and wellness.

From a 'technogenarian' perspective (see Chapter 1 of this book), we examine how anti-ageing medicine is a 'technology of the self' (Foucault 1988), as evident in the labels and practices noted above. The ageing body is in need of constant surveillance, intervention, maintenance, and management. Yet a fundamental irony is that anti-ageing providers, in delivering personalised medicine, claim to offer a return to the 'art' of medicine. Instead of working with pre-designed or prescribed treatment plans, these providers are concerned with the creation of medical care that is specific to the individuals they are treating, countering the trends of evidence-based medicine. In their minds, this makes a return to what they refer to as 'patient-centred care' more like the care given before the current era of managed healthcare. Many work outside traditional insurance arrangements, and many accept only out-of-pocket payments and offer off-label treatments, such as hormone therapies, that are not approved by the US Food and Drug Administration for anti-ageing purposes. Anti-ageing providers therefore employ rhetoric about a return to an earlier form of medicine, even though their approach may also embody some of the hallmark features of 21st century biomedicine. In the end, their approach represents an amalgamation of new and old forms of medical practice in order to appeal to patients who are looking for alternatives to conventional medicine, both in terms of the desired doctor-patient interactions and the kinds of services and therapies they seek. Anti-ageing medicine puts into practice a contorted and modified type of surveillance medicine, one that embraces a biomedicalisation of 'life itself' but in unconventional ways – through 'low tech' and 'holistic' approaches.

David Armstrong first described his concept of surveillance medicine in an article published in 1995 as a way of describing the historical shift from 'hospital medicine' in which the ill are the targets for medical intervention to a more general 'problematisation of the normal' that implicates the population at large (Armstrong 1995). By transforming signs and symptoms into risk factors for illness, everyone can be placed under surveillance. With everyone ripe for medical intervention, surveillance medicine turns 'increasingly to an extracorporeal space – often represented by the notion of 'lifestyle' – to identify the precursors of future illness' (Armstrong 1995: 401). Foucauldian theorists have similarly identified the expansion of the medical gaze to healthy, 'at risk' populations.

One of the unintended outgrowths of surveillance medicine has been the rise of evidence-based medicine, where knowledge about risk factors for illness is compiled in meta-analyses, turned into practice guidelines, and used to make medical decisions about diagnosis and intervention. Although evidence-based medicine was designed in part as a professionalising strategy to reduce medical uncertainty, it developed a reputation as achieving just the opposite, because of its purported potential for routinised care based on cost-effectiveness rather than individual need (Armstrong 2007). Polemicists might, for instance, pit evidence-based medicine against 'patient-centred care.' In fact, in the United States, rhetoric about evidence-centred medicine became conflated with health maintenance organisations' attempts to create efficient and cost-minimising care by reducing the number of 'unnecessary' diagnostic tests.

Anti-ageing providers are responding to this rhetoric and, moreover, to the rationalised and insurance-driven healthcare system in the US by rejecting the ideology behind evidence-based medicine, yet simultaneously embracing much of the ideology of surveillance medicine. In fact, we argue that they push the boundaries of surveillance medicine beyond just trying to treat risk factors for illness to improving and optimising one's health regardless of one's current health status. There is always room for improvement. 'Life itself' is a continually moving target for intervention. Yet, contrary to other forms of biomedicine that use the newest technologies for intervention, anti-ageing providers have turned to low-technological solutions – solutions that in their minds hark back to an earlier era of medicine which they associate with patient-centred care.

Methods

We interviewed a sample of 31 US-based anti-ageing providers drawn from the online directory of the American Academy for Anti-Aging Medicine (A4M) through which consumers can identify anti-ageing physicians, clinics, spas and products in their communities. The A4M is a professional organisation that claims to represent more than 28,000 physicians and scientists interested in anti-ageing. It organises and sponsors conferences all over the world to educate people and promote anti-ageing medicine and considers itself a 'global resource for anti-aging medicine' (American Academy for Anti-Aging Medicine 2008). It also has a fellowship and certification program for physicians to get training in anti-ageing medicine. It is in many ways one of the more public faces of anti-ageing medicine. Its website also has a directory of clinicians that anyone can search through and is the first hit in a google search of 'anti-aging medicine' (search conducted September 13, 2008). A total of 122 potential participants were identified within the category 'anti-aging health professionals' in the United States.

All potential participants were mailed recruitment packets that included information on the study, how to schedule an interview, and a small gift card for coffee. We conducted a total of 31 interviews, stopping after we met our goal for the sample size. Of the 31 participants, 19 (61%) were men and 12 (39%) were women. The majority (23, or 74%) reported themselves as White/Caucasian, three as Hispanic (10%), two as Black (6%), and one as Asian (3%). (Two respondents did not report their race and/or ethnicity.) Interviewees ranged from 33 to 71 years of age. Most (71%) reported a medical degree (MD) as their primary credential, with the remaining participants being Doctors of Naturopathy (ND), Doctors of Philosophy (PhD), Doctors of Osteopathic Medicine (DO), or Nurse Practitioners.

Semi-structured interviews were conducted by phone between March and August 2008 and ranged from 41 minutes to over two hours. Our inquiry draws heavily on sections of the interview that probe whether and how the term anti-ageing reflects the work of these providers, how their approach is similar to or different from 'conventional medicine', and what typical appointments and patients are like.

All interviews were fully transcribed and imported into Atlas.ti, a software program for qualitative data analysis. Codes were developed by drawing on existing scholarship and by building directly from the transcript text. First-level coding was done for particular questions (*e.g.* a reference to the provider's work as 'functional medicine' as a specific type of terminology), and similar first-level codes were collapsed into higher-order 'interpretive codes,' to use Huberman and Miles's (2002) term (*e.g.* references to specific terms were included in a larger code, 'objections to anti-aging'). Both types of codes were then applied to the entire interview. Using this 'grounded theory' approach (Charmaz 2006), codes were further sorted into broader conceptual categories and incorporated into the theoretical foundation of this project.

The transcripts were divided among three coders who had also conducted the interviews. A coding manual was developed in collaboration with the full research team. The manual included a specific definition of each code and how to apply them. A common set of interviews was initially coded by all three coders to establish reliability. Coded transcripts were also reviewed and discussed by the whole team. As new codes were developed, coders followed the same process to ensure consistent decisions and to fine-tune existing codes.

Framing their work: the significance of language

The majority of providers express some reservations about using the label 'anti-ageing' to describe their work. 'Anti-ageing' is viewed as 'a term that people get on a visceral level' – one that has meaning to the average person. It is not seen as an accurate descriptor of the daily work of most providers. Yet one of the most common objections of providers to the term 'anti-ageing' is that it is largely understood by the public to be aimed at making people *look* younger. Providers are quick to emphasise that aesthetic services are only a small part of what they do, if at all. One provider argues that 'anti-ageing' was once an accurate label for his work and the field, but its meaning had changed:

> In say '96 or '97, yes. Today, no. Anti-ageing, the term 'anti-ageing' has really been taken over by Oil of Olay and all sorts of not necessarily bad things, but it's really cosmetic. It's having people like chase the fountain of youth, things that I do not feel are part of our specialty at all (P21).

Regardless of whether providers offer aesthetic services, the 'anti-ageing' label is generally viewed as failing to reflect the breadth of their practices. One provider says: '[I'm] not just … balancing someone and their, you know, human growth hormone or whatever needs replacing, but [I'm] also spending a lot of time with emotional, you know, fostering spirituality, nutrition, and so yes, [anti-ageing] plus' (P4). This notion of 'anti-ageing *plus*' is important because it symbolises their work as far bigger than 'anti-ageing' alone.

For this reason, most providers opt for alternative labels, the most common being 'preventative medicine'. In positioning their work as preventative medicine, providers attempt to distance themselves from longstanding perceptions of anti-ageing providers as peddlers of the 'fountain of youth' or, worse still, as quacks or charlatans (see also Binstock 2003, Fishman *et al.* 2008). 'Functional medicine' (Settersten *et al.* 2008), another frequently used term, promotes the notion that these providers seek to *optimise* function, not merely maintain it – which also has the effect of preventing triggers of disease and age-related decline.

'Age-management medicine' is a term that seems to be gaining significant momentum as a replacement for 'anti-ageing medicine'. As one provider explained, 'age management tends to be a more muted way to say anti-ageing' (P10) – it is a safer way to describe the practice of anti-ageing medicine without carrying the same negative connotations. As we will later show, the 'management' descriptor is critical because it signals that ageing is a process that can and should be managed by providers and patients. Furthermore, it highlights the idea that the majority of anti-ageing patients are not the very old, but are, rather, middle aged, '45 and older' (P5).

Other commonly referenced terms include 'integrative medicine,' which providers describe as the integration of 'conventional' medicine with 'anti-ageing' practices; and 'longevity medicine,' which suggests that providers seek to extend the human lifespan – or at least the healthy portion of it (or 'health span'). Other terms that are raised by providers, but much less often, include 'complementary and alternative medicine', 'regenerative medicine', 'rejuvenating medicine', 'wellness medicine', and 'natural medicine'.

In the vanguard of biomedicine?

When providers are asked to compare their practices to 'conventional medicine', an almost uniform response results: that what they are doing is conventional medicine. This shocks the rhetoric of anti-ageing medicine as a cutting-edge and technologically-driven specialty of medicine. Most of our interviewees emphasise that they are not opponents of conventional medicine and, indeed, that the diagnostic techniques they use in their practices are staples of conventional medicine.

The major difference that sets them apart from conventional medical providers, in their estimation, has to do with the basic philosophy of their practices: they strive to deliver *personalised* and *individualised* care. This is a benefit for the provider as much as it is for the patient:

> [E]very physician, I think, should have his own practice, his own preferences, and in my understanding the patients should choose a physician according to his philosophy, rather than going to the McDonald-type physician which actually gives you the same product just in a different location (P2).

The scientific *methods* they use are consistent with conventional medicine, but *how* they deliver medicine is not – at least as they see it. In fact, the majority of providers say that they moved to anti-ageing medicine because the ethos and constraints of contemporary clinical medicine prevented them from delivering the type of care to which they are committed.

The emphasis on individualised care is evident from the first visit, with providers reporting that they spend between two and five hours with new patients. Providers take extensive histories that include things 'not stressed in traditional medicine', such as nutrition, exercise, sleep habits, supplements, and assessments of 'antecedents, triggers and mediators'. As a result, providers are less concerned about assigning a disease label to a patient's problems than they are about uncovering its etiology or underlying process:

> We look at the whole person, not necessarily a holistic approach, but we're looking at the entire person, all of the disease processes put together and trying to find out what is the core reason and the causative factors, whereas in conventional medicine we all work in a silo. I mean the orthopedists do theirs, and somebody's got a foot specialist and a hand specialist and an ear specialist, and right now the current medicine is just fragmental and everybody has their own thing. We try to put all those pieces of the puzzle together (P5).

The majority of providers stress the importance of taking an 'open-minded' approach that not only focuses on physical health, but also mental, emotional, sexual, and spiritual aspects:

> [W]e spend more time with our patients. We dig a little deeper. We're looking at the whole person. … A lot of conventional doctors would say 'Well it's in range. You're fine', and we have narrower ranges of what we consider normal. So we're kind of focused more on optimal health, versus just normal and, let's see, treating the underlying cause instead of just matching a drug with the bug, focus a lot on nutrition, lifestyle, which you know a lot of that is anti-ageing medicine anyway, supplements and the whole thing really. Just like basically it's your personal doctor (P4).

This provider's emphasis on 'optimal health, versus just normal' draws attention to a key way that anti-ageing providers see themselves as being in the vanguard of medicine (see also Mykytyn 2006). Their goal is to create optimal functioning, and not be satisfied when functioning falls within 'normal' ranges. Shrinking the range of 'normal' is a classic type of medicalisation – it makes pathological a set of parameters that were once normal and acceptable. In the case of anti-ageing medicine, the narrowing of an acceptable norm is a direct attempt to define (and strive for) an optimal state of being. It reflects one of the hallmarks of new forms of biomedicalisation in the 21st century: a movement away from the classification of diseases and towards the construction of an ever-improvable self (Clarke *et al.* 2003). Closely related to creating an optimal self is the emphasis that anti-ageing providers place on the goal of improving whole 'quality of life'. Their explicit attention to the spiritual, emotional, and physical aspects of their patients' lives is the full instantiation of a biomedicalisation of lifestyle. 'Life itself', following Rose (2006), is a worthy biomedical endeavour and part of the rhetoric of biomedicine – and anti-ageing providers are trying to fully implement this ideal.

Low-tech answers in high-tech times

Providers reject the traditional 'disease model' of medicine – one that focuses on standardised measures and tests and on uniform diagnoses – in favour of strategies that allow them to gain a deeper perspective on *why* patients have particular symptoms. It comes as no surprise, then, that the modes of treatment they choose are preventative ones, which they also say are not part of the repertoire of contemporary clinical medicine:

> There is minimal emphasis on prevention in medical school. … [N]o one cares about it and doctors don't know much about it, and it's also not very exciting. [They] are a lot more interested in learning how to do a bypass than they are in, you know, what the optimal dose of calcium is to prevent osteoporosis or, you know, things along those lines. … [T]he high tech stuff that's now available is much more interesting, so medical students and residents tend to gravitate towards the more interesting things (P8).

The fact that providers categorise anti-ageing medicine as a specialty that does not embody innovative high-tech developments is especially noteworthy, for anti-ageing providers do see themselves – and are promoted by the A4M – as being in the vanguard of medical knowledge and technology.

In an era in which high tech medical practices are touted as being synonymous with high-quality care, anti-ageing providers spend a great deal of time on decidedly less tech-heavy methods of treatment. They tend to rely on in-depth medical interviewing, repeated laboratory tests of hormone levels and other biochemical measurements, dietary and exercise regimens, supplements, and hormone replacement. And it is for this very counterintuitive reason that providers see themselves as 'revolutionary'. Even providers who rally to the cry that anti-ageing medicine is on the cutting edge of technology suggest that their principles are rooted in solid, traditional medicine:

> I think anti-ageing medicine is more on the edge. It's at the leading edge of medicine, okay, and it's like everything else in society. You have a subset of the population that's at the edge. You know they define science. They come up with methods, you know, technology, and then you have everybody else in the back. All right, the medical world, I look at it the same way. You have a set of doctors that are willing to leap that edge, you know, where it comes to anti-ageing. All it is is endocrinology, okay, and there's so much technology and new medications and things that you can do (P12).

Careful not to depict anti-ageing medicine as 'just endocrinology', this provider, unlike many of the providers we interviewed, does see anti-ageing as being 'on the edge', especially because of advances in endocrinology and hormonal treatments. All the providers we interviewed report using some form of hormone level assessment in their daily practice, and those who provide hormone replacement therapy use only bioidentical hormones. Yet bioidentical hormone synthesis is, on the face of it, neither new nor flashy. What is noticeably absent from these practices are advances in genetic science, particularly epigenetics. Only a few providers report that they use genetic testing, even when they acknowledge the significance of genetic predispositions for age-related diseases.

That a new medical specialty could arise without strong ties to new technology is peculiar – and an important commentary on the present state of biomedicine. Many social theorists have linked the turn in biomedicine to technologies of enhancement (*e.g.* Elliott 2003, Parens 1998) and optimisation (*e.g.* Rose 2006, Franklin 2003), but the emphasis there is primarily on biotechnologies that are part of the 'hybrid assemblages' of a regime of living (Rose 2006). Anti-ageing medicine embodies a regime that features an ever improvable and modifiable self, yet it does not carry with it the concomitant new technological developments that are present in other emergent fields of biomedicine. The representation of anti-ageing medicine by the A4M, the major professional organisation, however, capitalises on images of 'high tech' interventions: a DNA double helix; scientists in lab coats; magnified images of blood cells and neurons that are belied by what providers are actually telling us about daily clinical practice.

Anti-ageing practices are not only surprisingly low-tech. Providers are also reluctant to prescribe traditional pharmaceuticals, which they see as a key problem of mainstream medicine:

> I feel that there is a bias among conventional doctors to do a very sloppy job of prevention and instead just wait for disease to occur and then write a prescription. So rather than, you know, when someone comes in and their blood pressure is high or high normal, rather than reaching for the prescription pad right away, I will instead try to implement, you know, the lifestyle strategies that would bring that person's blood pressure down, like weight loss, exercise, stress management, diet, etc., rather than just giving them a prescription right off the bat (P8).

The use of pharmaceuticals in their own practices poses a dilemma: they are reluctant to use the same pharmaceutical drugs as conventional providers because those doctors and treatments represent the homogenised and routinised care that anti-ageing providers denounce. Given their mission of delivering individualised and personalised treatment, anti-ageing providers do not want to resemble 'ready made', factory-line medicine. They do use other synthetic pharmaceuticals in the form of bioidentical hormones, but these need to be compounded especially for the patient, which is consistent with their emphasis on customisation:

> Well, everybody has different hormonal differences. Everybody is absolutely different. Everybody is unique. So everybody is going to need a different level to get them where they need to be. So it's not a ready-made, it's not a pre-made dosage from a pharmaceutical company. It's going to be an individualised dose. The dose has to be compounded for that particular patient. So the usual idea is to start low and go slow. You start on the lower end of the dosage and slowly give it to them and recheck it, see it slowly kind of creeping up until their symptoms and, you know, their blood tests and saliva tests are over their optimal range (P10).

The above quote illustrates not only the resistance to 'ready-made' medicine driven by the pharmaceutical industry, but it again points to the goal of pursuing the 'optimal' over 'normal'.

Ironically, some of the largest technological advances in anti-ageing treatment are designed for cosmetic and aesthetic medicine, often in the form of pharmaceuticals. Several of the providers in our sample reported that they offer a variety of cosmetic procedures in their practice, ranging from hair and skin care (*e.g.* chemical peels, laser treatments) to wrinkle removal/filling (using injections of Botox or hyaluronic acid) to cosmetic surgery. For one provider, the aesthetic component of his practice is in addition to the 'anti-ageing' aspect of the practice:

> Again, my practice again does do, like I said earlier on, it's not just anti-ageing medicine. I also have an extent which is not particularly anti-ageing in the respect of a physiological level, but we're talking care of the outside, for instance. So we do laser treatments for skin care, also for skin conditions: Rosacea, sun damage, *et cetera, et cetera* (P1).

For others, aesthetic treatments are merely one option that anti-ageing providers can decide they want to provide:

> Anti-ageing is pretty broad-based. There's a lot of, in today's world, there's a lot of cosmetics, aesthetics in anti-ageing. I don't do those. I used to do facial cosmetic surgery for 15 years. I enjoy that. I like to do it. We used Botox for 30 years, but I'm not doing any aesthetics. I'm focusing primarily on comprehensive medicine. I don't do any mesotherapy. I don't do any acupuncture, don't do any massage. There's a lot of different … You know, anti-ageing is so multifaceted that you sort of have to pick out what you want to do, and so I'm primarily in the regenerative area (P5).

Clearly, cosmetic and aesthetic treatments are highly profitable. But they can also cast a long shadow on the professional legitimacy of providers. As a result, it is common for most anti-ageing physicians to distance themselves from dermatologists and plastic surgeons, whose work is restricted to improving 'the outside' of the human body without attention to 'the inside':

> There is this aesthetic component, aesthetic medicine component. Now aesthetic medicine in itself is not anti-ageing medicine, and any primary care doctor or

dermatologist or plastic surgeon can throw up a sign on their door, say 'We practice anti-ageing medicine', because they do Botox and facial fillers and laser therapies. That's *not* anti-ageing medicine. That's skin care. Anti-ageing medicine, you know this concept, is all about balancing of the physiology. Now you have the skin changes based on this, or it's based on the physiologic changes of the body, and most of that is endocrine, the loss of the hormones as we age. The hormones generally decline whether there's a medical issue or, you know, a non-medical issue. They're going to decline as we age, and along with decline of our supportive hormones, that's where we have enzyme failure, tissue failure and disease development (P6).

Here again, we see the provider alluding to the idea that anti-ageing medicine is about uncovering underlying etiologies rather than merely treating symptoms of ageing.

The lengths to which some anti-ageing physicians go to exempt themselves from, or at the very least de-emphasise, these more superficial modes of treatment only serve to elevate their personal sense of legitimacy as professionals. These dynamics are similar to what we have elsewhere identified as 'boundary work' in anti-ageing science and medicine, where in an emergent field of questionable credibility those within it feel the need to clearly demarcate themselves from those seen as less reputable (Fishman *et al.* 2008).

The collaborative management of ageing bodies

The emphasis on prevention, in particular, means that the prime targets for anti-ageing therapies are not individuals who are already old. Anti-ageing medicine is, ironically, mostly for middle-aged people – as one provider explains, 'generally speaking', anti-ageing medicine is for 'men and women ages 45 and older' (P5). Why this threshold? Because as individuals cross this threshold, they begin to experience significant bodily changes and become worried about growing older. Midlife patients come to anti-ageing practices because they have a growing awareness of not being 'up to speed', as one provider (P5) puts it, or of 'losing one's edge' and 'needing a hand up, not a push off a cliff', in the words of another (P3). Repeatedly, providers say that the most common reasons that patients seek their services are a 'pervasive sense of fatigue' and an associated desire to increase 'libido', 'energy', and 'cognition' (P10).

In identifying these 'symptoms' as part of ageing, providers and patients jointly engage in another aspect of surveillance medicine. Yet, they are neither interested in linking symptoms to illness categories nor trying to biomedicalise ageing. Rather, they use the language of maintenance, restoration, and optimisation to think broadly about the functioning of the whole body and the interconnectedness of systems, and to identify targets and treatments, which typically involve major changes in lifestyle. This is consistent with the growing legitimacy of improving lifestyle as an explicit goal of biomedicine (see *e.g.* Mamo and Fishman 2001, Marshall and Katz 2002).

The joint collaboration of providers and patients is based on the premise that ageing bodies can be effectively managed if a few conditions are met. One necessary ingredient for success is that individuals must have the right attitude and be truly desirous of change. One provider even opens his consultation by presenting a 10-point rating scale in which the patient must evaluate 'How ready are you to make changes in your life?' Effective treatments rest on the serious commitments of patients *and* of the people around them who must provide support. Lifestyle changes, in particular, do not occur in a vacuum, but involve spouses and partners, households, and extended families.

By the time patients end up in the waiting rooms of anti-ageing practices, their levels of commitment are generally high, they are informed, and they have specific concerns in mind:

Well, I think one of the nice things about, you know, not being [in an] HMO [health maintenance organisation] and everything else, whenever you walk in a room, the patient already knows where they are. ... I mean they know sort of what to expect. They've heard about it. You know they've been on the website or they've talked to a friend or something. They kind of know what kind of office they're walking into, and so right from the beginning they've got the idea (P13).

The magnificent thing about 'age management medicine' is that it's patient-driven. The patients want it. I do workshops and seminars throughout the year, and people who are interested in finding out about anti-ageing practices in medicine will come to those and they basically refer themselves ... So it tends to be driven by the patients (P20).

These patients have often reached the point where they realise it is their responsibility, even duty, to take personal control over their health, echoing the neo-liberal framework that has enveloped contemporary biomedicine. But they need help. Enter the provider, who becomes a guide or coach to facilitate it and has the knowledge and skill to do so. 'After all,' as one provider says, 'I'm a physician first, and an anti-ageing physician second' (P2). The first part (the physician) is the core part of the provider's knowledge and skill base:

My approach is integrative, you know, 'Let's bring everything in that I can possibly bring in to help the patient,' and so all [of the] traditional medicine that I've learned is fair game. ... [B]asically it's like going to war, okay? It's like as being a doctor you're in a strange war because you're going to lose. Everybody is going to die, so your job I think is to win as many battles as you can, and so the idea is use every weapon that's at your disposal. Now since I was able to actually go to medical school I've been given the legal right to use every weapon in the world, and that's what I'm going to do, you know (P13).

The second part (the anti-ageing specialist) is surprisingly much less about additional knowledge and skill and much more about the return to older ideals of medicine. The neo-liberal approach to health, in which one's health is a project to be constantly tended, is juxtaposed to older traditions that emphasise the doctor-patient dyad. Now the language has shifted, however, to reflect an emergent construct of doctor-patient *collaboration*. Altering the traditional medical paternalism, the anti-ageing provider takes on a new role as guide and mentor – just as the patient, too, must take on a new role as active participant and their own caretaker.

Founded on Foucault's analysis of the medical project, Armstrong (1995) described the 'new' regime of biomedicine as 'surveillance medicine'. Prescient of the hallmarks of anti-ageing medicine, Armstrong argued that preoccupations with diet, exercise, stress, sex, and the like, become 'vehicles for encouraging the community to survey itself,' and that the 'ultimate triumph of Surveillance Medicine would be its internalization by all the population' (1995: 399).

This sentiment is echoed in our interviews with providers, who say they do not simply 'tell' a patient what to do, but instead actively 'help' the patient do it and keep them on course. To be effective in this role, the provider must have intense personal knowledge about a patient and both provider and patient must spend significant time together – conducting full physical examinations, running many lab tests to create baseline data and monitor changes thereafter, and having follow-up meetings to discuss results and devise and revise treatment plans. This is, above all, a 'joint process between the physician and the patient' (P20). This process rests not only on the patient's willingness to submit themselves to the battery of tests, but to take responsibility for making significant lifestyle changes. The surveillance happens not only in the presence of the clinician's office, but thereafter in all aspects of the patient's life.

There is one other requirement that is not expressed explicitly (or at least voluntarily) in our interviews: most of the time, patients must be able and willing to pay on a cash-only basis – and given the intensity of these services, the price tag is high. Financial resources, therefore, become a significant barrier and only those who have resources can seek these services. When patients take control of their health, and are successful in their efforts, both patients and doctors are left with the sense that they are doing something of great import. Their joint work becomes what Williams (1998) calls a 'moral performance'.

Conclusion

Optimising health through individualised attention and manipulation is a hallmark of 21st century biomedicine, where the focus is less on norms and more on the customisation of care (Clarke *et al.* 2003). With its emphasis on small-scale practices and intimate knowledge of the patient, anti-ageing medicine embodies many of these ideals. In fact, much of anti-ageing medicine is an example of 'boutique medicine' and an instantiation of a backlash to corporatised, insurance-run American biomedicine.

These providers are, however, not necessarily setting the medical world on fire with the latest genomic or other cutting-edge technologies. In our study of anti-ageing medicine, practitioners use primarily 'low-tech' versions of technologies of the self. In contrast to popular images of anti-ageing medicine utilising the latest available technological advances, anti-ageing medicine, as described by our practising clinicians, relies on strategies that are surprisingly simple yet still reflective of the contemporary era of biomedicine through heightened surveillance, vigilance, and health management. This includes the emphasis on collaboration and co-operation between physicians and patients.

Anti-ageing providers consider their approaches cutting edge because they strive for personal and individualised treatment, with one eye on prevention and the other on optimisation. The rhetoric of customisation and optimisation are indeed part of the ideal practice of conventional medicine, and therefore considered an important part of healthcare in the 21st century. Its importance, however, stems in part from the idea that this is what patients *want*, and fulfilling consumer demand has become an integral part of healthcare delivery in the United States – at least for those who can afford it. The turn towards thinking of healthcare as a commodity and of patients as consumers is the crucial backdrop for thinking about the emergence of anti-ageing medicine.

In describing their practice as 'conventional' and their philosophy as 'medicine as an art', it is clear that practitioners are also trying to legitimise their work in the face of criticism. Anti-ageing medicine, with its dependence on hormonal supplementation, and the move away from the established insurance-based healthcare payment arrangements, is at great risk of condemnation and question. By positioning their work as a return to the 'golden age' of medicine based on intimate relationships between physicians and patients, anti-ageing practitioners effectively depoliticise their work through an appeal to medical professionalism.

The assembly-line approach to medicine that conventional providers describe is also what patients dislike. Anti-ageing providers attempt to meet consumer demand by returning to a practice of treating the patient as an individual. This is predicated on the need for an intimate provider-patient relationship that rests on collaboration and trust. The only way they see to ensure this is to take the time to 'get to know' patients, understand their particular circumstances, and develop an elaborate treatment program tailored to them.

In the end, responsibility for managing the ageing body is put in the hands of patients and providers themselves, particularly those of the patients who do all the work of adhering to the regimen. But anti-ageing medicine serves a set of larger social goods: As patients change their lives in these ways, and as providers deliver medicine in these ways, patients enact practices that serve medical institutions (in reinforcing norms of personal responsibility), society (in improving the health of the population), and individuals and families (in increasing lifespan and ensuring that those years are healthier).

The neo-liberal emphasis on individual responsibility for one's own health takes on a particular tone when it comes to preventing the diseases and disabilities of old age. Historically, the ideology for a civil society was that the welfare of older people was a state responsibility. Whether or not this was ever actualised is debatable, but the idea that the elderly should be cared for through state support has long been part of public discourse. Now, however, even the notion of public welfare for older people cannot be taken for granted, especially in the United States. With questions about the long-term viability of Social Security and Medicare, devolution of responsibility for care falls to older people themselves. And with sky-rocketing healthcare costs and the recent economic downturn that has drained stock market-based retirement accounts, individuals have good reason to worry about their ability to provide for themselves in old age, especially in the face of serious or chronic illnesses. Anti-ageing medicine patients are responding to this call and worrying early and often, with many patients seeking anti-ageing treatments while in their forties and fifties. The American backdrop for this analysis is clearly important. The practitioners we interviewed raised the issue of healthcare organisation in the US as an important consideration for their move to anti-ageing medicine. We would encourage other empirical studies of anti-ageing medicine in other national and cultural settings.

The impetus to stay healthy in middle and later life may indeed reflect new discourses about the presence and role of biomedicine in all aspects and periods of life. But we should also consider the other pragmatic, structural, and material reasons why individuals might seek out a medical specialty which, on the surface, seeks to control human ageing and stave off the challenges of old age. In societies that place a premium on staying as healthy as possible for as long as possible, the desire and demand for anti-ageing medicine is clearly rational, even if it comes with an equally premium price tag.

Acknowledgements

The authors wish to thank the other members of our research team for their integral contributions to the conceptualisations of the project and data collection: Eric Juengst, Marcie Lambrix, and Roselle Ponsaran. Support for this study and for the preparation of this chapter was provided by the National Institute on Aging (NIA) and the National Human Genome Research Institute (NHGRI), Grant 1R01 AG020916-04A1.

References

American Academy for Anti-Aging Medicine (2008) About A4M. http://www.worldhealth.net/pages/about accessed September 13, 2008.

Armstrong, D. (1995) The rise of surveillance medicine, *Sociology of Health and Illness*, 17, 393–404.

Armstrong, D. (2007) Professionalism, indeterminacy and the EBM Project, *Biosocieties*, 2, 73–84.

Binstock, R.H. (2003) The war on 'Anti-Aging Medicine', *The Gerontologist*, 43, 4–14.

Charmaz, K. (2006) *Constructing Grounded Theory: a Practical Guide through Qualitative Analysis*. New York: Sage Publications, Inc.

Clarke, A.E., Shim, J.K., Mamo, L., Fosket, J.R. and Fishman, J.R. (2003) Biomedicalization: technoscientific transformations of health, illness, and U.S. biomedicine. *American Sociological Review*, 68, 161–94.

Elliott, C. (2003) *Better Than Well: American Medicine Meets the American Dream*. New York: W. W. Norton and Company.

Estes, C.L. and Binney, E.A. (1989) The biomedicalization of aging: dangers and dilemmas, *The Gerontologist*, 29, 587–96.

Fishman, J.R., Binstock, R.H. and Lambrix, M.A. (2008) Anti-aging science: the emergence, maintenance, and enhancement of a discipline, *Journal of Aging Studies*, 22, 295–303.

Foucault, M. (1988) *Technologies of the Self: a Seminar with Michel Foucault*. Amherst: University of Massachusetts Press.

Franklin, Sarah. (2003) Ethical biocapital. In Franklin, S. and Rose, N. (eds) *Remaking Life and Death: Toward an Anthropology of the Biosciences*. Santa Fe: School of American Research Press.

Huberman, M. and Miles, M.B. (2002) *The Qualitative Researcher's Companion*. New York: Sage Publications Inc.

Mamo, L. and Fishman, J. (2001) Potency in all the right places: Viagra as a technology of the gendered body, *Body and Society*, 7, 13–35.

Marshall, B.L. and Katz, S. (2002) Forever functional: sexual fitness and the aging male body, *Body and Society*, 8, 43–70.

Mykytyn, C. E. (2006) Anti-aging medicine: a patient/practitioner movement to redefine aging, *Social Science and Medicine*, 62, 643–53.

Parens, E. (2003) *Enhancing Human Traits: Ethical and Social Implications*. Washington D.C.: Georgetown University Press.

Rose, N. (2006) *The Politics of Life Itself: Biomedicine, Power, and Subjectivity in the Twenty-First Century*. Princeton: Princeton University Press.

Settersten Jr., R.A., Flatt, M.A. and Ponsaran, R. (2008) From the lab to the front of the line: How individual biogerontologists navigate their contested field, *Journal of Aging Studies*, 22, 304–12.

Williams, S. (1998) Health as moral performance: ritual, transgression and taboo, *Health*, 2, 435–57.

4

Science, medicine and virility surveillance: 'sexy seniors' in the pharmaceutical imagination

Barbara L. Marshall

Introduction: sexualising seniors

It is not so long ago that studies of sexuality excluded older people. For example, the National Health and Social Life survey, one of the most widely cited studies on the prevalence of sexual dysfunctions in the US, surveyed only those between 18 and 59 years of age (Laumann *et al.* 1999).[1] The British National Survey of Sexual Attitudes and Lifestyles, data from which were published in 1994, also had a maximum age of 59 in the sample, with the rationale that 'many of the topics for which data were collected are known not to affect older people greatly' (Wellings *et al.* 1994: 23).[2] Even the Massachusetts Male Aging Study (Feldman *et al.* 1994), widely considered to have established the relationship between ageing and erectile dysfunction, did not include men over the age of 70.

More recently, increased interest in the sexuality of older people has been apparent both by their inclusion in surveys, and by the extent to which scientific findings about their sex lives have been reported in the mainstream press. In 2007, a study out of the University of Chicago (Lindau *et al.* 2007), published in the *New England Journal of Medicine*, spurred media headlines like 'Sexed up seniors do it more than you think' (MSNBC 2007) and 'Senior partners: still randy' (Agrell 2007). In 2008, it was a Finnish study, published in the *American Journal of Medicine* (Koskimaki *et al.* 2008), that had the press urging older men to 'have sex, and have sex often' (ABC/Reuters 2008) if they wanted to maintain their sexual function. Also widely reported on in 2008 was a Dutch study, published in the *Journal of Urology*, which was aimed at determining whether or not some common complaints of ageing – namely urinary, bowel and erectile problems – were part of the normal ageing process. They concluded that while deterioration of urinary and bowel function were not, an 'increasing prevalence of erectile dysfunction can be related to the "normal" aging process'. They go on to qualify this, however, by suggesting that 'normal aging does not necessarily mean healthy aging ...' (Korfage *et al.* 2008: 5). Clearly, new agendas have emerged which have put the relationship between ageing and sexuality at centre stage for both scientific research and public health promotion.

There is now a substantial body of research documenting the development of, and subsequent impact of, Viagra and other erectile dysfunction drugs (*e.g.* Loe 2004a, Mamo and Fishman 2001, Marshall 2002, Potts and Tiefer 2006). While historically sexual decline in both men and women was assumed to be an inevitable consequence of growing older, this assumption has now been reversed. Changing sexual capacities once associated with 'normal' ageing are now pathologised as sexual dysfunctions that require treatment. As with other aspects of health in contemporary societies characterised by 'healthism' (Crawford 1980) and 'surveillance medicine' (Armstrong 1995), individuals are encouraged to continually monitor their sexual function, manage risk, and seek medical treatment where indicated.

With age seen as the most universal risk factor for sexual dysfunction, the latter becomes re-framed as potentially progressive and as indicating 'unhealthy' ageing. As populations age, the prevalence of sexual dysfunction and the anticipated market for pharmaceutical solutions are predicted to increase dramatically. While currently a trend most notable in regions such as Europe, North America and Japan, the United Nations identifies population ageing as a global and accelerating trend, and notes that 'the population of most countries of the world is aging' (United Nations Department of Economic and Social Affairs, Population Division 2007: xxix). The pharmaceutical reconstruction of sexual lifecourses thus has the potential to become a global phenomenon, although local contexts will always shape the way that eldersex is discussed, sold and practised.

In this chapter, I explore the new place of sexuality in conceptions of 'healthy ageing'. First, I will briefly recount some key shifts in the sex/age problematic as it has been taken on by sexual science and sexual medicine. I will then turn to the emerging emphasis on 'virility surveillance' as sexual function is taken not only to be a marker of successful ageing in general, but as the 'canary in the coal mine'[3] with respect to health status. This will lead to a consideration of the place of sexual function in the biomedicalisation of ageing, and its relationship to what I call the 'pharmaceutical imagination'. Finally, I consider the status of sexualised ageing bodies in a global biotech market.

Sexual medicine and the sex/age problematic

> Genuine senile impotence can never be the subject of rational medical treatment, though one may sometimes pity an amorous old man (Vecki 1920: 409).

> Few fields in medicine can match the rapid progress that has been made in our understanding of male erectile function. ... The current state of the art is a pre-eminent example of what is achievable by systematic and conscientious application of basic research and clinical observation (Morales 1998: xv).

The currently hegemonic version of sexual medicine likes to tell a Whiggish history of progressive enlightenment (*e.g.* Goldstein 2004). Once upon a time, the story goes, doctors dismissed peoples' sexual problems as all in their heads, or, in the case of older people, as the result of natural decline that they should simply accept. Then, discoveries in the laboratory revealed the truth about how bodies worked, and drugs to fix their mechanical glitches were developed. Medicine finally shed its reticence to intervene in sexual disorders, and brought the arsenal of rational scientific treatment to an area of human life that was formerly shrouded in ignorance. The future looks bright, as the limitless horizons of pharmacological and gene therapy promise even greater treatment options. However, as studies of medicine from the social sciences and humanities have shown, medical histories are far more complex than this. The development of sexual medicine is no exception, with definitions of, and explanations for, sexual dysfunctions shifting in relation to both available treatments and cultural trends. Between the late 19th and the late 20th centuries, the aetiological pendulum for sexual dysfunctions swung from organic to psychological and back to organic causes.

The degree of medical importance accorded to age as a cause of sexual decline has varied historically. Common wisdom in the late 19th century often cited the age of 50 as that at which one should renounce physical love as one's desires and powers waned. Desire and power were separated out here (what sexologists would today treat as libido and function). Desire naturally waned, and while sexual powers (presumably erectile function) could be husbanded carefully to last as long as desire did, sexual excesses could easily deplete them. As William Hammond noted in 1887, 'No cause is ... so destructive to the happiness of the average man as the loss of his virile power while his desire still exists not measurably impaired' (1887: 93). But sex after 50 was often deemed to be exhausting and injurious to body and soul (*e.g.* Nichols 1873). It was nature's plan, for both men and women, to link peak sexual desire and power to the reproductive years, and these, once past, signalled a new, sexless phase of life (*e.g.* Drake 1902, Stall 1901).

The association of sexual vitality with youth (and the corresponding association of ageing with desexualisation) has long been integral to the general promotion of anti-ageing therapies (*e.g.* Sengoopta 2006). Part of the problem for earlier reincarnations of anti-ageing medicine – and especially for that related to sexuality – was a continuing association with quackery and the less-reputable rejuvenation enterprises that were seen to prey on the sexually weak. The reticence of mainstream medicine to promote sexual rejuvenation could be seen, for example, in the downplaying of the potential sexual benefits of testosterone supplementation in treating the 'male climacteric' in its American incarnation in the 1940s (Marshall 2007, Watkins 2007, 2008). Despite this, as those such as Susan Squier (1999) and Elisabeth Watkins (2008) have pointed out, throughout the 20th century the idea of rejuvenation – including sexual rejuvenation – continued to find resonance in the popular imagination despite the pooh-poohing of the medical establishment. Not until the latter part of the 20th century did mainstream medicine embrace the enterprise of sexual rehabilitation, especially with respect to ageing persons.

The clinical and market success of Viagra – introduced to the American market in 1998, and subsequently a global blockbuster – was pivotal in creating new institutional structures and health promotion discourses around sexual health and in constructing ageing bodies as sites of biomedical intervention. The enormous interest in sexual dysfunction by pharmaceutical companies and their eagerness to fund research, conferences, publications and 'disease awareness' has created for dysfunction-focused sexual medicine the same sorts of markers of disciplinary structure that other specialties have had for many years (textbooks, journals, institutional centres, CME programs). This interest has extended across the globe, as indicated by Viagra manufacturer Pfizer's sponsorship of a massive study of older adults' sexual experiences and attitudes in 29 countries (Nicolosi *et al.* 2004), and the establishment of global networks of researchers and organisations focused on sexual dysfunction, such as the International Society for Sexual Medicine.[4] The concept of sexual health itself, once defined as reproductive health and absence of sexually transmitted disease, has become increasingly focused on sexual desire and performance (Giami 2002). While those other agendas are still evident with respect to younger persons, when seniors are the concern, sexual 'health' is largely equated with 'sexual function', and new 'anti-decline' narratives have emerged (Potts *et al.* 2006). No longer constrained by the limits of 'normality', eldersex is opened up to the discourse of functionality (Katz and Marshall 2004).

Virility surveillance

Problematisation of the normal is central to what David Armstrong (1995) has called 'surveillance medicine'. In surveillance medicine, 'health no longer exists in a strict binary relationship to illness', and is characteristic of 'a world in which everything is normal and at the same time precariously abnormal, and in which a future that can be transformed remains a constant possibility' (1995: 400). As he describes it, 'in Surveillance Medicine each illness is simply a nodal point in a network of health status monitoring. The problem is less illness per se but the semi-pathological pre-illness at-risk state' (1995: 401). Signs of waning sexual function in ageing bodies act in precisely this manner.

In contemporary sexual medicine, 'sexual health' (particularly in ageing men) has been treated as a 'canary in the coal mine'; that is, as an indicator of their general health in mid-to late life. If the canary stops singing, it should be taken as a warning sign of imminent danger to health. As the keynote speech at the 2006 World Congress on the Aging Male put it, 'Sexual Health is the Portal to Men's Health' (Shabsigh 2006). An editorial in the *Journal of Men's Health and Gender* similarly proclaimed that '... sexual health is one of the gates to men's health in general!' (Meryn 2006: 318). The press release for the 2007 North American Congress on the Aging Male was headlined 'Failure to treat sexual dysfunction can pose serious risk for aging males' and warned that 'leading research scientists and clinicians from around the world are reaching the consensus that failure to treat decreased sexual function in aging males may actually put them at greater risk for heart disease and cancer' (Canadian Society for the Study of the Aging Male 2007). A recent article in the journal *The Aging Male* goes so far as to call men with erectile dysfunction 'lucky', suggesting that as an early indicator of testosterone deficiency or metabolic syndrome, it might bring them in for treatment at an earlier stage (Corona 2008).

While definitions of virility are generally associated with masculinity and masculine potency, I use it here as a more expansive standard for performative, phallocentric sexuality which includes women's sexual desire for, and response to, heterosexual intercourse in its purview. While women lack the external index of the erect penis to indicate their overall health, they are included in the project of virility surveillance by proxy, or with promissory claims that regular sex will boost their immune systems, their oestrogen levels, keep them young-looking, and prevent incontinence by exercising their Kegel muscles (BioSante Pharmaceuticals 2008, Ehrenfeld 2007). While not as dramatic as the warning messages regarding men, the promises to women still rest on a reinforcement of the benefits to general health (and in this case, beauty) of regular sexual activity (presumably intercourse) into late life, and suggest that women's sexual function also needs to be continually monitored.

The widespread media coverage of supposedly epidemic rates of sexual dysfunction has fostered an atmosphere of amplified risk for both men and women, and has intensified the move towards self-surveillance, monitoring and diagnosis. Versions of scales and indices assessing sexual function, originally developed in the context of clinical pharmaceutical research, are reproduced across a range of media as self-diagnostic quizzes, inviting individuals to screen themselves and consult their doctors for appropriate treatment options. For example, the Androgen Deficiency in the Aging Male scale, which was developed for clinical research on testosterone deficiency (Morley *et al.* 2000), has appeared as a self-screening quiz in newspaper articles (Black 2001), websites (http://www.andropause.com) and ads in magazines such as *Golf*. If individuals are negligent in screening themselves, doctors are encouraged to engage in 'pro-active questioning about a patient's sexual relations during routine consultations' (Kirby 2004: 256). They are told to monitor their patients for signs of sexual decline by conducting 'proactive sexual health' interviews (Nusbaum and Hamilton 2002) and by 'routinely asking about libido, sexual function and stamina' (MacIndoe 2003: 256). The lead author of the University of Chicago study mentioned earlier suggested in an interview that she would 'like to see physicians begin asking patients if they are sexually active, how their sex lives are going, or if there is anything preventing them from having sex' (Lindau, as cited in Agrell 2007). In short, ageing bodies have been reclassified as sexual bodies and targeted for rehabilitation.

This reclassification of ageing bodies is, however, far from a gender-neutral project. As Stephen Katz and I have argued elsewhere (Marshall and Katz 2006), the current pharmaceutical technologies of sexual enhancement are premised upon a *re-sexing* of ageing bodies. That is, ageing, which had traditionally been understood as weakening the conventional logic that the sexes were biological 'opposites', is now the basis on which sexual difference is re-instated. If the shifts in sexuality once associated with normal ageing were taken as signifying de-masculinisation and de-femininisation, then reversing the effects of ageing requires re-sexing bodies and identities to align them with culturally dominant notions of heterosexuality and the hegemony of penetrative sex.

Sexual function and biomedicalisation: tales from the pharmaceutical imagination

Carrol Estes and Elisabeth Binney (1989), in their prescient paper on the biomedicalisation of ageing, argued that ageing was increasingly becoming defined as a medical pathology requiring intervention, with widespread consequences for how ageing bodies were known, treated and experienced. Revisiting that thesis some years later, Kaufman and colleagues (2004) confirmed that biomedical advances continue to shape knowledge about ageing bodies, and crucially influence public opinion and personal expectations regarding 'normal' ageing and medical intervention in later life. As we have seen, 'normal', when it comes to ageing, and especially when it comes to ageing and sexuality, is not what it used to be.

Centrally implicated in the contemporary biomedicalisation of ageing and sexuality is the expansion of pharmaceutical culture, although not as a simple process of pharmaceutical imperialism. As Nikolas Rose (2006: 480) suggests, 'it is too simple to see actual or potential patients as passive beings, acted upon by the marketing devices of Big Pharma who invent medical conditions and manipulate individuals into identifying with them'. I suggest that the concept of the 'pharmaceutical imagination' might capture the contemporary orientation of biomedical research into sexual function and dysfunction, and the manner in which it provides an important set of resources for understanding and managing sexuality (Marshall 2009). The pharmaceutical imagination frames a range of possible narratives whose common thread is the assumption of a linear model of scientific progress which proceeds towards physiological explanations and results in pharmacological solutions. In this framing, knowledge about drug effects (either already existing or anticipated) is incorporated into the production of knowledge about bodies (including sexual bodies). As applied to sexuality, the pharmaceutical imagination defines 'sex' in terms of the physiological capacity for intercourse, largely interpreted in terms of youthful bodily standards. As such, it trades in a rather narrow understanding of what counts as sex and sexual pleasure. The pharmaceutical imagination assumes that the biological body is a realm unto itself, neatly separable from its cultural materialisation or subjective experience. It circumscribes what is to be considered problematic, valorises particular kinds of solutions and accords significance to some agents over others in constructing explanatory narratives for the success or failure of those solutions. But bodies are, of course, never outside culture, and it is from this point that the pharmaceutical imagination draws its gendered (and ageist) character. Assumptions about 'naturally' (hetero)sexual bodies whose essential properties can be known and then restored obscure the hegemonic conceptions of gender and sexuality upon which they rest.

The pharmaceutical imagination also embodies a future-orientation: there is an optimism linking patients, practitioners, researchers and industry that, whatever the problem, a better chemical solution is on the horizon. It is this optimism that provides a key point of articulation between sexual medicine and anti-ageing medicine (see *e.g.* Mykytyn 2006). Articulating a similar point, Kaufman and her colleagues conclude that, 'knowledge of aging and disease today, like knowledge of life itself, is intrinsically linked to interventions' and 'the coupling of hope with the normalization of life-extending interventions affects our understandings of a 'normal' and therefore desired old age' (Kaufman *et al.* 2004: 735–6).

As Stephen Katz and I (2004) have argued, the binary of 'functional and dysfunctional' appears to be supplanting that of 'normal and abnormal'. The pharmaceutical imagination underpins this binary as it links clinical scientists, medical practitioners and patients pursuing treatments to manage sexual dysfunction.

First, there is an important distinction to be made between 'functional' and 'normal'. For example, it may be 'normal' for erectile function or testosterone levels to decline in ageing men, or for libido or lubrication to vary in women at different life stages (or even on different days of the week). However, because functionality does not have to correlate with normality, standards of sexual function can redefine what is statistically normal as dysfunctional, and hence treatable. Clearly, sexual function is more of a cultural ideal than a biological 'norm' or capacity. But, because treatments to produce functionality are premised on the biological effects of drugs, they link these fluid cultural ideals to perceived biological capacities. For example, the clinical success of drugs like Viagra in producing erections has been instrumental in reinforcing a notion of male sexual function as a strictly physiological capacity that can be manipulated and enhanced. That they can do this so effectively is related to the fact that conceptions of functionality are premised upon measurability and standardisation.

Thinking about 'function' in terms of measurability and standardisation is required by the logic of pharmaceutical testing. Functional states must be quantified and stabilised as endpoints for evaluating interventions. The measurement of functional states is directed at quantifying drug effects, and the effects that drugs produce become the endpoints against which their success as interventions is measured. For example, a drug aimed at treating erectile dysfunction is evaluated by how much it increases penile rigidity. However, the indices designed to measure drug effects, as components of clinical trials (which require standardised and measurable data to report to regulatory bodies), also then circulate as diagnostic tools. For example, the International Index of Erectile Function was a 15-item index developed to measure the efficacy of treatment for erectile dysfunction in clinical trials (Rosen *et al.* 1997). After demonstrating its ability to detect 'real treatment effects' in those clinical trials, it was shortened to five items to make it better suited for use as a self-administered screening tool for erectile dysfunction (Rosen 1999). The end result is that standards of function become inseparable *from* treatment effects. Therefore, if a drug effect is to produce increased penile rigidity in men or increased lubrication in women, these become the standards for evaluating sexual function, and those from which 'dysfunctions' are distinguished.

Once functional states are accepted as adaptable states, the transformation of previously normative experiences into dysfunctions or pathologies demands intervention. Thus, drugs and their effects become important points of articulation between cultural ideals and bodily capacities. Acknowledging the latter by exploring the manner in which particular narratives materialise them in no way means resurrecting a 'natural body' separated off from culture. Rather, it takes up the challenge articulated in recent science studies, to confront 'how matter comes to matter' (Barad 2003). This work suggests a more complex understanding of the biology/culture interface which recognises that biology is better understood as a source of variation and diversity than it is of uniformity (Hird 2004). As feminist critics have rightly pointed out, the standardisation of sexual function central to sexual pharmacology pathologises the heterogeneity of sexual bodies and experiences (see *e.g.* Koch *et al.* 2006, Potts *et al.* 2004, Tiefer 2006a).

Simon Williams has suggested that a productive point of departure for those thinking through the biological/social nexus might be 'to deconstruct the apparent unity of 'biology' as a disciplinary matrix and to think instead of anatomy, physiology, neurobiology, endocrinology, genetics and so on, thereby reducing the risk of simplistic resolutions or realignments of biology and sociology' (2006: 15). Yet such deconstructions, already the stock in trade of scientific medicine, may be enfolded into marketing logics of unending frontiers of discovery, as fungible aetiologies are promoted for loosely bounded and vaguely defined disorders. Leonore Tiefer, for example, has traced how endocrinology quietly replaced vascular biology as the presumed explanatory paradigm for female sexual dysfunction, illustrating well how 'the effort to match up some drug with FSD moved freely among symptoms and labels' (Tiefer 2006b: 439). Treatments for sexual dysfunctions in ageing men have also seen shifting, and more precise justifications, as erectile function and libido become tied to different physiological anchors variously conceptualised as vascular or hormonal (Marshall 2007, Watkins 2008) and increasingly, genetic (Kendirci et al. 2006). All of these demonstrate the varying ways in which sexual dysfunctions and the sexual bodies that suffer from them are materialised and accorded facticity and explanatory power. Furthermore, these shifting aetiologies have visceral effects: understanding one's sexual experiences as vascular or neurochemical or hormonal has implications for the way they are experienced, and the steps that might be taken to try and change them. One does not need to actually use pharmaceutical remedies to experience this aetiological shift: revised standards of sexual functionality, premised on biotechnical possibilities, reconstruct sexual lifecourses in such a way as to set new expectations and create new sites for anxiety about our ability to meet them.

Sexy technogenarians?

It is widely recognised that '[A] massive and growing market for drugs and devices to treat sexual problems targets older adults' (Lindau et al. 2007: 762). Thus, age still matters when it comes to sexuality, but the meanings and practices associated with ageing sexuality have been radically reconfigured. Revised standards of functionality have reshaped norms of ageing, and biomedical interventions are integral to this reconfiguration and reshaping. Since these very standards are premised on drug effects, then drugs are deemed to be 'what works'. Normality becomes fluid, defined by the pharmaceutical possibilities for optimising function, fuelled by the optimism of limitless potential.

Pharmaceutical industry reports continue to see a large global market for treating both men's and women's sexual dysfunctions (Spectra Intelligence 2006). In the wake of Pfizer's market success with Viagra, competing pharmaceutical companies have brought their own erectile drugs to market – Levitra and Cialis. Lilly, the makers of Cialis, has begun marketing a once-daily version of their medication as an alternative to the current on-demand version now available, transforming erectile capacity into a continually biochemically modifiable state (Berenson 2006). While erectile drugs continue to dominate the market, new multi-million dollar market opportunities are seen in treating hypoactive desire disorder in women and androgen deficiency in ageing men. A 2005 report in *Science* suggested that two dozen companies have sexuo-pharmaceuticals for women in development (Enserink 2005), and commentators continue to predict a growth market for treatments for 'andropause', premature ejaculation, and erectile difficulties (*Biotech Week* 2003). Underlying this optimism is an assumption that more knowledge about the physiology and neurochemistry of sexuality will advance the linear model of scientific progress that underpins the pharmaceutical imagination. And, as noted above, as populations age, the corresponding markets for biotechnologies aimed at enhancing their sexual function grow ever larger.

There is an urgent need for more qualitative research to provide some narrative resources that can broaden our understanding of ageing and sexuality beyond the crudely reductive 'use it or lose it (and ask your doctor to provide our remedy so you can use it)' script provided by pharmaculture. While there are now a number of studies exploring the meaning and experience of sexuality in the lives of older people which provide a richer, more complex perspective on sexuality and ageing (Gott 2004, Kleinplatz *et al.* 2009a, 2009b, Loe 2004b, Potts *et al.* 2006, Vares *et al.* 2007), there is still much to be learned. For example, about half of Viagra prescriptions are not renewed (Nehra *et al.* 2003), but little is known about *why* those prescriptions are not renewed. Some practitioners of sexual medicine speculate that the reasons for 'non-compliance' with such drug therapy might include inadequate patient instruction on how to use the medication (Gruenwald *et al.* 2006), and low success rates due to complicating factors such as 'androgen deficiency', requiring co-treatment with testosterone (Shabsigh *et al.* 2008). Assumptions are made about 'unmet needs' as the basis for future sexuo-pharmaceutical development.[5] However, what qualitative research is available with older men and women, including Viagra users, suggests that they have not entirely bought into the decline/anti-decline narratives offered by the pharmascript (see for example Potts *et al.* 2004, Potts *et al.* 2006, Vares *et al.* 2007). For example, as Potts *et al.* summarised the findings from their research:

> Some of the men in our study relay a progress story associated with adapting to, enjoying, and even preferring, sexual experiences and practices that are quite different from their preferences when they were younger, and/or when they were able to readily experience erections; these alternative stories are not necessarily related to erections, male orgasm or coital sex. Such accounts disrupt the arguably common-sense notion that healthy meaningful sex for life for men (and their partners) requires the maintenance of 'rock hard' erections and frequent penetrative sex (2006: 325).

Another study by Canadian psychologist Peggy Kleinplatz and her colleagues (2009a, 2009b) confirms that for many older men and women, sex improves with age and experience. Based on interviews with men and women over the age of 60 who had been in long-term relationships, they found that conventionally defined sexual 'function' (*i.e.* intercourse to orgasm performed by erect penises and lubricated vaginas) is neither necessary nor sufficient for 'great sex'. Instead, such factors as communication, connection, intimacy and fun were repeatedly stressed as defining optimal sexual experiences (2009a). Participants in their study told them that 'the quality of their sex lives had changed over time as well as perceptions of what sex might be or could become' (2009b: 16). Such accounts remind us that, despite the best efforts of pharmaceutical marketers, technologies will never be taken up uniformly or without active engagement on the part of users, and that 'technogenarians' are no exception.

Conclusions

In this chapter, I have suggested a recent and significant shift in understandings of the place of sexuality in the biology of 'healthy' ageing. Whether sexual function is seen as an indicator of overall health and/or a warning sign of disease, the enfolding of compulsory sexual activity into health promotion signals a new regime of virility surveillance. The question is no longer whether or not changing sexual capacities are an aspect of normal ageing or a health problem requiring intervention: contemporary sexual medicine suggests they are both.

While a more positive image of elder sex than has held sway in the past is certainly welcome, implicit is an underlying assumption that those who choose to opt out of conventionally-defined sexual activity as they age are victims of a pathology. Subtly reiterated is the message of risk and decline in the absence of appropriate intervention. The emphasis on reliability and standardisation of sexual function promoted by sexual medicine pathologises the heterogeneity of sexual experiences and sexual bodies, especially where age is concerned. Everyone wanting or being able to 'do it' in the same way, for all time, hardly seems to acknowledge a diversity of experience across the lifespan. As long as being sexualised means adhering to youthful norms of sexual attractiveness and prioritising sexual intercourse as the gold standard of sexual function, 'it is not old age that is being sexualised but rather an extended middle age. The incompatibility of sexuality and old age is hence reinforced' (Gott 2004: 2). On the contrary, as Kleinplatz *et al.* (2009b: 15) suggest, 'it stands to reason that individuals and couples ... who have developed the capacity over the years to experience optimal sexuality have much to teach the rest of us'.

Against the backdrop of work on the biomedicalisation of ageing, I have used the concept of the 'pharmaceutical imagination' to explore how drug effects, either existing or just anticipated, are implicated in the production of knowledge about sexual function and sexual bodies. As the ageing population represents a critical and growing biotech market, the meaning of 'normal' ageing, including sexual ageing, stands to be radically reconfigured. The discursive shape of that meaning, as circumscribed by the clinical research, media reports, and health promotion literatures that I have reviewed here, is also shaped by the embodied, lived experience of ageing men and women, and I endorse Clarke and colleagues' call (among others) for 'case studies that attend to the heterogeneities of biomedicalization practices and effects in different lived situations' (2003: 185).

In 2006, an article on the potential applications of gene therapy for treating erectile dysfunction concluded that:

> Although preclinical studies have highlighted the application of local gene therapy as a viable treatment option for ED in *diverse pathologic conditions including diabetes, ageing, hypercholesterolaemia, and cavernous nerve injury*, this therapeutic approach still requires more clinical studies in humans (Kendirci *et al.* 2006: 1218, emphasis added)

What is remarkable here is not the extension of gene therapy into the treatment of sexual performance problems – that has been on the horizon for at least a decade – but the explicit inclusion of 'ageing' itself as a generalisable 'pathologic condition'. As sexual medicine and biogerontology join forces, the remarkable disassembling and reconstitution of ageing, sexualised bodies that has occurred over the last 150 years seems headed for some new frontiers. A key task of critical studies of science, health and ageing is surely to open up to scrutiny the stories about sexuality and ageing narrated by the pharmaceutical imagination.

Acknowledgements

Many thanks to Meika and Kelly for all their work pulling this volume together. Both their comments as editors, and those of two anonymous referees, were invaluable in sharpening my analysis. The research on which this paper is based was supported by a grant from the Social Sciences and Humanities Research Council of Canada. Finally, I'm grateful for the insights of my colleague Stephen Katz, with whom I originally developed some of the ideas developed in this chapter.

Notes

1   This study is the source for the infamous and widely repeated 'fact' that 43% of women suffer from sexual dysfunction. For a good critique, see Bancroft, Loftus and Long (2003).
2   While the National Health and Social Life survey excluded people older than 64, despite its explicit 'life-course' perspective, the British National Survey of Sexual Attitudes and Lifestyles focussed on sexually transmitted diseases, particularly HIV/AIDS, which influenced the age profile of the sample.
3   Early coal miners would take canaries down into the mines with them, as these birds were particularly sensitive to the dangerous gases which could accumulate. As long as the canary was singing, they could be assured of their safety. If the canary died, it was a harbinger of serious risk to the miners, and prompted their evacuation.
4   The International Society for Sexual Medicine includes affiliated regional societies in Africa, Asia-Pacific, Europe, Latin America and North America (http://www.issm.info, last accessed May 14, 2009).
5   David Healy (2008: 221–31) draws on Kalman Applbaum's (2004) argument that the concept of 'unmet needs' is the lynchpin of marketing, including pharmaceutical marketing. While Healy is writing in the context of psychotropic medications, his insights regarding market segmentation and the extent to which 'anthropological' rather than therapeutic research underpins drug development and marketing are equally applicable to sexuo-pharmaceuticals.

References

ABC/Reuters (2008) Older men told to 'use it or lose it', http://www.abc.net.au/science/articles/2008/07/08/2297561.htm?site=scienceandtopic=health, last accessed October 23, 2008.

Agrell, S. (2007) Late-life lovin' governed by health, not mojo, *Globe and Mail*, Toronto. L.1., August 28.

Applbaum, K. (2004) *The Marketing Era: from Professional Practice to Global Provisioning*. New York: Routledge.

Armstrong, D. (1995) The rise of surveillance medicine, *Sociology of Health and Illness*, 17, 3, 393–404.

Bancroft, J., Loftus, J. and Long, J.S. (2003) Distress about sex: a national survey of women in heterosexual relationships, *Archives of Sexual Behavior*, 32, 3, 193–208.

Barad, K. (2003) Posthumanist performativity: toward an understanding of how Matter comes to matter, *Signs*, 28, 3, 801–31.

Berenson (2006) A daily pill to combat impotence? *New York Times*, New York, June 13.

BioSante Pharmaceuticals (2008) Let's get it on, *MarketWatch*. http://www.marketwatch.com.

Biotech Week (2003) Sexual dysfunction and andropause lead strong growth in men's segment, 289, September 10.

Black, D. (2001) Hormone-deficient men deserve a little sympathy, *Toronto Star*, Toronto. C1, C4, June 8.

Canadian Society for the Study of the Aging Male (2007) 'Failure to treat sexual dysfunction can pose a serious risk for aging males' (press release, 5 February, 2007).

Clarke, A., Shim, J.K., Mamo, L., Fosket, J.R. and Fishman, J. (2003) Biomedicalization: Technoscientific transformations of health, illness and U.S. biomedicine, *American Sociological Review*, 68, April, 161–94.

Corona, G., Forti, G. and Maggi, M. (2008) Why can patients with erectile dysfunction be considered lucky? The association with testosterone deficiency and metabolic syndrome, *The Aging Male*, 11, 4, 193–99.

Crawford, R. (1980) Healthism and the medicalization of everyday life, *International Journal of Health Sciences*, 10, 3, 365–88.

Drake, E.F.A. (1902) *What a Woman of Forty Five Ought to Know*. Philadelphia: Vir Publishing.

Ehrenfeld, T. (2007) Six reasons to have sex every week, *Newsweek*, web exclusive. http://www.news-week.com/id/74575.

Enserink, M. (2005) Let's talk about sex – and drugs, *Science*. V.308, June 10, 1578–80.

Estes, C. and Binney, E. (1989) The biomedicalization of aging, *The Gerontologist*, 29, 587–96.

Feldman, H.A., Goldstein, I., Hatzichristou, D.G., Krane, R.J. and McKinlay, J.B. (1994) Impotence and its medical and psychosocial correlates: results of the Massachusetts Male Aging Study, *Journal of Urology*, 151, 54–61.

Giami, A. (2002) Sexual health: the emergence, development and diversity of a concept, *Annual Review of Sex Research*, 13, 1–35.

Goldstein, I. (2004) Editorial: The Inaugural Issue of the Journal of Sexual Medicine, *Journal of Sexual Medicine*, 1, 1, 1–2.

Gott, M. (2004) *Sexuality, Sexual Health and Ageing*, Buckingham: Open University Press.

Gruenwald, I., Shenfield, O., Chen, J., Raviv, G., Richler, S. and Cohen, A. (2006) Positive effect of counseling and dose adjustment in patients with erectile dysfunction who failed treatment with sildenafil, *European Urology*, 50, 1, 31–3.

Hammond, W.A. (1887) *Sexual Impotence in the Male and Female*. Detroit: George S. Davis.

Healy, D. (2008) *Mania: a Short History of Bipolar Disorder*. Baltimore: Johns Hopkins University Press.

Hird, M.J. (2004) *Sex, Gender and Science*. New York: Palgrave MacMillan.

Joyce, K. and Mamo, L. (2006) Graying the Cyborg: New directions in feminist analyses of Aging, science and technology. In Calasanti, T.M. and Slevin, K.F. (eds) *Age Matters: Realigning Feminist Thinking*, New York: Routledge.

Katz, S. and Marshall, B.L. (2004) Is the functional 'normal'? Aging, sexuality and the biomarking of successful living, *History of the Human Sciences*, 17, 1, 53–75.

Kaufman, S.R., Shim, J.K. and Russ, A.J. (2004) Revisiting the biomedicalization of aging: clinical trends and ethical challenges, *The Gerontologist*, 44, 6, 731–38.

Kendirci, M., Teloken, P.E., Champion, H.C., Hellstrom, W.J.G. and Bivalacqua, T.J. (2006) Gene therapy for erectile dysfunction: fact or fiction? *European Urology*, 50, 1208–22.

Kirby, M. (2004) Erectile dysfunction: a model for men's health, *Journal of Men's Health and Gender*, 1, 2–3, 255–58.

Kleinplatz, P.J., Menard, A.D., Paquet, M-P, Paradis, N., Campbell, M., Zuccarino, D. and Mehak, L. (2009a) The components of optimum sexuality: a portrait of 'great sex', *Canadian Journal of Human Sexuality*, 18, 1–2, 1–13.

Kleinplatz, P.J., Menard, A.D., Paradis, N., Campbell, M., Dalgleish, T., Segovia, A. and Davis, K. (2009b) From closet to reality: optimal sexuality among the elderly, *The Irish Psychiatrist*, 10, 15–18.

Koch, P.B., Mansfield, P.K. and Wood, J.M. (2006) Women's sexual desire: a feminist critique, *Journal of Sex Research*, 43, 236–44.

Korfage, I.J., Roobol, M., de Koning, H.J., Kirkels, W.J., Schroder, F.H. and Essink-Bot, M.-L. (2008) Does 'normal' aging imply urinary, bowel and erectile dysfunction? *A general population survey, Urology*, 72, 1, 3–9.

Koskimaki, J., Shiri, R., Tammela, T., Hakkinen, J., Hakama, M. and Auvinen, A. (2008) Regular intercourse protects against erectile dysfunction: Tampere Aging Male Urologic Study, *The American Journal of Medicine*, 121, 592–96.

Laumann, E.O., Paik, A. and Rosen, R.C. (1999) Sexual dysfunction in the United States: prevalence and predictors, *Journal of the American Medical Association*, 281, 6, 537–44.

Lindau, S.T., Schumm, L.P., Laumann, E.O., Levinson, W., O'Muircheartaigh, C.A. and Waite, L.J. (2007) A study of sexuality and health among older adults in the United States, *New England Journal of Medicine*, 357, 8, 762–74.

Loe, M. (2004a) *The Rise of Viagra: How the Little Blue Pill Changed Sex in America*. New York: NYU Press.

Loe, M. (2004b) Sex and the senior woman: pleasure and danger in the Viagra era, *Sexualities*, 7, 3, 303–26.

MacIndoe, J.H. (2003) The challenges of testosterone deficiency, *Postgraduate Medicine*, 14, 4, 51–62.

Mamo, L. and Fishman, J. (2001) Potency in all the right places: Viagra as a technology of the gendered body, *Body and Society*, 7, 4, 13–35.

Marshall, B.L. (2002) 'Hard science': gendered constructions of sexual dysfunction in the Viagra age', *Sexualities*, 5, 2, 131–58.

Marshall, B.L. (2007) Climacteric redux? (Re)medicalizing the male menopause, *Men and Masculinities*, 9, 4, 509–29.

Marshall, B.L. (2009) Sexual medicine, sexual bodies and the pharmaceutical imagination, *Science as Culture*, 18, 2, 133–49.

Marshall, B.L. and Katz, S. (2006) From androgyny to androgens: resexing the aging body. In Calasanti, T.M. and Slevin, K.F. (eds) *Age Matters: Realigning Feminist Thinking*. New York: Routledge.

Meryn, S. (2006) Why a theme issue on sexual health, *Journal of Men's Health and Gender*, 3, 4, 317–19.

Morales, A. (1998) Preface. In Morales, A. (ed.) *Erectile Dysfunction: Issues in Current Pharmacotherapy*. London: Martin Dunitz Ltd.

Morley, J.E., Charlton, E., Patrick, P., Kaiser, F.E., Cadeau, P., McCready, D. and Perry, H.M.I. (2000) Validation of a screening questionnaire for androgen deficiency in aging males, *Metabolism*, 49, 9, 1239–42.

MSNBC (2007) Sexed up seniors do it more than you think, http://www.msnbc.msn.com/id/20395061/, last accessed 23 October, 2008.

Mykytyn, C.E. (2006) Anti-ageing medicine: a patient/practitioner movement to redefine ageing, *Social Science and Medicine*, 62, 643–53.

Nehra, A., Steers, W.D., Althof, S.E., Andersson, K.-E., Burnett, A., Costabile, R.A., Goldstein, I., Kloner, R.A., Lue, T.F., Morales, A., Rosen, R.C., Shabsigh, R., Siroky, M.B. and King, L. (2003) Third International Conference on the Management of Erectile Dysfunction: linking pathophysiology and therapeutic response, *Journal of Urology*, 170, S3–S5.

Nicolosi, A., Laumann, E., Glasser, D.B., Moreira, E.D., Paik, A. and Gingell, C. (2004) Sexual behavior and sexual dysfunctions after age 40: the global study of sexual attitudes and behaviors, *Urology*, 64, 991–97.

Nichols, T.L. (1873) *Esoteric Anthropology (the Mysteries of Man): a Comprehensive and Confidential Treatise on the Structure, Functions, Passional Attractions and Perversions, True and False Physical and Social Conditions and the Most Intimate Relations of Men and Women. Malvern*. Available from Kessinger Publishing, LLc (pb, 2003).

Nusbaum, M.R.H. and Hamilton, C.D. (2002) The proactive sexual health history, *American Family Physician*, 66, 9, 1705–12.

Potts, A., Grace, V., Gavey, N. and Vares, T. (2004) 'Viagra stories': challenging 'erectile dysfunction', *Social Science and Medicine*, 59, 489–99.

Potts, A., Grace, V.M., Vares, T. and Gavey, N. (2006) Sex for life? Men's counter-rhetoric on 'erectile dysfunction', male sexuality and ageing, *Sociology of Health and Illness*, 28, 3, 306–29.

Potts, A. and Tiefer, L. (2006) Special issue on Viagra culture, *Sexualities*, 9, 3.

Rose, N. (2006) Disorders without borders? The expanding scope of psychiatric practice, *BioSocieties*, 1, 465–84.

Rosen, R.C. (1999) Development and evaluation of an abridged, 5-item version of the International Index of Erectile Function (IIEF-5) as a diagnostic tool for erectile dysfunction, *International Journal of Impotence Research*, 11, 319–26.

Rosen, R.C., Riley, A.J. and Wagner, G. (1997) The International Index of Erectile Function (IIEF): a multidimensional scale for assessment of erectile dysfunction, *Urology*, 49, 822–30.

Sengoopta, C. (2006) *The Most Secret Quintessence of Life: Sex, Glands and Hormones, 1850–1950*. Chicago: University of Chicago Press.

Shabsigh, R. (2006) *Sexual health is the portal to men's health*, 5th World Congress on the Aging Male, Salzburg, Austria.

Shabsigh, R., Kaufman, J.M., Steidle, C. and Padma-Nathan, H. (2008) Randomized study of testosterone gel as adjunctive therapy to sildenafil in hypogonadal men with erectile dysfunction who do not respond to sildenafil alone, *Journal of Urology*, 179, (5 supplement), S97–S103.

Spectra Intelligence (2006) *The World Market for Sexual Disorders, 2005–2012: Traversing New Frontiers in Sexual Chemistry*. London: Spectra Intelligence.

Squier, S. (1999) Incubabies and rejuvenates: the traffic between technologies of reproduction and age-extension, In Woodward, K. (ed.) *Figuring Age: Women, Bodies, Generation*. Bloomington, Indiana: Indiana University Press.

Stall, S. (1901) *What a Man of Forty-Five Ought to Know*. Philadelphia: VIR Publishing Co.

Tiefer, L. (2006a) The Viagra phenomenon, *Sexualities*, 9, 3, 273–94.

Tiefer, L. (2006b) Female sexual dysfunction: a case study of disease mongering and activist resistance, *Public Library of Science Medicine*, 3, 4, 0436–39.

United Nations Department of Social and Economic Affairs, Population Divison. (2007) *Population Ageing: 2007*. New York: United Nations.

Vares, T., Potts, A., Gavey, N. and Grace, V.M. (2007) Reconceptualising cultural narratives of mature women's sexuality in the Viagra era, *Journal of Ageing Studies*, 21, 2, 153–64.

Vecki, V.G. (1920) *Sexual Impotence*. Philadelphia: W.B. Saunders Co.

Watkins, E.S. (2007) The medicalisation of male menopause in America, *Social History of Medicine*, 20, 2, 369–88.

Watkins, E.S. (2008) Medicine, masculinity and the disappearance of the male menopause in the 1950s, *Social History of Medicine*, 21, 2, 329–44.

Wellings, K., Field, J., Johnson, A.M. and Wadsworth, J. (1994) *Sexual Behaviour in Britain: the National Survey of Sexual Attitudes and Lifestyles*. London: Penguin.

Williams, S.J. (2006) Medical sociology and the biological body: where are we now and where do we go from here? health: An Interdisciplinary Journal for the Social Study of Health, *Illness and Medicine*, 10, 1, 5–30.

5

Time, clinic technologies, and the making of reflexive longevity: the cultural work of *time left* in an ageing society
Sharon R. Kaufman

Introduction

> Biomedicine, throughout the twentieth century and into our own, has thus not simply changed our relation to health and illness but has modified the things we think we might hope for and the objectives we aspire to. That is to say, it has helped make us the kinds of people we have become.
>
> Nikolas Rose (2007) *The Politics of Life Itself*

Developments in clinical intervention are having a profound impact on health and health behaviours in late life, on understandings of 'normal' old age and on ideas about longevity and the appropriate time for death. The fact that the *timing* of death is even considered to be a controllable event is a relatively new cultural phenomenon (Kaufman 2005). Surgery, drugs and implantable devices for those already old are ubiquitous. Diagnostic tests and disease prevention interventions are ordinary activities well into late life. Life-prolongation in the later years is generally considered positively everywhere, yet the ethical, existential and practical challenges which accompany the biotechnological extension of the oldest lives in the US continue to emerge.

Medical treatment at all ages is more complex than ever before, a result of the proliferation of diagnostic techniques. Greater diagnostic capability leads to ever more finely tuned therapeutic intervention which, in turn, often requires repeated decision making about whether to pursue aggressive, possibly life-prolonging treatments. In addition, medicine now offers many older persons a dual offering – the choice between (potentially) life-extending *and* palliative options. These developments open up a reflexive, ethical field in which clinical options give rise to two pressing questions in which the management of life itself is increasingly understood (for many) as an imperative: *How much more time do I want to try to live?* And, *How do I want to live the remainder of my life, given what the clinic offers?* These questions are linked to how we think about medicine's successes, standards and promises. This chapter explores the reflexive and socio-ethical terrain that patients, families and physicians enter when those two questions about longevity-making become central. *Reflexive longevity* characterises that terrain, and it refers to an emergent form of life, a mode of knowledge, reasoning and embodiment that older persons and their families come to inhabit at the site where ethics, ageing, clinic technologies and life itself meet.

The activities that comprise longevity-making, like other medical practices scrutinised by social scientists, organise and inform the governing of life and the emergence of new forms of social participation in which at least several subject-making processes occur.

Theorists have provided useful groundwork here, stressing the ways in which strategies for living and life planning are open to continual revision and how those strategies, more and more often, emphasise the relationship between identity and 'the biological' (Giddens 1991, Rose 2007). The future is 'colonised' in this scheme, collapsed into the present through both knowledge of the unavoidability of risks (known and unknown) and mechanisms for their calculation and assessment. Health risks have come to take centre stage through new knowledges about the genome, the environment, food, etc. Foundational to the site of longevity-making and to the question, *How to live*, is the idea that risk, responsibility for health (Crawford 2006) and opportunity for self-reinvention all become located within individual bodies and lives (Beck 1992). Prevention and risk reduction become important life strategies for many in which self-surveillance and its technologies are emphasised (Armstrong 1995).

Medicine in the US, unlike in Europe, exists in a cultural milieu that stresses longevity by any means and at any cost, and it both shapes and responds to emerging notions of subject-making and time. Technologies of the clinic organise the ways in which life planning strategies, risk awareness and prevention are embodied and lived. Their use links the notion of progress to each individual's (malleable and risk-aware) lifecourse. Ideals about the body, late life and the lifespan become then, also, the potentialities and promises of medicine (Shim and Russ *et al.* 2007). The clinical encounter thus serves as a mirror, reflecting back to us our hopes for the regeneration and continued health of the body / self and our assumptions that we can 'add time' through biotechniques. The information gleaned through the clinical encounter, together with the options generated by ever-advancing biomedicine, de-emphasise the inevitability of biological senescence that (eventually) leads to death.

Subjects of 'technological modernity' (Lash 2001) engage these reflexive self-making processes. The difference for old people, who are enabled to access much that the clinic offers by Medicare (the US government program that pays for acute medical care for persons aged 65 and over) is this: the clinical encounter forces an additional calculation about *how much time left* is wanted – years, months, weeks – in relation to age and in the face of the fact that one is already closer to the end of the 'natural' lifespan than to the beginning or even middle. The future has a short horizon *already*. And that future is brought into the present in the joined scenarios that medicine sets up for the seriously ill old – the risk of death *and* the potentiality of avoiding death a bit longer; the condition of being *already* (relatively) near the end of the 'natural' lifespan and the hope for extended life through biotechnological intervention. Medicine thus materialises time (Wilk 2007) in its interventions that offer the possibility of a certain number of additional weeks, months or years. But, as part of the lure of 'more' future, the clinic also problematises *time left* through the tension it creates between the fact of advanced chronological age and the idea that the amount of *time left* might be negotiable.

The ethical demand: imagining and choosing the future

Much of the work of medical sociologists and anthropologists over the last two decades has addressed the ways in which medicine and its rationality impinge deeply on the conduct of individual lives, showing how clinical technique contributes to moral sensibility (Brodwin 2000) and that 'technological reason' shapes ethical practice (Lakoff and Collier 2004). In cases of serious and chronic illness, clinical practices contain at least two temporal challenges for those who are ill – imagining certain kinds of futures in which one's corporeality is central (Mattingly 1998), and choosing among medical options in order to move toward one kind of future instead of others (Maynard 2006). These challenges constitute a particular multi-faceted ethical demand for older persons and for an ageing society that takes for granted the technologies of the clinic. That demand is organised as follows: how long to try to live via medical technique when one is already nearing the end of the 'natural' lifecourse; how to weigh both medical risks and suffering against the meanings of potentially 'added' time; and how much the value of life is determined by the amount of it perceived to be remaining. The value of the amount of *time left* and the value of life itself must be weighed against each other and against the powerful progress narratives of science and biomedicine, including shifting ideas of standard treatment and emerging notions of 'normal' ways of growing old. This is a complex set of challenges which inform subject-making in an ageing society.

The emergence of 'the timing of death' as a focus for individual-clinical control, the desire to grow older without ageing and the creation of *time left* as an ethical problem to be grappled with in the clinical sphere are contemporary dimensions of a dynamic modern temporality which has been broadly characterised, first, by the 'emptying out of time and space' (Giddens 1991: 17), in which the 'lifting out' of social relations from local context, the stretching of interpersonal and institutional relations across time and space, and the co-ordination of activities among persons physically absent from one another represent the hallmarks of modern social organisation. This 'lifting out' is accompanied by 'time-space compression,' the simultaneous speed up of the time it takes to traverse space and the overcoming of spatial barriers by diverse technologies (Harvey 1990: 240). As a result, theorists of modernity note that the time horizons of public and private decision making have shrunk; the foreseeable future is foreshortened toward the present (Guyer 2007) and decisions take place immediately (Harvey 1990: 147). Within this sensibility that emphasises the control of time, insurance becomes a primary technology and framework through which individuals and institutions calculate risk, thereby attempting to govern time and discipline the future (Ewald 1991). The future is brought into the present ('colonised') through the experience of ongoing risk calculation (recognised as imperfect and limited), in all spheres of life. I explore how, in an ageing society, the site of longevity-making provides a dramatic illustration of the contours of contemporary temporality.

The twin dimensions of the transformation of time highlighted here – the control over the timing of death and the creation of *time left* – are particularly salient to identity, sociality and ethics in affluent sectors of industrial and post-industrial societies (Clarke *et al.* 2003). This chapter begins to map the cultural work that the concept, *time left*, does, the socio-medical ways in which that notion is talked about, organised and calculated in the clinic today. It works there in several ways: as a rationale for choosing one intervention over another (and thus gives shape to clinical practice and its tensions); as the catalyst for self-bargaining about the value of life in relation to time and age; and as a reflexive tool for confronting or ignoring mortality.

In performing this multiplex work, *time left* exposes a number of features of the ethics and politics of life itself. It elicits, for example, negotiations about 'quality of life',[1] loss of meaning and the costs and worth of life-extension, especially in the face of scarce medical resources and uneven access to them. It promotes debates about what constitutes 'normal,' 'natural' and acceptable old age and infirmity. It highlights cultural ambivalence about how much to do, how far to go, in extending life. Perhaps above all, *time left* draws attention to the emphasis, especially in the US but also elsewhere, on individual responsibility not only for health but also for the quality of one's own ageing experience. Longevity has become a reflexive endeavour for those who can access clinical offerings.[2]

In the pages that follow I explore how the tools, talk and routines of the clinic shape ways of knowing the body/self, and then how those ways of knowing contribute to a subjectivity in which older persons consider and confront the value of life in relation to *time left*. I ask, what kind of subject emerges when longevity becomes a reflexive practice and an object of technological intervention and apparent choice?

Methods

This chapter is part of a larger anthropological investigation of the ways in which longevity-making practices and the ethics and existential conditions associated with them are changing. The project explores how persons aged 70 and beyond, their families and their doctors understand, deliberate and respond to the use of (potentially) life-extending procedures. It describes what 'choice' between and among therapeutic options is entailed for different actors, and it questions the ways in which value, debates about value and subjectivity are being remade in light of constant biotechnological innovation.

Here I begin to explore the socio-clinical production of *reflexive longevity* as an emergent form of life. This chapter draws from observations of more than 100 older persons who were patients in major medical centres of cardiology, cancer and transplant clinics in 2007 and 2008. Those clinics serve urban, multi-ethnic populations of insured and uninsured patients. The author observed cardiology and transplant clinics; a collaborator observed cancer clinics.[3] Both ethnographers took long-hand notes, verbatim as far as possible, of clinic exam conversations (which ranged from a few minutes to about half an hour) among patients, family members and physicians. The only exclusion criterion was age; observations included only patients aged 70 and older. The study did not stratify or organise observations by gender, class or ethnicity, however defined. We conducted open-ended follow up interviews (audio-recorded and later transcribed) in the homes of 25 patients and their family members. Those interviews ranged from 30 minutes to over an hour and probed patient and family reflections on clinical offerings, their own clear or ambivalent decision making and the kinds of quandaries they faced both during and after interventions.

The forging of older person/patient sensibility

Three stories illustrate different aspects of the temporal challenges commonly faced by older persons who arrive in the American clinic. The stories exemplify the kinds of futures that become 'present' in the form of decision-making imperatives, and they show that the risks and timing of death, pain and suffering must be considered though they cannot be pinned down. Those risks must be weighed against the potentiality, but not certainty, of longer life. The imminence of death is confronted via probabilities. The varied embodiments – of worsening health or better health or death – must be imagined because there are options. And, control over *time left* through *technological choice* is the patient's (or the family's) responsibility. These challenges – in which self-knowledge, risk assessment and the confrontation with mortality merge – are ordinary accompaniments to preventive and life-extending medical interventions for older persons in the US today. The scenarios below can happen at any age in adulthood. The point I wish to emphasise is that these scenarios become more common, indeed, have become ordinary, in an ageing society. Reflexive longevity becomes the way we live.

Together, these stories reveal the modes of knowing and reasoning that are made pos-sible, indeed, are emphasised, for older persons by technologies of the clinic. The clinic demands from seriously ill patients a sense of lived knowing through the imagination of an embodied condition (*i.e.* the effects of life-prolonging treatment, the natural course of disease, dying) that is not (yet) real. For older persons that practice of calculating *time left* – in relation to age, risk of death, and the unknown outcomes of procedures – structures decision making and meaning. That practice constitutes reflexive longevity.

Mr. A: technology organises the apprehension of risk
Mr. A, aged 86, was not feeling well following a bout of pneumonia. He asked his daughter to take him to the local hospital and he was 'shipped' to this hospital from there. Mr. A has congestive heart failure and recently suffered a heart attack. At his bedside, the cardi-ologist emphasises that he 'does not have to make a decision today' regarding what to do after the cardiac catheterisation diagnostic procedure[4] he is about to undergo. The doctor does not want to rush the patient into making treatment decisions.

When catheterisation laboratories came into being about 25 years ago their single purpose was diagnostic angiograms. Proportionally fewer patients had the procedure. The only treatments for cardiac disease were medications and coronary bypass operations. Today, cath lab procedures are curative and preventive as well as diagnostic – balloons and stents routinely open up clogged coronary arteries, enabling patients to breathe more easily and live longer. Four times as many patients have procedures now compared with two decades ago, and the patients are older, often in their eighties and early nineties, with mul-tiple health problems in addition to cardiac disease. The cardiologist I am following will do four to six procedures this day. The hospital she works in will do more than 3,000 cardiac catheterisation procedures in 2008. Approximately 10 per cent of the patients here are aged 90 and older.

Mr. A is wheeled on a gurney into the cath lab and I watch the procedure from behind a window in a lead-shielded 'control' room where technicians monitor the patient and the procedure. The patient is lying on his back and he can turn his head to watch a big screen at his side. The doctor takes pictures – still and moving – throughout the procedure which are displayed there. The patient's beating heart and coronary arteries are clearly visible on the screen, larger than life, in black and white, as is the placement and movement of the catheter. The patient and the rest of us can view his own constricted arteries and muse, along with the doctor, about how to interpret the facts of his body and his disease. The medical truths of the body have never been more prominently displayed, more 'in your face', than here.[5]

Forty-five minutes after the procedure begins, the doctor says to Mr. A, 'There is a tight narrowing in the left main coronary artery due to plaque. It is very dangerous. The right artery is also completely blocked – it is not supplying any blood to the heart. This is a dangerous matter. Typically, bypass surgery is considered the safest. But, technically, we could use stents [placed by a catheter] to open the arteries. But if there is a problem it could be fatal; it is high risk for both procedures. You can think about it. If we're going to treat it, we should do something before you leave the hospital. Unless, philosophically, you want to let nature take its course. And then we can treat it with medications'.

Mr. A responds, as do so many patients who are faced with choices that are frightening, possibly life-threatening and nearly impossible to make, 'What would you advise?' The doctor says it is hard to know what to advise in this case. Bypass surgery is, theoretically, the safest. But the stent procedure has a lower morbidity than open heart surgery. In the stent procedure blood flow in one major artery would be clamped for a few seconds. Since the other major artery is also completely blocked, Mr. A could die in those few seconds without blood flow to and through the heart.

The doctor continues. The surgeons will not want to do bypass surgery; it is major surgery. It requires general anesthesia. The patient has had pneumonia for two weeks, so he is not in great condition for major surgery. Mr. A could decide to opt out of any procedure. In that case medications, such as nitroglycerin, are palliative. They can help leave the arteries open a little bit, for a short time. 'But if he goes home and has the big one, that's it'.

Knowing these details creates the need to anticipate, think about, and decide certain matters, to consider life in corporeal terms and to imagine how things might proceed – both to better health and to death. Mr. A simply didn't feel well. He had a cough, pneumonia. He had asked to be taken to the hospital. The diagnostic workup there led to the cath lab procedure here. And that procedure produced the knowledge – experiential for the patient, clinical and ordinary for the medical team – of being between a rock and a hard place. Decisions must be made.

The option of *no decision* is not allowed in this case, because standard hospital procedure, indeed, good medicine, creates an awareness, a list of risks which must be acknowledged, and provides an array of interventions that must be decided among – by physicians and patients alike. The problem in this case is that all options seem equally risky. A hierarchy of risk is not apparent. Yet paradoxically Mr. A cannot go home without articulating a desire for one thing over another. That is how 'patient autonomy', 'informed consent' and 'ethical practice' operate today. The clinic sets up a deliberative process and Mr. A must engage it (or someone must do it in his stead). He must apprehend the likely or possible scenarios of his life-time future. If he does choose to go home without having anything else done in the hospital, it will be, can only be, with the knowledge that it was a decision on his part – to take his chances about the relative nearness of a fatal heart attack. It would also be with the knowledge that the other two procedures (bypass surgery or stents placed via catheter) could bring about immediate death or could, instead, relieve his condition and stave off death.

The dark side of patient autonomy is revealed here. The doctor wants the patient to know which medical interventions are possible and available. That is, she guides Mr. A to consider the risks of death and the risks of life-extension and then to voice an opinion. The following day, Mr. A rejects the surgical bypass operation. Three days later Mr. A elects medical management only and is discharged from the hospital.

The tools of the clinic provide, simultaneously, bodily knowledge, risk awareness and the imperative of 'choice'. Mr. A's 'choice' which is not a choice depends on a lived knowledge of his bodily condition together with an appreciation for the unknowns about the offered interventions. He is asked to imagine death, which of course is impossible to do, and also to imagine longer life, which in his case, involves life-threatening risk, regardless. The clinic demands this particular imaginative process, and it sets up this choice as a (potential) means for controlling the timing of death. At the same time, the doctors acknowledge that they cannot know, in advance, the outcome of whatever he chooses; they cannot control that timing. Yet, paradoxically, the clinic asks the patient to attempt that control. This kind of impossible choice, which demands reflexive engagement with control over *time left*, is becoming more ordinary in late life.

Mrs. B: The naturalness of controlling time left
Following several years of worsening symptoms, Mrs. B, aged 75, was referred to a gynecological surgeon and diagnosed with ovarian cancer. That physician discussed with Mrs.

B and her husband the possibilities of both surgery and chemotherapy and Mrs. B decided to proceed with surgery. Mr. B recalls, 'My wife felt that the operation was the way she wanted to go. If the tumour could be removed, it should be removed. She wanted to treat it aggressively.'

Immediately after the surgery Mrs. B and her family learned that the cancer had spread to other organs and was inoperable. Mrs. B died six weeks later. A week following her death, her husband and daughter reflected on that six-week period in an interview. Their story recalls the way in which the divergent, fraught and now ordinary scenarios of hospice care and aggressive treatment emerged, scenarios that, on the one hand, acknowledge the outer limits of therapeutics and thus death's inevitability (though not knowing when it will occur) and, on the other hand, seek the continuing pursuit of interventions that can potentially 'add' to the future. The story exposes a remembered sensibility about how the clinic shapes consideration of *time left*.

Mrs. B's husband and daughter reported that, right after the surgery, the surgeon discussed with them both chemotherapy and hospice care. The doctor had made it very clear to the patient and family that the medical team could not cure her. He had brought up the topic of hospice care right away, yet then he pulled back, the family said, and, at the end of the conversation, he began to talk about chemotherapy. Mrs. B's husband and daughter remember Mrs. B being offered 'two options' by the surgeon. She could consider hospice care, which she did, thinking, 'I've had a good life. I've done a lot of things. This is it'. Or, she could try chemotherapy. They recall the surgeon telling them, 'You can always just try it out, see if anything happens. We should have some response by the third or fourth treatment.' Both the husband and daughter stressed that the surgeon made it very clear that he was making no promises – Mrs. B could spend the last year of her life in chemotherapy treatments.

Many cancers have become chronic illnesses today, manageable well into late life (though not curable) because of better treatments, including surgery, chemotherapy infusions, oral medications and radiation. These treatments have become a normal part of living for many (Brody 2008), and not only in the US. In addition to augmenting time 'naturally' through standard or new treatments, the clinic also often makes a dual offering – aggressive, potentially life-prolonging treatment *and* palliative care that anticipates the end of life. Without medical guidelines or regular, explicit discussions between doctors and patients about the end of life or toxicity of treatments, patients have no basis on which to make decisions, that is, whether to acknowledge and accept the nearness of death or aggressively fight the natural course of the disease, for an undetermined amount of time, in the attempt to stave off death. Recent medical literature reveals an emergent concern about the growing numbers of patients who receive aggressive chemotherapy treatments up to days and weeks before death (Earle *et al.* 2004, Matsuyama *et al.* 2006), though the practice itself has been in existence a long time.

When patients are over 70 or so that dual offering is ethically and practically complicated by the fact that more of life is behind than is ahead, and that the future, despite interventions, may be only days or weeks. Yet, as medicine extends lives routinely, death in the seventies, eighties or even early nineties appears no longer acceptable, usual, indeed 'natural', to a large segment of society. That cultural phenomenon is born out in recent studies showing that many patients proactively choose aggressive, toxic and costly treatments up to the time of death (Harrington and Smith 2008, Matsuyama *et al.* 2006) instead of hospice care.

To complicate matters, the idea of 'palliative chemotherapy' (Harrington and Smith 2008) is not well understood by patients and families, and physicians do not necessarily take the time to explain that it is not curative. The goal is to provide better quality of life, for a time, until death from the disease occurs. There was no question for any of the doctors involved in the care of Mrs. B that she would die of her disease. The family, on the other hand, hoped for 'remission' that would add time to life.

Mrs. B's first and only chemotherapy infusion took place while she was still hospitalised. Extremely debilitated, she was discharged to a rehabilitation facility for post-operative care where she decided that she wanted to move forward with more chemotherapy. Two and a half weeks later Mrs. B came to the clinic with her husband and daughter to assess her condition for proceeding with a second chemo treatment. Weak from the cancer, the surgery and the first chemotherapy session, Mrs. B was at a 'crossroads' moment, which, importantly, no health professional explicitly discussed with her.

At the clinic, Mrs. B and her family aired their first ambivalence about whether to continue treating her cancer aggressively. Her husband said that now, following the first chemo infusion, 'we don't know if we'd do the same thing'. Mrs. B said, 'I'm not sure. I was under the impression that I should do the chemo, but I don't think I want it. I'm thinking about hospice'.

Her daughter, clearly advocating additional chemotherapy, remarked, 'You're okay, considering it's only been a couple of weeks since the chemo'. Her husband retreated from his ambivalent position and wanted her to move forward with treatment. The physician said, 'We can delay it a week. It's appropriate to continue with one more treatment, and then see what happens ... Our recommendation is to do it, because the majority of people respond'. By the time Mrs. B and her family left the clinic they all felt strongly that she should and would continue treatment.

But two weeks later, Mrs. B's husband called the clinic to report that they cancelled Mrs. B's chemotherapy appointment. She was now home with hospice care. The daughter said, 'At the most it was going to be a year, and when she thought about it, when she thought about what she and we had already been through, my mother decided that she really wanted to be home. I was angry that that she didn't want to continue on with chemotherapy. She was utterly exhausted that day at the clinic. It was only later that she said she didn't want to go through the rigours of going back and forth for chemotherapy. Once she was convinced that nothing was going to improve, she made the decision that she wanted to give up the treatment and come home'. Mrs. B's husband added, 'She was very weak. She had been prepared to take the chemo, to see if it would do any good, if it would prolong her life and reduce her pain. But neither happened. She decided to elect hospice. I was pretty upset about her decision. But the decision was hers. I accepted whatever she wanted'.

Mrs. B died at home a month later. Her husband mused, 'Would it have added anything to my wife's life, if she had the chemo? I don't know. I have no idea. The chemo might have killed her'.

Because there are treatment options, augmenting *time left* seems always to be a possibility and is thus impossible to ignore. No one could guarantee how much *time left*, if any, would have been added to Mrs. B's life if she had continued treatment, yet she and her family were guided to dwell within that hope during the clinic visit. After a period of ambivalence, in which she had to weigh the value of time 'added' but through the adverse effects of more treatment, Mrs. B acknowledged that any 'added' time might not result in 'good' time and thus *time left* did not seem worth extending. She chose, or rather yielded to, hospice care. After her death her husband remained ambivalent. The fact that medicine can so routinely attempt to augment *time left* promotes an open-ended and uneasy feeling about the end-point of one's decisions – could I have added time (for myself, my family member) if I (or she) made another choice? Even when augmenting *time left* consists of adding weeks or months only, with uncertain 'quality of life' as in this case, the disquiet about the lost possibility of proactively lengthening the future – a particular fantasy about time – remains salient for this family, as it does for many. Although ultimately, time itself did not trump 'quality of life' as a value for Mrs. B, it did so for her family as it does for many, which is why so many 'choose' aggressive therapies even close to death (Kaufman 2005, Matsuyama and Reddy *et al.* 2006). The dual offering of aggressive versus palliative care sets up potentially long-term anguish for family members, regardless of the 'choice' patients and families make, in part because controlling *time left* is perceived as a 'natural' act. The unwillingness to attempt to do so can seem like a failure and can remain unsettling for survivors.

Mr. C: Self-bargaining: linking the value of life to age and time left

Mr. C, aged 78, has liver cancer which he and his physicians are monitoring with vigilance by periodic blood tests and scans. He has had two rounds of chemotherapy infusion treatments directly into the liver in the past year to shrink the tumours while he waits for his name to rise to the top of the national waiting list for a liver transplant. Mr. C has been seeing one liver specialist for a decade. When that specialist began to talk about transplant as his 'best option' Mr. C was enthusiastic.

His daughter accompanies him on every clinic visit. She will support any decision he makes. His wife, also present, does not want him to have a transplant because she fears for his life in surgery. In the exam room, the physician reviews the most recent CT scans and remarks that there is a new cancer tumour, in a new location. The doctor comments, 'One of the tumours has grown a little in size. We're going to have to go again and repeat the chemo procedure. This is telling us that you have a liver that is prone to making tumours. And this tells us that a transplant is the best way to manage your cancer. These treatments can't control it.'

The physician continues, 'You could get an offer for a transplant in a couple of months. You should have the treatment in the next couple of weeks.' The daughter asks how the cancer is treated if her father does not have a transplant. The doctor replies, 'One of the risks is that the cancer can get ahead of us, and then the pace speeds up, and we can't control it and we can't predict how it will behave'.

He shifts the topic to speak about age and risk. 'When we started with liver transplant, we didn't have any patients over 55, then 60. Now, there is no limit. But the older you are, the greater the risk. They have to clamp the largest vein in your body for 45 minutes. And that puts a stress on your heart. So, we want to do more tests, to see if you can withstand the surgery. If others on the team think he's a good candidate for a transplant, he should have one, and the sooner, the better ... The fact that they treated the tumour a couple of months ago and didn't knock it out – that edges me over toward a transplant. In my experience you'd do well with a transplant'.

Another doctor comes in to discuss the different types of 'high-risk' cadaveric livers that patients may 'choose' among. There is a 'high-risk donor form' to fill out. There are 'in-between' livers from persons with Hepatitis B or C; from patients who died a 'cardiac' rather than 'brain' death; from older donors. 'In order to use as many livers as possible, we use some of those in-between livers. They might not look good, but they might work well. We use our judgment. But the surgeon will give you the option – they will call you about these less-than-perfect livers and you can decide if you want it'. He adds that when you get a call that a liver has been found, the surgeon does not bargain with you. You have 15 minutes to decide.

Mr. C comments, 'I've lived a good life to age 78. Now I leave it to the doctor'. The doctor replies, 'We won't offer you a liver that isn't good. You have to trust the surgeons.

The science isn't perfect. The surgeon judges the context of the donor liver and your age and everything, and decides if the liver is good for you'.

When the doctor leaves the exam room Mr. C reflects on the discussion. 'Maybe I should wait for a perfect, healthy liver. I want to wait. If I get a healthy liver, and it gives me five years, that's okay. If I live five years. My father died at 77. If I live to 82, that's good. If I had stayed in [another country], I wouldn't live this long. The medicines here have helped me live longer'.

Mr. C's daughter notes, 'You have two things going against you if you wait for a 'healthy' liver. First, the cancer will grow, and second, you'll be older. If you turn down the first offer you get, and then need another infusion treatment, before they offer you a 'healthy' liver, what would that be like? Healthy liver offers are more infrequent'.

Mr. C muses, 'To live past age 80 would be good'. After a few seconds of reflection he changes his mind and says, 'If I could get two added years with a non-perfect liver, living to age 80, that would be okay'.

How much potential additional time is worth the risks of surgery? Mr. C answers rhetorically, five years, but then he quickly reconsiders and says that two years of life, from a donor liver, would be enough for him. Both his range (two to five years) and his recalibration (from five to two) are not unusual for older persons considering major interventions, whether in transplant, cancer, or cardiac therapy. It seems that in their self-negotiations, older persons who seriously consider life-extending treatments confront all at once: the limits of medicine yet the fact that life-extending interventions are normal and occur successfully every day; that even a relatively short future is worth the pain and risk of death involved in major interventions; and that *time left* is a mandatory variable in calculations about risk, worth, and the best thing to do.

When the physician re-enters the room the daughter has questions. Can one have as long a life with a 'high-risk' liver, as with a 'perfect' liver? The doctor replies that generally, the longevity with a high-risk liver is as good as that from a perfect liver. But there are more technical problems, up front, that need to be taken care of. Does he only get one shot, because of his age? 'It depends. If he gets a bad organ, and it's technical, he'd get another organ. If things go wrong later he'd probably not get another organ'. What about cancer again, from his own or from a high-risk donor who had cancer? The doctor notes that one can have a recurrence of the cancer in the liver. 'Even though this is the best treatment, we can't guarantee that he won't get a recurrence. But it's only a 10 per cent or 20 per cent chance of recurrence. If we don't do a transplant, we know his cancer will progress. The transplant is mostly curative, and we hope the cancer won't come back'. What if the tumours get bigger? 'We can't do a transplant if the tumours are bigger than five centimeters. Right now they are smaller and we can control it'.

Two weeks after that clinic visit Mr. C had another chemotherapy infusion to reduce the size of the tumours. Four weeks later he had a successful liver transplant. He never filled out the 'high-risk' donor form. He does not know what kind of liver he received vis a vis that form.

Mr. C confronts risk by negotiating with himself how much *time left* is important to him. He calculates *time left* – and wanted *time left* – in terms of age. He negotiates with himself about the value of life in relation to the amount of future he thinks would be acceptable, given his current age, his growing cancer, the risks of surgery, and the age of his father at death (a very common comparative point). He ponders and then decides quickly that the risks of transplant surgery would be worth it if he gains even two 'additional' years of life. The socio-economic structure of American healthcare delivery, together with the medical emphasis on individual choice, supports his calculation.

Conclusion: living (and) the future

Of the three stories, that of Mr. C illustrates the clearest life strategy and the most well-articulated calculation about amount of *time left* in relation to age and risk. Important, too, is the fact that his doctors were unanimous and vocal that transplant would extend his life and was the right thing to do. Such a straightforward opinion was not given to Mr. A, who was told that all moves risked death, or to Mrs. B, whose surgeon initially waffled between chemotherapy and hospice and did not explain the purpose or meaning of 'palliative chemotherapy.' As a result, Mrs. B had to dwell in the tension between the words of the palliative care specialist about limited *time left* and the desires of her family for more life via more treatment.

The opening epigraph of this chapter challenges ethnographers to question the ordinariness of clinical norms and to describe the changing conditions of time, self and ethical practice that the clinic organises, indeed demands. These scenarios exemplify the lure of 'more' future, the role of the *time left* calculus and ideas of the malleable body in shaping who we have become and who we are becoming in an ageing society. Fifty years ago, medicine was characterised by waiting – for death, for the acute disease to pass, for the body to recover or not. Today all of medicine is characterised by risk calculations, which are coloured (or displaced) by hope, and by decisions within decisions about interventions. Diagnostic procedures lead to treatment options. In late life, those options force consideration of the worth and amount of *time left* to live and compel clinicians, patients and families to attempt to govern time. All of these interventions create a stark imperative to imagine and then choose among future scenarios in which procedural risks, roads to death, biomedical progress and ideas about the naturalness of control over the timing of death and the 'natural' adaptability of the body are invoked.

In its work over the past several decades of re-calibrating the boundaries and signs of what is considered treatable and worthwhile to treat at ever-older ages, medicine both nurtures and extends into ever-later life the already widespread existential and societal condition of hyper-reflexivity so well documented among medical ethnographers and theorists, such that risk is an individual, embodied condition, selfhood is increasingly considered in somatic terms and health promotion strategies are intensified throughout the lifecourse. I have elaborated here on one feature of that self-awareness that the clinic both offers to and imposes on older persons turned patients: the need to calculate *time left* – as a source and effect of a new form of relentless future thinking about life itself. This reflexive longevity emerges every day in clinics across the US. It is evidence of the centrality of contemporary temporality to desire, decision making and the apprehension of risk, and to sensibility about the malleable arc of human life. It shows, too, how the nature and practice of life – including responsibility about lengthening it or allowing its end – are being (re-) constituted in relation to emergent, ordinary biotechnologies.

Acknowledgements

This research was funded by the National Institute on Aging, grant RO1AG28426, to Sharon R. Kaufman, Principal Investigator. I thank the health professionals, patients and families who allowed observations of clinic visits in 2007–08 and who spoke candidly about medical conditions and treatment decisions. Vincanne Adams, Lakshmi Fjord and Jodi Halpern offered useful comments on earlier drafts. Sarah Lochlann Jain, Kelly Joyce,

Meika Loe and two anonymous reviewers provided thoughtful suggestions that helped shape the final version.

Notes

1   'Quality of life' is impossible to define or evaluate because it has no empirical basis. It refers to a variable set of attributes based on different perceptions (Kaufman 2005: 151, 210).
2   Those who come to major medical centre clinics are a self-selected group and Medicare enables access to treatments. People who choose not to come to the clinic do not engage the particular futures that the clinic fosters. Those who cannot access the clinic were not part of this study.
3   Data for the stories of Mr. A and Mr. C that follow were collected by the author. Data for the story of Mrs. B were collected by Lakshmi Fjord.
4   in which a catheter is inserted through the groin and threaded through blood vessels up and into the heart.
5   Yet see Cartwright 1995, Joyce 2008 and Van Dijck 2005 for analyses of the variable mediating effects of body imaging technologies.

References

Armstrong, D. (1995) The rise of surveillance medicine, *Sociology of Health and Illness*, 17, 3, 393–404.
Beck, University (1992) *Risk Society*. London: Sage.
Brodwin, P.E. (2000) Introduction. In Brodwin, P.E. (ed.) *Biotechnology and Culture*. Bloomington: Indiana University Press.
Brody, J.R. (2008) In cancer therapy, there is a time to treat and a time to let go. *New York Times*, 8/10/08 (http://www.nytimes.com/2008/08/19/health. Accessed 9/24/08.)
Cartwright, L. (1995) *Screening the Body*. Minneapolis, MN: University of Minnesota Press.
Clarke, A.E., Shim, J.K., Mamo, L., Fosket, J.R. and Fishman, J.R. (2003) Biomedicalization: technoscientific transformation of health, illness, and U.S. biomedicine, *American Sociological Review*, 68, 2, 161–94.
Crawford, R. (2006) Health as a meaningful social practice, *health*, 10, 4, 401–20.
Earle, C.C., Neville, B.A., Landrum, M.B., Ayanian, J.Z., Block, S.D. and Weeks, J.C. (2004) Trends in the aggressiveness of cancer care near the end of life, *Journal of Clinical Oncology*, 22, 315–21.
Ewald, F. (1991) Insurance and risk. In Burchell, G., Gordon, C. and Miller, P. (eds) *The Foucault Effect*. Chicago: University of Chicago Press.
Giddens, A. (1991) *Modernity and Self-identity*. Stanford: Stanford University Press.
Guyer, J.I. (2007) Prophecy and the near future, *American Ethnologist*, 34, 3, 409–21.
Harrington, S.E. and Smith, T.J. (2008) The role of chemotherapy at the end of life, *Journal of the American Medical Association*, 299, 22, 2667–78.
Hartocollis, A. (2008) Rise seen in medical efforts to improve very long lives, *New York Times*, 7/18/08 (http://www.nytimes.com/2008/07/18/health. Accessed 8/18/08.)
Harvey, D. (1990) *The Condition of Postmodernity*. Cambridge MA: Blackwell.
Joyce, K. (2008) *Magnetic Appeal*. Ithaca, NY: Cornell University Press.
Katz, S. (2005) *Cultural Aging*. Peterborough, Canada: Broadview Press.
Kaufman, S.R. (2005) ... *And a Time to Die*. New York: Scribner.
Lakoff, A. and Collier, S.J. (2004) Ethics and the anthropology of modern reason, *Anthropological Theory*, 4, 4, 419–34.
Lash, S. (2001) Technological forms of life, *Theory, Culture and Society*, 18, 1, 105–20.
Matsuyama, R., Reddy, S. and Smith, T.J. (2006) Why do patients choose chemotherapy near the end of life? *Journal of Clinical Oncology*, 24, 3490–6.

Mattingly, C. (1998) *Healing Dramas and Clinical Plots*. Cambridge: Cambridge University Press.
Maynard, R.J. (2006) Controlling death – compromising life, *Medical Anthropology Quarterly*, 20, 2, 212–34.
Rose, N. (2007) *The Politics of Life Itself*. Princeton: Princeton University Press.
Shim, J.K., Russ, A.J. and Kaufman, S.R. (2007) Clinical life, *health*, 11, 2, 245–64.
Van Djick, J. (2005) *The Transparent Body*. Seattle, WA: University of Washington Press.
Wilk, R. (2007) It's about time. *American Ethnologist*, 34, 3, 440–43.

6

Aesthetic anti-ageing surgery and technology: women's friend or foe?

Abigail T. Brooks

Introduction

Feminist ageing studies scholars and critical gerontologists highlight the need to examine ageing as a socially constructed phenomenon (Cruikshank 2003, Holstein and Minkler 2003) and to explore how the social meanings ascribed to ageing interact with individuals' lived experiences of the ageing process (Oberg 2003, Woodword 1999, Featherstone and Hepworth 1991). Feminist ageing studies scholar Margaret Morganroth Gullette (2004) prompts us to ask: how are we 'aged by culture'? This study explores some of the different ways that American women experience and construct understandings of ageing in an expanding and increasingly normalised culture of aesthetic anti-ageing surgeries and technologies. Television, internet, newspaper, and magazine coverage of women's health and age-related illnesses (Covello and Peters 2002), and of age-related changes in the body such as the menopause (Gannon and Stevens 1998, Gonyea 1998, Topo 1992), are fast replacing the mutual communication of shared experience as women's primary source of information about ageing (Davis 1997). The recent overturning of the American Medical Association's longstanding ban on soliciting business by advertising or otherwise, combined with the Food and Drug Administration's eroded capacity to regulate the pharmaceutical industry, has produced a culture of commercialised medicine in the United States (Relman 2005, Sullivan 2001, Cohen 2001).[1] Fierce competition between medical professionals who advertise their products and services to solicit patients, direct-to-consumer pharmaceutical advertising, and the fast-track approval process for new pharmaceutical drugs means that older Americans are increasingly targeted as potential recipients of anti-ageing technologies and medications.

Recent scholarship analyses the cultural messages contained within anti-ageing advertising (Croissant 2006, Calasanti and King 2007, 2005, Marshall 2002a, 2002b) and investigates the impact of the marketing and use of anti-ageing technologies, particularly Viagra, on women and men's perceptions of gender identity, ageing, and sexuality (Loe 2004, Potts *et al.* 2003). With the exception of the work of Meika Loe, Annie Potts *et al.* and several others, however, there remains little empirical research to date that explores the influence of the growing advertising, availability, and use of anti-ageing surgeries and technologies on living, breathing individuals. Empirical scholarship on the content and impact of women-centred anti-ageing advertising, and on how women's use of aesthetic anti-ageing surgeries and technologies interacts with their understandings and experiences of the ageing process, is near to none.[2] In the tradition of the scholarship of Meika Loe and Annie Potts, my research aims to contribute to our general knowledge of 'how the design and marketing' – and I would add, use – 'of technologies reproduce and, at times, reconfigure cultural understandings of ageing' (Joyce and Mamo 2006: 110) in the United States. More specifically, through illuminating what women themselves have to say about their relationship to the growing field of aesthetic anti-ageing surgeries and technologies, I hope to enlighten our understanding of how aesthetic anti-ageing surgeries and technologies inform women's attitudes about, and experiences of, growing older.

Successful ageing and agelessness

The 'successful ageing' paradigm, part of a larger movement in gerontology and geriatrics termed the 'new gerontology', focuses on health and active participation in life, and counters traditional conceptualisations of ageing as a time of disease and decline (Calasanti *et al.* 2006, Bayer 2005, Holstein and Minkler 2003). Successful ageing, according to Rowe and Kahn (1998, 1997, 1987), is dependent upon individual choice, effort and behaviour, and can be achieved through the positive influence and adoption of several extrinsic factors, from psychosocial aspects to personal habits. Diet and disciplined physical activity – the embodiment of what Stephen Katz terms 'busy bodies' (Katz 2000) – are two essential methods by which individuals can age 'successfully' and increase the likelihood of a healthy, active old age (Holstein and Minkler 2003: 787). Successful ageing mirrors our contemporary era of late consumer capitalism in which individuals are free to shape, mould, design, and choose their bodies (Giddens 1991), and finds fertile ground within our increasingly individualised discourse on healthcare (Williams and Bendelow 1998) whereby ageing is portrayed as a private problem that individuals are responsible for fixing (Debert 2003). Indeed, the individualist focus of successful ageing mirrors the rhetoric of choice and self-determination that permeates late consumer capitalism, finding easy resonance with a contemporary American popular and media culture in which we are constantly told that we can choose our own bodies (Bordo 2003 [1993]: 247).

A practice that counters prevailing 'decline narratives' (Gullette 2004, 1997) and challenges widespread cultural equations between age and decay, successful ageing can empower women to re-define ageing beyond limiting, negative, 'identity stripping' (Gullette 2004: 9) stereotypes. For members of marginalised groups, self-definition can be an act of resistance and power (Browne 1998: 220, cited in Morell 2003: 71). Older women who track-run for example, refute the notion that older women's bodies are weak and should be hidden from view (Hayles 2002). In her interviews with women in their nineties, Carolyn Morell (2003) found that her respondents' identities centred on the defiance of decline – of able bodies and sharp minds, her respondents' experiences contradicted old age stereotypes.

'Successful ageing' engenders resistance towards the stigmatisation of old age; however, it may also contribute to it. As successful ageing is increasingly equated with anti-ageing (Bayer 2005: 14), with 'not aging, not being 'old' or, at the very least, not looking old' (Calasanti *et al.* 2006), the process of ageing itself is reviled. Further, the characteristic aspect of successful ageing – that of individual choice and responsibility – can increase the likelihood of blame and shame placed upon older individuals (simply for being and growing old). Carolyn Morell (2003: 83) argues that the individualistic ethic of successful ageing provokes antagonism towards signs of physical ageing. Martha B. Holstein (2006) echoes this concern, particularly as it applies to women:

> If we older women fail to care for our bodies so that we can meet normative expectations to 'age successfully', we may be viewed askance – at the simplest level for 'letting ourselves go' when 'control' is putatively within our grasp – and, more problematically, as moral failures for being complicit in our own aging (Holstein 2006: 316).

The women in my sample exhibit a shared commitment to taking good care of their bodies through healthy eating and physical exercise and, thereby, embody key aspects of the successful ageing paradigm. But how, and in what ways, does the growing prevalence of aesthetic anti-ageing surgeries and technologies interact with women's successful ageing ideologies and practices? And how does it inform their understandings of ageing more generally? Are aesthetic anti-ageing surgeries and technologies experienced as a new and welcome method for ageing successfully? Or are they creating more stringent requirements for successful ageing and restricting women's capacity to equate ageing with a broad range of positive elements? These questions provide the context for my data analysis below.

Some ageing studies scholars suggest that 'successful ageing' increasingly connotes a quest for *agelessness*, or what Molly Andrews (1999) calls the 'seductiveness of agelessness'. Stephen Katz and Barbara Marshall (2003) argue that the optimistic cultural imagery of successful or 'new ageing' reflects the postmodern fantasy of constructing and reconstructing the self and body outside time, in the continuous present, and the posthuman desire to live in bodies that are 'never really born and never really die' (Katz and Marshall 2003: 4–6). The 'seductiveness of agelessness' informs my respondents' attitudes about, and experiences of, anti-ageing surgeries and technologies in myriad ways. For some, the seduction of agelessness merges with the seduction of technology – technology becomes a means-to-agelessness – as they speak of age-touched flesh being 'whisked away' and 'cheating mother nature'. For others, this seduction is met with suspicion, ambivalence, and doubt. Still others reveal an underside of this seduction, an underside rife with increased anxiety about, and vulnerability to, biological age-related changes that remain beyond technology's influence. Zygmunt Bauman (1992a: 18) argues that the modern/postmodern obsession to deny the body's limits makes confronting death particularly difficult; Chris Shilling (1993: 189) articulates the related assertion that our increasing belief in our ability to control and discipline our bodies leaves us uncertain and socially unsupported when it comes to dealing with death. My respondents' anxieties and vulnerabilities mark a fundamental contradiction that I will analyse against the backdrop of Bauman's and Shilling's hypotheses.

Successful ageing and femininity

The individual choice, effort, and responsibility that the paradigm of successful ageing demands – particularly as directed towards the maintenance of a healthy and active body – parallel the cultural expectations of individual responsibility and effort that inform the 'disciplinary practices of femininity' (Bordo 1993, Bartky 1990). A woman engages in daily work on her 'defective body' to achieve a feminine appearance (Smith 1990: 189); the feminine beauty ideal in the United States – White, heterosexual, thin, young – makes its attainment difficult – and impossible – for many. In a culture wherein women's femininity, a 'chief marker' of which is the 'capacity to draw admiring glances from others' (Bartky 1999: 67), serves as a significant measure of their worth, aesthetic anti-ageing surgeries and technologies offer women new choices and opportunities (or pressures and responsibilities) to mould and shape their faces and bodies in compliance with the feminine imperative of a youthful appearance. Because women's value is more commonly rooted in their physical appearance and sexual attractiveness than men's (men's value is determined more by 'what they do then how they look') *and* because women's sexual eligibility depends on meeting much 'stricter 'conditions' related to looks and age', women are 'more heavily penalised than men' (Sontag 1997: 23) for the normal changes that age inscribes on the human face and body. It is not difficult to imagine, then, how successful ageing for women can come to signify not only healthy body practices, but the successful 'doing of femininity' (Smith 1990) as well.

Women's naturally ageing faces and bodies – deviations from the dominant youth/beauty imperatives of femininity – provide a particularly lucrative market for aesthetic anti-ageing surgeries and technologies in the United States: 'Let's face it. Older women are a growth industry!' (O'Beirne 1999: 114).[3] Medical/pharmaceutical/cosmetic advertising that targets older women projects a powerful youth/beauty/sexual desirability imperative, reinforcing the equation between a woman's societal value and worth and the sexual attractiveness and reproductive viability of her body. Older women are taught about what to do, what to buy, and what to put in and on their bodies in order to remain young, beautiful, and sexually desirable. In my analysis below, I explore how the growing availability, advertising, and use of aesthetic anti-ageing surgeries and technologies both challenge and strengthen dominant cultural assumptions about ageing and femininity in the United States. In what ways do aesthetic anti-ageing surgeries and technologies inform women's understandings of their own physical attractiveness? Does the growing availability of these surgeries and technologies fuel new desires (or pressures) among women to continue to meet and comply with feminine beauty norms as they age? Do women find the growing availability and accessibility of aesthetic anti-ageing surgeries and technologies empowering or oppressive or both? These are some of the questions that are addressed through my respondents' articulations of their perspectives on and experiences of aesthetic anti-ageing surgeries and technologies.

Data and analyses of the study

My research is based on 44 in-depth interviews, ranging from one and a half to four hours in length, with American women between the ages of 47 and 76. My sample is purposive (Neuman 2000, Gamson 1992) and strategic (Rubin 1992). The women in my sample share a common concern for the health of their bodies and a commitment to taking good care of them through physical exercise; yet they also inhabit a variety of attitudes and approaches to growing older. I utilised the snowball sampling technique (Neuman 2000, Ostrander 1984) to recruit women who participate in some type of physical exercise on a regular basis – including gym workouts, walking, running, yoga, and pilates – and to select women who have different views on aesthetic anti-ageing surgeries and technologies. My sample consists of 16 women who are having and using aesthetic anti-ageing surgeries and technologies, 22 women who have not had/used aesthetic anti-ageing surgeries and technologies and articulate an active resistance to having them in the future (these women often describe themselves as growing older 'naturally'), and 6 women who are undecided about whether they will or will not have/use aesthetic anti-ageing surgeries and technologies in the coming years. For the purposes of this study, aesthetic anti-ageing procedures, including plastic surgery (i.e. neck lifts, eye lifts, brow lifts, face lifts, tummy lifts) and what have come to be known as the 'injectables' (i.e. Restylane, Botox, Collagen, Perlane, Juvaderm).

Most of the women in my sample reside in the Northeastern United States, with the exception of two who live in the Midwest, and one who lives on the West Coast. They have a diversity of lifestyles (some live in urban centres, others in suburbs, still others live in small towns in rural settings) and livelihoods (some are retired and some are stay-at-home mothers) and work in a variety of professional fields, from education to business, from social work to psychology, from real estate to journalism, from art and music to physical fitness and dance. All but one of the women in my sample, who is Latina, are White. Approximately three-quarters of the women enjoy financial security – some inhabit upper and middle-upper class positions, others can be described as comfortably middle class; approximately one-quarter are less economically privileged, and fall within the socio-economic categories of middle, to lower middle, to working class. The cost of aesthetic anti-ageing surgery and technologies, like most cosmetic surgery procedures in the United States, is not covered by medical insurance – they range in the hundreds of dollars for injectables to the thousands of dollars for surgeries.[4] While there are no official statistics on class and cosmetic surgery in the United States, the monetary expense of cosmetic procedures tells us that their use is a predominantly privileged practice. On the other hand, the widespread advertising and marketing of aesthetic anti-ageing surgeries and technologies in print media, on television, and in doctors' offices, and the availability of long-term financing and payment plans, means that more women are aware of these surgeries and technologies and makes these procedures more accessible to greater numbers of women across class lines. The majority of the women in my sample who are having and using anti-ageing surgeries and technologies are easily able to afford them. Yet others with lower financial means, including a musician, a childcare worker, and a woman who is currently unemployed, also partake of them, albeit at considerable financial sacrifice: they have scrimped and saved money over a period of years, borrowed money from family, friends, and/or lending institutions, utilised long-term payment plans, and incurred financial debt as a result of their anti-ageing surgery and technology use.

Despite the growing normalisation and mainstreaming of cosmetic surgery in the United States, however, it continues to be practised overwhelmingly by Whites: Hispanics account for only nine per cent, African Americans six per cent, Asians five per cent, and other non-Whites two per cent, of the total number of recipients of cosmetic procedures (American Society for Aesthetic Plastic Surgery 2007). The demographics of the women in my sample who are having and using anti-ageing surgeries and technologies (all are White) reflect the reality that cosmetic surgery, at least at present, remains largely the prerogative of Whites in the United States. The medicalisation of non-White facial and bodily features in the discourse and publications of American cosmetic surgery practitioners (Eichberg 2000), combined with the popularity of surgeries that promote a White aesthetic among women of colour (Kaw 1993), suggest that the practice of cosmetic surgery in the United States reinforces cultural ideals of whiteness and conflations between whiteness, heterosexuality and femininity (Wepsic 1996). The themes of race and body image among older women are starting to be explored (see, for example, Reel *et al.* 2008) and the intersections of gender, race, and class in the contexts of ageing and cosmetic surgery are ripe for further analysis. Race is not an explicit focus of my study; yet, the fact that all my respondents who have and use aesthetic anti-ageing surgeries and technologies are White bespeaks the powerful absent-presence of race that haunts the cultural phenomenon of cosmetic surgery in the United States.

Faith and comfort in new technologies

Many of my respondents represent themselves as empowered consumers who can access an increasingly appealing range of new and exciting technologies with which to fight, and even conquer, the ageing process. As Maya, a homemaker, aged 49, puts it:

I feel like 'oh, there's a whole arsenal out there, great, no problem!'

Maya also finds comfort in the increasing advertising of new anti-ageing products and technologies. First, the advertisements reassure her that many other people are suffering the same ageing 'symptoms' that she is:

I think that so much more advertising is being done, marketed towards, you know, the older ageing population. Which I think is very helpful in terms of being more comfortable, knowing that many more people in this world have, you know, reflux or bladder control or ... it's so helpful knowing that other people are going through the same thing that we might be going through.

Secondly, these new products and technologies being advertised offer her a constructive course of action to 'do something' to conquer the symptoms of ageing:

Yeah, I think it's great. So you got reflux, so does everybody else. You know, deal with it. Isn't it great, we can, some of these drugs aren't even prescription anymore, you know, it's like 'okay, we can take care of this ourselves'.

Julia, a homemaker, aged 47, also feels comforted by increasing availability of anti-ageing technologies, and the power of these new technologies to 'fix' aspects of her ageing face that she is unhappy with:

I feel like it's comforting in the back of my mind to know like, okay, if I get to the point where I'm horrified by something, I can go fix it.

Caroline, a radio producer, aged 47, is reassured not only by the increasing availability of anti-ageing surgeries and technologies, but by the fast pace of technological advancement. She expresses faith and confidence in on-going user-friendly innovations that will enable her to stave off ageing without having to do any 'major work':

I think it's great that they [cosmetic surgeries and technologies] are out there. We [my friends and I] always say, 'yeah, it's great, who knows what they'll have in 10 years'. I think the less invasive the better. All these little advances mean that you can keep tweaking, without really, you know, having to do major work. You know, why not? 'Keep working in your labs, that's all I have to say! Keep at it!'.

Technological power, magic, and seduction

Some of my respondents express an almost heady excitement as they recount their past experiences and future hopes for new anti-ageing surgeries and technologies. Amy, aged 48, who recently left the business world to become a stay-at-home mother, describes, with wonder and amazement, the way her surgery made her 'sagging stomach' like new again:

I was *very pleased* with the results. I mean I just felt like a million bucks. I mean I felt like, 'oh my god, it's amazing this thing that I never could get rid of is gone!'

While Amy resisted the surgeon's pressure to have 'a lot more done' at the time – including liposuction on her hips, thighs and vaginal area – she explains that she certainly will take advantage of more anti-ageing surgery and technology in the future:

It's almost like magic and I *totally* can see how women, especially as we age, get seduced into 'oh, let me do a little bit of this', because it is *very enticing* ... Going in [to surgery] my line was 'this is all I'm ever going to do' like I've drawn the line and that was it. [But] afterwards I kind of sat there and thought, 'oh, you know, I might get an eye job at some point' and 'yea, I mean, never a full face lift, but I can see, you know, a little bit here and there ...'

In the recovery room, in fact, Amy experienced some pangs about not having had more surgery done. She muses that maybe if her husband hadn't been opposed to her having surgery in the first place (due to his worries about the potential health risks of surgery, Amy's husband was against her having plastic surgery of any kind) she would have woken up to the pleasure of even more of her age-touched flesh having been magically 'whisked away':

> But I *do remember* when I was recovering in the recovery room, there was a woman next to me who also had the same doctor operate on her in our drugged state and had had a tummy tuck, and she said, 'you know what? I did the full thing.' She did the thighs, she did the hips and everything … And I don't know how she looked because I was too drugged and I never saw her afterwards. But to a certain extent, if Daniel [Amy's husband] hadn't been so adamant about 'I don't even want you to do it', to a certain extent I could see it. You're under [anesthesia], it's not that much more in terms of money, I mean just, the recovery I can't imagine is *that much worse*. So, I don't know. I could've, afterwards I definitely sort of thought, hmmm maybe I … I mean, you know, cause it is nice to think of this notion that it can just sort of be all *whisked away*.

For Janet, a retired airline ticket agent, aged 68, the power and magic of anti-ageing surgery and technology equals, even surpasses, that of Mother Nature. Through accessing these new technologies, Janet feels confident that she can almost cheat, or at least get a handle on, and ultimately reverse, the natural ageing process:

> You don't exactly cheat on Mother Nature, but you kind of, you know, get a handle on this particular aging process by getting rid of all that skin. And I felt like I could go back a few years and look the way I used to look, you know.

Technology as life-renewing, death resistant

My respondents often equate their surgeries and technologies with the achievement of a more youthful, more healthy, more rested, more energised look. Outside the achievement of more youthful look, however, 'going back a few years' or 'turning back the clock' can also signify a belief in actually becoming younger. Some of my respondents experience anti-ageing surgery and technology as energy producing and life giving; they come out of surgery feeling pleased not only with their younger look, but also with their literally de-aged faces, bodies, and souls. Amy, aged 48, (quoted above), is especially excited by the reversal of the ageing process that her surgery has engendered – surgery has re-charged her body *and* changed its direction:

> All of a sudden something feels drastically *better* and it's kind of like 'wow I can keep going'. With the ageing process you feel like you're going in a good direction from many respects, but from your body's respect, it's tough. And all of a sudden something's been reversed and it's like 'wow, I can really go off in this direction!'

Anti-ageing surgeries and technologies contribute to a general optimism among several of my respondents about an increasingly realisable potential for eternal youth. As Maya puts it:

I love the idea that, you know, 60 is the new 50. I think that's the best attitude going ... It's a really great way of thinking. And people do live longer and, you know, there's so much more you can do [referring to anti-ageing surgeries and technologies].

Faith in contemporary technological and surgical advancements and progress is also evident in the way several respondents favourably compare their own generation to that of their parents. Unlike their parents, who were 'old before their time', these women strive to look and feel young for as long as possible – fitness, surgery, and other advancements in medicine and health awareness make extended youth possible. Nora, aged 62, a restaurant owner who has had eye-lift surgery, distinguishes herself from her parents at her age, and even from when they were younger than she is now:

My mother already started acting old ... well, actually they both [her mother and her father] did, like when they were 40. Oh, you know, you just didn't do certain things [at a certain age] then.

Lisa, a retired financial planner, age 58, who has had neck-lift and eye-lift surgeries, also distinguishes herself, and her generation, from that of her mother's. While Lisa describes her mother as someone who 'always looked nice', 'made herself look attractive', and didn't 'totally let herself go', she stresses that, unlike herself and her friends, her mother 'never *worked* on her body'. In contrast to Lisa and her friends, her mother did not have facials or manicures or pedicures – she cut her own hair and did her own nails – and she let her hair go gray. Lisa identifies her mother's lack of 'work' on her body as evidence of her mother's acceptance of growing older and compares this acceptance with her own (and her friends') resistance to it:

I think of my mother talking much more like 'okay, now we're old'. I always got the sense she was *much* more accepting. For years, she would say, 'I'm ready to die, I'm ready to go'. Whereas everyone I know is like 'can we just stop the clock here?'.

Lisa also understands her mother's lack of interest in plastic surgery as a reflection of her mother's comfort with growing older and wonders aloud whether she and her friends' embrace of anti-ageing surgeries and technologies signifies the opposite:

My mother would never, I mean she *would never*, she wouldn't have done that [have plastic surgery]. She would have thought it was unnecessary ... She was more accepting of 'that's *just the way I am*'. I mean, there is something about this [having anti-ageing surgery] that I'm sure that has to do with, you know, you're almost 60 years old. And my mother's generation thought 60 was *old*. And my generation is *primarily* trying to make 60 young.

Although Lisa's initial explanation for her neck and eye-lift surgeries is that she didn't like the way she looked, the more she thinks about it, the more she is convinced that her surgeries also represent her desire to stay young, her desire to fight off ageing for as along as possible. Indeed, upon greater reflection, Lisa admits that perhaps what she hated most about her face was simply that it looked old:

So I mean I talk about it [her surgery] in terms of, I didn't like the way I looked. But the way I looked is a normal ageing process for some people.

Lisa's neck and eye-lift surgeries have come to serve as a buffer between herself and her fears of growing older. Her surgeries obscure the facial changes that, in her mind, signify ageing, deterioration, even death:

> There is no question that my friends will say 'hey I'm not old' and we *hate* the fact that we are, *hate* it. *I really, really* don't like thinking about the fact that in twenty years I'll be 80. I mean I *really* don't like thinking about that. I *really* don't want to die. I really don't want to get old ... I think that it's [her surgeries] about not wanting to become frail, not wanting to become, not wanting to die. Not wanting to *leave*, not wanting to have things end. I don't like things *ending* ... What I mind is that it's going to end. I'm not accepting of that in a way that I think my mother was.

Several other respondents also express a visceral hatred of ageing and, like Lisa, link aesthetic, exterior changes to physical deterioration and death. Claire, a physical trainer, aged 49, who has on-going Botox treatments and claims she will take advantage of anti-ageing surgery later on, puts it like this:

> There's not one good thing about it [ageing]. It completely 100 per cent sucks. I mean, *what's* good about everything ageing? I mean, what's good about it? I'm not talking mentally and spiritually, I'm talking about physically. I mean your internal organs are ageing – I mean nothing's going in the positive direction. ... So, um, what I'm not okay with is I have a huge fear of death. And it's something I'm trying to work on. It's like one of my biggest goals right now, to work on doing some work around that. In that regard I can't totally separate ageing from the fear of death.

Claire struggles with the tension between warding off visible signs of ageing and overcoming her fear of death so that she can fully experience and enjoy the present moment:

> I'd like to be able to embrace that [fear of death] a little bit more so that I can let that go. And, you know, fully be present in the age that I'm at.

And yet, it may be harder for Claire to confront her fear of death and let it go when she is ever more distracted by the noise and youthful promises of anti-ageing surgery and technologies.

The technological imperative

Many of my respondents find the increasing availability of anti-ageing surgeries and technologies (and their capacity to choose these increasingly user-friendly surgeries and technologies as consumers) comforting and empowering. For others, however, the increasingly inevitable exposure to anti-ageing surgeries and technologies, through media coverage, television/print advertising, and even billboards in doctor's offices, makes them uncomfortable. Such exposure can lead women to feel worse about ageing and to feel increasing pressure to 'do something' about the age-related changes in their faces and bodies. What had been felt and perceived to be a natural, normal, and even universal process (ageing) is increasingly experienced as pathological, as a problem in need of fixing and repair. The existence of these surgeries and technologies – the very fact that women can make the choice to have and use them – makes some women feel personally responsible for their ageing faces and bodies. Ageing becomes *their fault*.

For Lucy, a recently retired shop owner, aged 62, it seems that the advertisements for new anti-ageing technologies are 'in your face a lot' and are pointing out problems 'I didn't know I had'. Lucy also talks about being bombarded with new anti-ageing procedures at her local doctor's office. She understands that doctors make a lot of money from these procedures and therefore have an incentive to pressurise women into having them. Even so, seeing the billboards in the waiting room makes her feel worse about her own ageing body and worry that everybody else is doing it – should she be doing it too? As she puts it:

> You go in [to her local doctor's office at her Health Maintenance Organization] and there's this huge sign in the hall about all the cosmetic surgeries they offer now ... It makes you stop and think about 'oh, my God, everybody must be doing this'.

Mia, a real estate agent, aged 59, offers a nuanced critique of direct-to-consumer anti-ageing advertising, describing it as creating an 'artificial demand' and as 'morally wrong'. Despite portraying herself as 'fairly immune' to such advertising, however, she begins to wonder whether she *should* be worried about her naturally ageing face and body as a result of her exposure to it:

> You see it all the time and it makes you think: 'Oh, is that something I should be thinking about?' Or, 'Am I so out of the mainstream or am I so weird, that I don't care about this?'

Knowing that she could 'do something' to 'fix' the age-related changes in her face and body makes Mia feel 'apologetic' for what was once simply a natural process, beyond her control:

> I think it [anti-ageing product advertising] does make one aware of what the possibilities are. And I think that now one has to make a conscious choice not to use them. Whereas before it wouldn't have been on one's radar screen. I think it does make one feel worse about getting older, because these products are designed to make one look younger. I think it makes one feel either apologetic or gee, I'm getting older and things are just getting worse. It does not help one's self esteem.

Laura, an education advisor, aged 51, laments the fact that she doesn't live in a culture that 'supports her' and just allows her to 'relax' about ageing. Instead, modern science harasses her with formulas to look younger, with ammunition to fight the ageing disease, and it becomes harder and harder to age without stigma, without guilt:

> It's hard to feel good about ageing, having your body do what it naturally does around this age, when the culture is telling you that that's not necessarily so. It'd be much easier if I had a culture supporting me, saying relax, women your age are supposed to look like that. But no, modern science tells me no, that's not true, that it could be otherwise. And there's a sense of guilt, an added sense of guilt for women, I think, to say you're choosing this because *we've proven otherwise.*

Laura continues to assert her belief in ageing as a 'normal' process that is 'happening to me' and that 'happens to everybody':

> I think things like your face growing lined, and the thickening of the middle if you've had children, and all that stuff is *normal.*

And yet, increasingly, Laura feels that American culture 'doesn't allow aging' and teaches her that 'aging is not good'. She wistfully wonders about other cultures, outside the United States, where perhaps you can simply 'get old' and 'slow down' because that's just 'what happens':

> The choice in all the matter can be a burden because we constantly feel that when we age, or get older looking, it's partly our fault and there are things that you can do to undo effects of ageing. And so there's just more guilt there. I don't think other cultures have that. You get old, that's what happens. You slow down. But we have this feeling that it's bad to do that.

Laura, Mia and Lucy have not had or used anti-ageing surgeries or technologies; Mia and Lucy are fairly convinced they will not partake of them in the future, whereas Laura is 'on the fence' about whether she will or will not have/use anti-ageing surgeries and technologies in coming years. Discomfort with the growing prevalence and accessibility of aesthetic anti-ageing surgeries and technologies is not limited to my non-user respondents, however. Several of my respondents who are generally embracing these surgeries and technologies articulate ambivalence about the increasingly ubiquitous nature of these surgeries and technologies, and the subsequent pressure they feel to use them. These women convey feelings of nostalgia (if only they could 'just accept' the natural ageing process) as well as exhaustion and frustration with the constant expectation to resist and fight the ageing process that the widespread availability and advertising of anti-ageing surgeries and technologies promotes.

Julia, a homemaker, aged 47, has had several rounds of sclerotherapy (varicose vain removal treatments via laser), laser treatments to remove age spots on her face, and plans to move on to Botox, collagen, and probably even surgical anti-ageing procedures in the future. She struggles to sort out whether her motives for having these procedures are self-driven or whether her negative feelings about her face and body stem from her increasing exposure to anti-ageing surgeries and technologies:

> What I resent is that I can't look in the mirror and just be happy. I have to look and think, 'Oh, Are these too saggy?' 'Do you think I should be doing something down the road?' Or, 'Should I fix this?' ... I can't read the Boston Globe magazine without seeing all these ads: *Before, After*. So I don't know what comes first, the chicken or the egg. Am I dissatisfied with myself and I want to fix it? Or, am I minding my own business, the media is showing me all these ads, and I'm thinking, 'Oh, maybe I need to do this?'.

The more she talks about it, the more Julia seems to become convinced that she wouldn't be so worried about her ageing face and body if she wasn't surrounded by a plethora of anti-ageing technology options and choices. If the 'products and services weren't available', she posits, 'I wouldn't be thinking about it'. Even when she goes in for routine check ups at her gynecologist's office she is bombarded (and tempted) by new anti-ageing procedures: it is her gynecologist, she explains with some incredulousness, who performs her laser hair and age spot removal treatments.

Like Laura (quoted in the preceding section) Julia appears to feel some wistfulness for what her ageing process might be like if she didn't have the choice of having and using anti-ageing surgery and technologies. She explains that ageing could really be a 'beautiful process' and that she would be more likely to accept looking in the mirror and seeing wrinkles – to feel like that's just what happens – if everybody else would just let her 'be okay with it'. Yet, even the reality of several 'wonderful' women role models who are ageing 'naturally', including her own mother, fails to insulate Julia from the cultural pressures to look young and to interrupt her pull towards anti-ageing surgery and technologies:

> I'm lucky that I have wonderful role models. My mother is so adorable. She's 71. She's kind of dumpy. She doesn't do any exercise, her body is all flab and she's a little overweight. And she's ... everybody says, 'Oh, she's so young looking'. And I think that's because of her personality, she's so happy and twinkly. And so I feel like she's beautiful. And I go to committee meetings and there are older women. I see the most beautiful women that are white haired lately. They're fit, they twinkle, they're alive. So I think that it [ageing] could be a really beautiful process and I think it's mostly the culture around us that makes us feel badly. Because I could look in the mirror and see these wrinkles and think *okay*, that's what's happening, if everybody else would *let me be okay with it*.

My respondents' sentiments and experiences discussed here, and in the preceding section, illuminate some of the conflicts women face as they encounter anti-ageing surgery and technologies. Even among some of my respondents who use/have anti-ageing surgery and technologies, and/or are convinced that they will have and use them in the future, feelings of ambivalence surface. And yet, it seems that most are somewhat resigned to being caught up in the anti-ageing surgical and technological cycle. As Julia puts it: 'I've seen those barriers [to anti-ageing surgery and technologies] break down in me.'

The feminine imperative

As women grow older, most confront a 'double standard of ageing' (Sontag 1997 [1972]). Unlike men, who are valued for capacities such as individual agency and for unique thoughts and actions, women's value is more likely to be linked to their sexual attractiveness and reproductive viability. A man's social value, and even his perceived physical desirability, often increases with age, while a woman's decreases. As Sandra Bartky explains:

> The loss of an admiring gaze falls disproportionately on women. We need to see but also to be seen and to be seen as attractive ... a woman's worth, not only in the eyes of others, but in her own eyes as well, depends, to a significant degree, on her appearance (1999: 67).

Women can experience shame when they 'lose their ability to conform to dominant standards of femininity' and when their bodies no longer represent 'important feminine qualities, such as sexual attractiveness, youth, and slenderness' (Furman 1999: 10). Aesthetic anti-ageing surgeries and technologies offer older women new opportunities to embody the youthful characteristics of traditional femininity and thereby to challenge the stigma, shame, and invisibility that many encounter as they age. Certainly, for some of my respondents, feelings and experiences of being ignored, negatively stereotyped, and cast aside as older women influenced their decision to have and use anti-ageing surgeries and technologies. For these women, looking more youthful after surgery can be an empowering and self-esteem building experience. Achieving smoother skin, flatter stomachs, and perkier breasts makes them feel more 'attractive' and 'sexually desirable', and means receiving increased attention from others, helping, therefore, to lessen the painful invisibility they endured as naturally ageing women. Yet others resent the prospect of continuing to meet the 'disciplinary practices of femininity' (Bordo 1993, Bartky 1990) just at a time when they are beginning to enjoy some freedom from the pressures to conform to traditional feminine aesthetics. Further, while anti-ageing surgeries and technologies make the 'doing of femininity' (Smith 1990) possible at an older age, more time, work, money, and pain is required to mould the older face and body in compliance with feminine beauty standards. The opportunity for re-claiming, or maintaining, feminine beauty and sexual desirability via anti-ageing surgery and technology increases the pressure some women feel to conform to feminine norms and practices they find limiting and confining.

The potential, as a woman, to look younger, and therefore more 'attractive', through anti-ageing surgery and technology use can translate into a kind of moral, feminine imperative. According to Mary, aged 72, a semi-retired commercial property agent who has had a face lift, it is a woman's responsibility to look as physically attractive as she can, within her power (especially if she hopes to attract and hold on to a man), and for women of a certain age this means having surgery:

> I think it's stupid not to do everything you can, particularly if you're single. You just have to do what you can with what you have ... I mean, why not [get a face lift]? You might as well do what you can.

Laura, however, feels differently:

> Why should an older woman be expected to be sexually attractive and have a hot body? I shouldn't feel badly if people don't find my 91-year-old mother-in-law sexually attractive. She *is attractive*, just in a *different way*.

Laura, like many of my respondents who are resisting anti-ageing surgeries and technologies, and who are on the fence about whether or not they will have/use anti-ageing surgeries and technologies in the future, strives to re-conceptualise attractiveness outside the rigid youth/beauty confines of traditional femininity. In addition to re-defining physical beauty to include age-related characteristics, and finding beauty in realms outside appearance altogether, these respondents also begin to explore and develop new aspects of themselves, and to find value and self-worth in their capacities beyond physical attractiveness and reproductive viability. Yet, realising the potential for new freedom with age (a freedom, that, in part, can be attributed to the release from the admiring/objectifying male gaze) becomes more difficult as anti-ageing surgeries and technologies gain ground and offer more and more avenues for older women to continue to comply with, and conform to, the normative and disciplinary practices of femininity.

Conclusion

My data suggest that the growing availability, marketing, and use of aesthetic anti-ageing surgeries and technologies in the United States both 'reproduce' and 'reconfigure' (Joyce and Mamo 2006) mainstream American cultural attitudes about women and ageing. As my respondents' experiences and perspectives illuminate, aesthetic anti-ageing surgeries and technologies project a new paradigm of ageing, one that echoes the successful ageing directives of individual responsibility, effort, and work on the body, but also intensifies and expands these directives and contributes more ambitious goals. Ageing successfully, in light of the increasing prevalence of aesthetic anti-ageing surgeries and technologies, comes to mean not only maintaining a healthy, active body through diet and exercise, but a young-looking body (and face) through surgery and injectables. My respondents articulate an aesthetic anti-ageing surgery-and-technology-driven paradigm that edges out successful ageing in favour of a kind of feminised agelessness – health work on the body in the context of ageing is subsumed into youth/beauty work on the body that aims to minimise, reverse, and even prevent signs of ageing altogether.

The prospect of being able to shed age-related characteristics in the face and body, and thereby to conserve traditional feminine attributes – to conform to the feminine norm of youthfulness *despite* growing older – explains much of the appeal that aesthetic anti-ageing surgeries and technologies hold for the women who have and use them. Through achieving younger, tighter-looking skin, flatter stomachs and perkier breasts, my respondents seek to lessen some of the (unjust) invisibility and stigma they encountered as naturally ageing women. The increased attention and praise my respondents receive for their (post-surgeried, post-injected) appearance is a confidence and self-esteem booster; such attention and praise also debunks the belief that older women cannot be sexy and physically attractive. Finally, aesthetic anti-ageing surgeries and technologies offer women the opportunity to assert some control over the biological process of natural ageing. (My respondents commonly describe once familiar faces and bodies becoming alien due to age-related changes – it's as if they are no longer at the helm of their own faces and bodies but instead, nature, or the ghost of ageing, is.) Many express heady excitement about these surgeries and technologies as a means to erase age-related changes in their faces and bodies, as a means to *fight back against nature with the power of technology*. In this way, aesthetic anti-ageing surgeries and technologies enable my respondents to inhabit new agency in and through their bodies. As Kathy Davis explains, cosmetic surgery can provide women with an empowering 'different starting position' in relationship to her body:

> Cosmetic surgery can provide the impetus for an individual woman to move from a passive acceptance of herself as nothing but a body to the position of a subject who acts upon the world in and through her body. It is in this sense that cosmetic surgery can, paradoxically, provide an avenue toward becoming an embodied subject rather than an objectified body (1997: 114).

The capacity for maintaining a youthful appearance engendered by aesthetic anti-ageing surgeries and technologies proves agenic for many; yet, the controllability of the body made possible by aesthetic anti-ageing surgeries and technologies also pathologises the naturally ageing female body with new virulence. The older woman's face and body has always been rejected for failing to meet the feminine cultural expectations of sexual attractiveness and reproductive viability. However, with the increasing availability and accessibility of aesthetic anti-ageing surgeries and technologies, with the possibility to continue to mould, shape, and discipline their faces and bodies in accordance with feminine youth imperatives as they age, older women are penalised not only for having faces and bodies that exhibit natural signs of ageing but also for failing to *do something* to repair them. Despite the fact that age-related changes, in one respondent's words, 'happen to everybody', and are a reflection of the body 'doing what it naturally does', the growing prevalence of aesthetic anti-ageing surgeries and technologies can make women feel they are 'choosing' the inferior path of natural ageing over and above the superior route of femininity-maintenance and age-prevention. Aesthetic anti-ageing surgeries and technologies are contributing to a culture that, as she puts it, 'doesn't allow ageing'. Women are made to feel 'guilty' for failing to uphold their femininity (or social value) and culpable for the age signs on their faces and bodies. As another respondent proclaims, 'if women can afford to do it [have anti-ageing surgery] *they should do it*'.

My respondents' articulation of an aesthetic anti-ageing surgery-and-technology-driven ideology of agelessness and femininity (whether they subscribe to this ideology through embracing these surgeries and technologies, or resist it through refusing them, all express a keen awareness of its existence) echoes Martha Holstein's prediction that anti-ageing medicines will 'devalue old age and intensify [negative] cultural attitudes about aging' (2002: 38). Aesthetic anti-ageing surgeries and technologies make women who are growing older naturally feel worse about their ageing faces and bodies. Women who have and use these surgeries and technologies feel better about ageing precisely *because* they are able to minimise the age signs on their faces and bodies. Only when we understand that the body is 'not controllable', Carolyn Morell (2003) argues, 'will those who cannot control their bodies no longer be perceived as responsible for their limitations or as examples of 'unsuccessful ageing' (2003: 80). But aesthetic anti-ageing surgeries and technologies connote an increasing controllability of the body and, with that, the perception of the ageing body as the 'rejected body' (Wendell 1996, 1999) and of old bodies as 'problem bodies' (Oberg 2003) intensifies, particularly if they belong to women.

Aesthetic anti-ageing surgeries and technologies reinforce the cultural understanding of growing older – and for women, specifically, looking older – as an inherently undesirable and negative experience. To feel better about ageing means minimising age signs on the face and body; in short, *looking younger*. Women are empowered in and through their use of aesthetic anti-ageing surgeries and technologies as they slow, stop, and even reverse what had previously been endured as unwelcome age-driven changes beyond their control. These women realise the role of technogenarian as they reconstruct their naturally ageing bodies with age-erasing technology, replacing undesired ageful faces and bodies with youthful ageless ones. The recent cultural ascendance of the successful ageing paradigm – with its focus on the maintenance of active, healthy bodies through diet and exercise – restricts not only popular understandings of how to age 'successfully', but limits understandings of positive ageing to the directives of successful ageing as well (Holstein 2006, Gergen and Gergen 2001). The technogenarian model of ageing (via anti-ageing surgeries and technologies) narrows understandings of positive ageing yet further; indeed the 'positive', 'successful', pay off for adopting this model connotes wiping out indicators of ageing altogether.

Aesthetic anti-ageing surgeries and technologies are welcomed by many as a cheering alternative to natural ageing ('who wouldn't take advantage of surgery?' one woman asks, incredulous at the thought that any woman would not do just that). There are women, however, who reject the anti-ageing technogenarian model in favour of ageing naturally, and who gain new freedom, agency and empowerment in and through their embodiment of natural ageing – women, in short, who resist negative and limiting ageist and sexist stereotypes, who 'redefine *old*' as inclusive of positive aspects, 'without adopting the normative rubrics of 'successful' and 'productive'. (Holstein 2006, Holstein and Minkler 2003). My respondents who are ageing naturally enjoy a wealth of positive benefits as a result of being liberated from the feminine mandates of youth and beauty and from the socially prescribed feminine roles of sex object, nurturer and reproducer. Technogenarians may lose out on many benefits of natural ageing – less anxiety about physical appearance and about attracting the male gaze and, therefore, less effort and pain caught up in beauty work; more freedom to observe others; more diverse and inclusive definitions of beauty; re-claiming the body for oneself after years of making it available for the pleasure and nurturance of others; discovering and developing new parts of oneself outside the role of sex object/wife/mother – yet, perhaps most detrimental, is the erasure of age signs from the face and body that mark the inevitable passage of time. My respondents who are growing older naturally struggle, at times, with accepting and adapting to the age-related changes in their faces and bodies. These changes, however, signal the positive growth and memories that accompany life experience; they can also prove useful strategies that, as one woman puts it, 'remind me of the preciousness of life', and that 'help me prepare for the next stage', in the words of another. Technogenarians' young-looking faces and bodies distract them from the reality of biological ageing and disguise its signs. While these (aesthetic anti-ageing surgery and technology produced) distractions and disguises are welcomed by many women, they may also leave them less able, in Lisa's words, to accept the reality of 'things ending', than their naturally ageing counterparts.

Acknowledgements

I am grateful to the anonymous reviewers for useful comments on an earlier draft of this chapter.

Notes

1   In 1982, the Supreme Court upheld the Federal Trade Commission ruling overturning the American Medical Association's ban on direct advertising and patient solicitation, initiating the deregulation of medicine in the United States. Federal Trade Commission rulings, Congressional mandates, and pressures from pharmaceutical companies throughout the 1990s have dramatically cut back on the time allotted to the Food and Drug Administration to test and approve new pharmaceutical drugs (drug approval times have been reduced 50% since the enactment of Congressional legislation in 1992) and have curtailed the power of the FDA to regulate the advertising and marketing of these drugs. Direct-to-consumer pharmaceutical advertising, in print media, on television, and on the internet, began in 1998. The FDA is not legally mandated, nor does it have the legal jurisdiction, to review the accuracy of these advertisements before they reach the public. (Please see Deborah Sullivan's *Cosmetic Surgery: The Cutting Edge of Commercial Medicine in America* (2001), Jay S. Cohen's *Overdose. The case Against the Drug Companies: Prescription Drugs, Side-Effects, and Your Health* (2001), and Arnold S. Relman's 'The Health Care Industry: Where is it taking us?' (2005) in *The Sociology of Health and Illness: Critical Perspectives*, for more in-depth analysis of the history and current manifestations of the deregulation and commercialisation of medicine in the United States.)

2   The exception here is the recent scholarship of Clarke and Griffen (2007).

3   It is worth noting that women-centred products continue to make up the lion's share of anti-ageing advertising in the United States, and that the vast majority of cosmetic surgery consumers are women. In 2007, women had nearly 10.6 million procedures, or 91% of the total number of cosmetic procedures performed, while men had nearly 1.1 million procedures, only 9% of the total number of cosmetic procedures performed (American Society for Aesthetic Plastic Surgery 2008.) Despite recent survey data that indicates that men increasingly approve of cosmetic surgery (according to the American Society for Plastic Surgery 38.8% of men have more favorable attitudes towards cosmetic surgery than they did ten years ago), the rate of increase in numbers of male patients remains strikingly low. In fact, the total percentage of male patients has decreased from its high of 13% in 2003. Finally, anti-ageing procedures continue to account for the majority of non-surgical procedures, and for half to two-thirds of surgical procedures, among women in the United States (American Society for Aesthetic Plastic Surgery 2008).

4   In the United States, the average cost of a Botox injection is $417, for an eye lift, $2,882, and for a face lift, $6,532. These figures do not include fees for surgical facilities, anesthesia, and other miscellaneous costs related to surgery (The American Society for Aesthetic Plastic Surgery 2006). The vast majority of cosmetic surgeries and injectables are not covered by medical insurance; several exceptions include eye lifts for visual improvement purposes, breast lifts for back pain, and Botox injections for migraines.

References

American Society of Aesthetic Plastic Surgery (2006, 2007, 2008) Statistics (summary with links to other pages) http://www.surgery.org/media.statistics

Andrews, M. (1999) The seductivenss of agelessness, *Ageing and Society*, 19, 301–18.

Bartky, S.L. (1990) *Femininity and Domination: Studies in the Phenomenology of Oppression (Thinking Gender)*. New York: Routledge.

Bartky, S.L. (1999) Unplanned obsolescence: some reflections on aging. In Walker, M.U. (ed.) *Mother Time: Women, Aging, and Ethics*. Oxford, England: Rowman and Littlefield Publishers, Inc.

Bauman, Z. (1992) *Intimations of Postmodernity*. London: Routledge.

Bayer, K. (2005) Cosmetic surgery and cosmetics: redefining the appearance of age, *Generations*, Fall, 13–18.

Bordo, S. (2003 [1993]) *Unbearable Weight: Feminism, Western Culture, and the Body*. Berkley, Los Angeles, and London: University of California Press.

Browne, C.V. (1998) *Women, Feminism, and Aging*. New York: Springer.

Calasanti, T.M. (2004) New directions in feminist gerontology: an introduction, *Journal of Aging Studies*, 18, 1–8.

Calasanti, T.M., (2005) Ageism, gravity, and gender: experiences of aging bodies', *Generations*, Fall, 8–12.

Calasanti, T.M. and Slevin, K.F. (2001) *Gender, Social Inequalities, and Aging*. Walnut Creek, CA: AltaMira Press.

Calasanti, T.M. and King, N. 2005. Firming the floppy penis: age, class, and gender relations in the lives of old men, *Men and Masculinities*, 8, 1, 3–23.

Calasanti, T.M. and Slevin, K.F. 2006. Introduction: age matters. in Calasanti, T. M. and Slevin, K.F. (eds) *Age Matters: Realigning Feminist Thinking*. New York and London: Routledge.

Calasanti, T.M., Slevin, K.F. and King, N. (2006) Ageism and feminism: from 'et cetera' to center, *NWSA Journal*, 18, 1, 13–30.

Calasanti, T.M. and King, N. (2007) Beware of the estrogen assault: ideals of old manhood in anti-aging advertisements, *Journal of Aging Studies*, 21, 4, 357–68.

Clarke, L.H. and Griffen, M. (2007) The body natural and the body unnatural: beauty work and aging, *Journal of Aging Studies*, 21, 187–201.

Cohen, J.S. (2001) *Overdose. The case Against the Drug Companies: Prescription Drugs, Side-Effects, and Your Health*. New York: Jeremy P. Tarcher/Putnum.

Covello, V.T. and Peters, R.G. (2002) Women's perceptions of the risks of age-related diseases, including breast cancer: reports from a 3-year research study, *Health Communication*, 14, 3, 377–95.

Croissant, J. (2006) The new sexual technobody: Viagra in the hyperreal world, *Sexualities*, 9, 3, 333–44.

Cruikshank, M. (2003) *Learning to be Old: Gender, Culture and Aging*. Lanham, MD: Rowman and Littlefield Publishers.

Debert, G.G. (2003) Old people in advertising, *Cadernos pagu*, 21, 133–55.

Dillaway, Heather E. (2005) Menopause is the 'good old': women's thoughts about reproductive aging, *Gender and Society*, 19, 3, 398–417.

Featherstone, M. and Hepworth, M. (1991) The mask of ageing and the life course. In Featherstone, M., Hepworth, M. and Turner, B.S. (eds) *The Body: Social Process and Cultural Theory*. London: Sage.

Eichberg, Sarah Lucile. (2000) Bodies of work: cosmetic surgery and the gendered whitening of America, *Dissertation Abstracts International, A: The Humanities and Social Sciences*, 60, 12, 4610-A.

Furman, F.K. (1997) *Facing the Mirror: Older Women and Beauty Shop Culture*. New York and London: Routledge.

Furman, F.K. (1999) There are no older Venuses: older women's responses to their aging bodies. In Walker, M.U. (ed.) *Mother Time: Women, Aging, and Ethics*. Oxford, England: Rowman and Littlefield Publishers, Inc.

Gannon, L. and Stevens, J. (1998) Portraits of menopause in the mass media, *Women and Health*, 27, 3, 1–15.

Gamson, W. (1992) *Talking Politics*. Cambridge: Cambridge University Press.

Gergen, M.M. and Gergen, K.J. (2001) Positive ageing: new images for a new age, *Ageing International*, 27, 1, 3–23.

Giddens, A. (1991) *Modernity and Self Identity: Self and Society in the Late Modern Age*. Cambridge: Polity Press.

Gonyea, J.G. (1998) Midlife and menopause: uncharted territories for baby boomer women, *Generations*, 22, 1, 87–89.

Gullette, M.M. (2004) *Aged by Culture*. Chicago and London: The University of Chicago Press.

Gullette, M.M. (1997) *Declining to Decline: Cultural Combat and the Politics of the Mid-Life*. Charlottesville and London: University Press of Virginia.

Hayles, C. (2002) Ladies of the track: femininity and sport in later life, Conference Paper, *International Sociological Association*, Brisbane, Australia.

Holstein, M.B. (2001–2002) A feminist perspective on anti-aging medicine, *Generations*, 25, 4, 38–43.

Holstein, M.B. (2006) On being an aging woman. In Calasanti, T.M. and Slevin, K.F. (eds) *Age Matters: Realigning Feminist Thinking*. New York and London: Routledge.

Holstein, M.B. and Minkler, M. (2003) Self, society, and the 'new gerontology', *The Gerontologist*, 43, 6, 787–96.

Hurd, L.C. (2002a) Older women's bodies and the self: the construction of identity in later life, *The Canadian Review of Sociology and Anthropology*, 38, 4, 441–64.

Hurd, L.C. (2002b) Beauty in later life: older women's perceptions of physical attractiveness, *Canadian Journal on Aging*, 21, 3, 429–42.

Hurd, L.C. (2000) Older women's body image and embodied experience: an exploration, *Journal of Women and Aging*, 12, 3/4, 77–97.

Joyce, K. and Mamo, L.(2006) Graying the cyborg: new directions in feminist analyses of aging, science, and technology. In Calasanti, T.M. and Slevin, K.F. (eds) *Age Matters: Realigning Feminist Thinking*. New York and London: Routledge.

Katz, S. (2000) Busy bodies: activity, aging and the management of everyday life, *Journal of Aging Studies*, 14, 2, 135–52.

Katz, S and Barbara, L.M. (2003) Is the functional 'normal'? Aging, sexuality, and the bio-marketing of successful living, *History of the Human Sciences*, 17, 1, 53–75.

Kaw, E. (1998) The medicalization of racial features: Asian American Women and Cosmetic Surgery. In Weitz, R. (ed.) *The Politics of Women's Bodies: Sexuality, Appearance, and Behavior*. Oxford and New York: Oxford University Press.

Loe, M. (2004) Sex and the senior woman: pleasure and danger in Viagra, *Sexualities*, 7, 3, 303–26.

Marshall, B.L. (2002a) 'Hard science:' gendered constructions of sexual dysfunction in the 'Viagra age', *Sexualities*, 5, 2, 131–58.

Marshall, B.L. (2002b) Forever functional: sexual fitness and the aging male body, *Body and Society*, 8, 4, 43–70.

Morell, C.M. (2003) Empowerment and long-living women: return to the rejected body, *Journal of Aging Studies*, 17, 1, 69–85.

Neuman, L.W. (2000) *Social Research Methods: Qualitative and Quantitative Approaches*. Needham Heights, MA: Allyn and Bacon.

Oberg, P. (2003) Image versus experience of the aging body. In Faircloth, C.A. (ed.) *Aging Bodies Images and Everyday Experience*. Walnut Creek, Lanham, New York, Oxford: Alta Mira Press.

O'Beirne, N. (1999) The 'docile/useful' body of the older woman. In Onyx, J., Leonard, R. and Reed, R. (eds) *Revisioning Aging: Empowerment of Older Women*. New York: Peter Lang Publishing Inc.

Ostrander, S. (1984) *Women of the Upper Class*. Philadelphia: Temple University Press.

Potts, A., Gavey, N., Grace, V.M. and Vares, T. (2003) The downside of Viagra: women's experiences and concerns, *Sociology of Health and Illness*, 25, 7, 697–719.

Reel, J.J., Soohoo, S., Franklin Summerhays, J. and Gill, D.L. (2008) Age before beauty: an exploration of body image in African-American and Caucasian adult women, *Journal of Gender Studies*, 17, 4, 321–30.

Relman, A.S. (2005) The health care industry: where is it taking us? In Conrad, P. (ed.) *The Sociology of Health and Illness: Critical Perspectives*, 7th Edition. New York: Worth Publishers.

Rowe, J. and Kahn, R. (1987) Human aging: usual and successful, *Science*, 237, 4811, 143–49.

Rowe, J. and Kahn, R. (1997) Successful aging, *The Gerontologist*, 37, 433–40.

Rowe, J. and Kahn, R. (1998) *Successful Aging*. New York: Random House.

Rubin, L. (1994) *Families on the Fault Line: America's Working Class Speaks about Family, the Economy, Race, and Ethnicity*. New York: Harper Collins Publishers.

Shilling, C. (2003 [1993]) *The Body and Social Theory*. London, Newbury Park. New Delhi: Sage Publications.

Smith, D.E. (1990) *Texts, Facts, and Femininity: Exploring the Relations of Ruling*. London: Routledge.

Sontag, S. (1997) The double standard of aging. In Pearsall, M. (ed.) *The Other Within Us: Feminist Explorations of Women and Aging*. Boulder, CO: Westview Press.

Sullivan, D. (2001) *Cosmetic Surgery: the Cutting Edge of Commercial Medicine in America*. New Brunswick, NJ: Rutgers University Press.

Topo, P. (1997) Climacteric hormone therapy in medical and lay texts in Finland from 1955–1992, *Social Science and Medicine*, 45, 5, 751–60.

Tunaley, J.R., Walsh, S. and Nicolson, P. (1999) I'm not bad for my age: the meaning of body size and eating in the lives of older women, *Ageing and Society*, 19, 6, 741–59.

Wendell, S. (1996) *The Rejected Body: Feminist Philosophical Reflections on Disability*. New York: Routledge.

Wendell, S. (1999) Old women out of control: some thoughts on aging, ethics, and psychosomatic medicine. In Walker, M.U. (ed.) *Mother Time: Women, Aging, and Ethics*. New York: Rowman and Littlefield Publishers.

Wepsic, R.M. (1996) Cosmetic surgery and images of aging women: constructing difference by race and class, *Society for the Study of Social Problems* (conference paper).

Williams, S.J. and Bendelow, G. (1998) *The Lived Body: Sociological Themes, Embodied Issues*. London and New York: Routledge.

Woodward, K. (1999) Introduction. In Woodward, K. (ed.) *Figuring Age: Women, Bodies, and Generations, ix–xxix*. Bloomington and Indianapolis: Indiana University Press.

Wray, S. (2004a) Women growing older: agency, ethnicity, and culture, *Sociology*, 37, 3, 511–27.

Wray, S. (2004b) What constitutes empowerment and agency for women in later life? *The Sociological Review*, 52, 1, 22–38.

7

'A second youth': pursuing happiness and respectability through cosmetic surgery in Finland

Taina Kinnunen

My second youth started after my first facelift (Hilja, 84, two facelifts).

When you get older, the corners of the mouth hang down; you look very ill-humoured. I am not an ill-humoured person at all so I don't want to look like an angry old maid (Liisa, 56, a facelift and two upper eyelid surgeries).

Cosmetic surgery is frequently justified as a quality of life investment: ageing people who choose it often wish to feel happier by looking younger. People at times describe cosmetic surgery as an action that brings a new phase of life – one that brings a 'second youth'. The belief that one's state of mind could be manipulated by appearance was systematically developed by late 19th century plastic surgeons who compared the practice with psychiatric therapy; psychiatrists were also enthusiastic about the comparison (Gilman 1998). Since early modernity, youthful appearance has been an ideal in European and North American countries.

Cosmetic surgery is a form of biomedical practice aimed at preventing ageing and thus the unhappiness associated with it. It is one of the fastest growing fields of commercial medicine in which patients' subjective needs are understood as proper indications for medical interventions. Instead of one procedure, many choose a set of procedures. Cosmetic surgery is one tactic people use to pursue what is commonly called positive ageing. Positive ageing promotes the idea that one can defy ageing by purchasing products or services that will help one look young, healthy, and happy (see Bytheway 2003, Featherstone and Hepworth 1995).

Studies of cosmetic surgery and beauty culture discuss the growth in this field as both outcome and producer of an anti-ageing society (ageism). Ageing is thought to have a particularly stigmatising effect on women, who are viewed in terms of appearance throughout their lives. Thus, most cosmetic surgery patients have historically been female. Women are socially defined by and pressured to be concerned about their appearance (which includes a fear of ageing), and cosmetic surgery provides a technological response to this pressure (*e.g.* Balsamo 1996, Davis 2002, Fraser 2003, Jones 2004, Haiken 1999). Critical feminist research deconstructs gender power relations in practices and representations of cosmetic surgery, considering it as a form of objectification and subordination of women (*e.g.* Bordo 1993, Kinnunen 2008, Morgan 1998, Negrin 2002). On the other hand, some researchers emphasise cosmetic surgery's potential to empower women who suffer ageist, sexist forms of discrimination (Blum 2003, Davis 1995, Gagne and McGaughey 2002, Gimlin 2002, Holliday and Sanchez Taylor 2006).

Although many studies provide insightful analyses of the cultural meanings of ageing, gender and cosmetic surgery, and some utilise interviews with ageing women consumers of cosmetic surgeries (*e.g.* Davis 1995, Sleven 2007), the discussion of lived experiences of elderly cosmetic surgery customers is insufficient, especially outside the Anglo-American context. Further, discussion of surgeons' views is limited although their role in setting norms for bodily ageing is notable (*cf.* Blum 2003). In addition, older men are mostly excluded from published studies. This chapter contributes to the literature on cosmetic surgery by analysing why women and men over 55 choose cosmetic surgery. I argue that cosmetic surgery is believed to be a way to obtain happiness (which is equated with youth); emotions are embedded in this embodied practice. I also show how cosmetic surgery must be understood as part of national and global processes. In Finland, surgical manipulation of perceived 'Finnish' features results from an effort to be more 'American' and more 'white'. Interviews with Finnish people between 55 and 84 years old who chose cosmetic surgery form the basis of the analysis presented. Here it must be noted that while generally people over 70 are considered old, in the world of beauty culture and cosmetic surgery those in their 30s undergo their first rejuvenation operations. That said, the vast majority of procedures are requested by people over 50.

This chapter analyses the motives that interviewees expressed for choosing surgical procedures. The theoretical perspective of the body follows Arthur W. Frank's (1991) notion of the human body as constituted always in the *intersection* of subjective experiences, cultural discourses and institutional practices. In this case, patients and surgeons in dialogue with cultural and national discourses create a bodily ideal of ageing that highlights how cosmetic surgery is used to counter what are perceived as undesirable physical and mental features of being Finnish. Each dimension is important to include in the discussion of embodied meanings of rejuvenation surgery. After introducing the research material and methodology, I describe beauty culture and cosmetic surgery in Finland. Although cosmetic surgery is a global phenomenon, and I refer to the predominantly Anglo-American published research, it is important to keep in mind the Finnish context of the discussion. Finland represents a periphery of the cosmetic surgery world; surgical intervention is far from normative in this context, and thus arouses strong suspicion in many people's minds.

Research material and methods

I conducted 23 interviews in 2003–2004 with 55–84 year-old women (21) and men (2) who had chosen to undergo cosmetic surgery. Nine belonged to the 55–59 age group, five were between 60–64 years old and six were in the 65–74 age bracket. Three interviewees were older than 75. All were of Finnish ethnic origin. Half of the interviewees had a bachelor or upper degree and the rest had basic or upper secondary education or had completed vocational training. The material discussed here comprises part of a larger study on embodied meanings of cosmetic surgery.[1]

Beyond cosmetic surgery users, I interviewed 12 plastic surgeons and two cosmetic surgery consultants who provided customers to Estonian surgeons.[2] Most of the procedures discussed here are categorised as rejuvenation surgery, which includes upper or lower eyelid surgeries, forehead lifts, facelifts, injections for wrinkles (*e.g.* Botox and Restylane) and lipo-transfers.[3] Even the label 'rejuvenation' shows the ageist ideal at work. The ideal body is youthful and ageing men and women should rejuvenate their bodies to mimic youthful qualities. Breast operations, rhinoplasty and liposuction are typical for younger customers, but some individual procedures are represented in the research group as well.

The semi-structured interviews were conducted around five main themes: (1) background knowledge and procedures performed (when and where), (2) the criteria for choosing the surgeon or clinic and the level of satisfaction with the service, (3) the decision-making process ending up in opting for the surgery and its social sharing, (4) satisfaction with one's own appearance, and (5) views about contemporary beauty culture and cosmetic surgery. Aesthetic, psychic and social expectations and results regarding the surgery were also explored.

Surgeons and consultants were asked about their career choice, cosmetic surgery as a medical specialty and personal attitudes about this field. Surgeons generally described a typical 'good' and 'bad' patient and talked about rewarding and frustrating experiences during their careers. One question asked surgeons to recommend procedures for an imaginary patient (the researcher) facing a mid-life crisis in her forties.

All interviews were tape-recorded and transcribed. In the first phase, the gathered material was read through so as to understand each interview as an individual story of cosmetic surgery. In the second phase, the material was analysed through interview themes. Thereafter modes of experiences recurring throughout the interview were abstracted to find out the key meanings attached to the operations. On this basis it was also possible to characterise some patient types and isolate discourses of ageing and social control.

My interview approach was phenomenological-hermeneutic. This enabled the adoption of a position of pause and amazement in the face of the *reflected* experiences[4] the interviewees offered to me (*cf.* Moustakas 1994, Van Maanen 1990). The final aim of the act of interpretation, for me, is to construct a credible narrative of the interviewee's words or, as Charles Taylor (1987) puts it, to hermeneutically find the 'sense' of them. Still, instead of open questions and minimal reacting to the interviewee's speech in the orthodox phenomenological sense, I understand phenomenological-hermeneutic interviewing as encouraging the interviewee to analyse their key experiences on the basis of shared cultural meanings (*cf.* Saukko 2002). Besides listening intensively, it demands using emphatic, ironic, provocative, exaggerating or understating comments to facilitate discussion. A researcher can even offer pieces of his/her own experiences and conceptions as tools for reflection. Thus, the phenomenological-hermeneutic method is understood to be fully realised in this study in dialogue with the interviewees.

Beauty culture and cosmetic surgery in Finland

Finland is one of the most sparsely inhabited, rural countries in Europe. It has also had very little immigration compared to neighbouring countries. Finland is marked by conservative values such as limiting the rights of sexual minorities, encouraging gender segregation of work and limiting women's career possibilities. Among the Western countries, Finland leads the statistics of violence towards women in intimate relationships. Despite these indicators of gender inequality, the myth of the strong Finnish woman persists in post-war Finland. The myth exerts its influence on the beauty culture as well. In the Finnish countryside, a woman's diligence has always been valued more than beauty, and the strong rural woman has been distinguished from the pretty, weak and clumsy city woman (Vakimo 1999: 139–40). Ageing rural women tend to complain more of the deterioration of their bodies' functionality rather than their appearance (Palomäki 2004: 107). In North American and European countries, ageing has traditionally worried the members of the urban middle class more than rural or working class people (Botelho and Thane 2001, Featherstone 1987).

The work-centredness of Finnish women across social class categories means that they have not invested in their appearance as eagerly as, for example, their European, Russian or American sisters (Halonen 2004: 73). The stereotype of the functional Finnish woman in her shell suit and low-heeled shoes, contrary to the Estonian or Russian traditionally feminine and sexy woman, is widely shared in Finland. In 2004, Dove, a cosmetics company, conducted an international research project in co-operation with academics.[5] The research compared 18–55 year old women's conceptions of beauty in 15 countries. Approximately 300 women from each country participated. Finnish women tended to be more critical about the beauty culture than the average by claiming, for example, that the media set an unrealistic and narrow beauty ideal. In the Dove study, one in four Finnish women had sometimes considered cosmetic surgery, whereas in Sweden the proportion was one in three and in Brazil one in two. The view of cosmetic surgery, in particular within the post-war generation, has long been negative. It is no wonder that in my study only one-fifth of the patients felt that they could talk openly about their surgery. For many participants, I was the first to know about their surgery. In 2000, former Miss Finland, Lola Odusoga, sparked a wild public debate over her silicon breast implants. The act was reported to 'divide the nation' over opinions of Odusoga's morals and intelligence.[6] Since then cosmetic surgery has become more visible in the media, which can be easily seen, for example, in the increased advertising of surgical services in the leading paper *Helsingin Sanomat*. According to surgeons' estimation, thousands of procedures are performed yearly.

Still, cosmetic surgery triggers strong reactions. Surgeons I interviewed complained that Finland is at the periphery of cosmetic surgery, a fact which they linked with 'backwardness', 'primitiveness' and the 'ideal of indifference'. Interviewees who had undergone surgical procedures discussed general attitudes about cosmetic surgery. They linked several negative attributes to people with negative attitudes to cosmetic surgery, such as totalitarianism, fundamentalism, ugliness, feminism, malevolence, bitterness, peasantry, timidity, depression, ignorance, psychic instability, backwardness, and failure. In contrast, they linked positive attitudes to cosmetic surgery with tolerance, individualism, femininity, courage, carefulness, development, cosmopolitanism, happiness, joyfulness, realism, curiosity, education, responsibility, freedom and success.

According to the statistics of the International Society of Aesthetic Plastic Surgery (*ISAPS*), the number of cosmetic surgery procedures increases globally by 20 per cent per year.[7] More and more middle-aged and retired women, for example, have the money needed for cosmetic surgery. On the other hand, 'low price, low risk' procedures, such as laser techniques and injections, are constantly developed to lower the threshold for buying surgical services (*cf.* Brooks 2004). Therefore, the global increase is also likely to concern Finland, as the surgeons that I interviewed believe. They had also noticed a gradual change in general attitudes; for some, cosmetic surgery represented a new exciting technology to pamper oneself. Some male surgeons and patients even pleaded a rational viewpoint of consumption, stating that cosmetic surgery freshened up the domestic economy. Currently, clinics are heavily centred around the area of the capital city in southern Finland. Some services are offered in smaller towns, where indications for procedures, *i.e.* the threshold for choosing surgery, however, are much 'higher' than in the capital area, as the interviewed surgeons underlined.

Curing the melancholic Finnish body

It is a Finnish national disease that the forehead droops (Surgeon).

A belief in the physical inferiority of the Finnish body has long troubled Finns. In the 19th and early 20th centuries several foreign scientists categorised Finns as of Eastern Mongolian origin instead of as European in origin. Finnish sports journalists countered this idea by, for example, maintaining that one reason for the Finnish athletes' success was belonging to the 'white race' (Tervo 2002). The pathologisation of the Finnish body still exists and some interviewees evoked it as a justification for their surgical operation. Raija, 60, told me that her father – who happened to be a doctor – had always made it clear that he admired 'slim and long-legged Scandinavian' type women instead of 'short-legged and round Finnish' women. As a young adult, her father's opinion had pushed her to seek a breast reduction. The Finnish 'potato' nose is one problematic feature, as one of the interviewees who underwent a rhinoplasty described:

> Last summer we had a meeting between my maternal cousins and I remember particularly when one of my cousins said that he does not reveal his surname because one can recognise it from the big ... Savonian[8] nose. Finns have this in their genes, it is not beautiful.

This pathologisation of the nose can be seen in a discussion on an internet cosmetic surgery site:

> The hypothetical patient asks: My nose is otherwise straight but its tip has the typical Finnish 'bulb': in other words, it is the potato nose ... Could it be reduced without surgery reaching the bone? ...

> The surgeon answers: The nose and its tip can be modified, reduced and extended. Fixing the rounded tip of the Finnish nose, the so-called potato nose, is one of the most common domestic procedures.[9]

In interviews, some surgery customers blamed their family genes for their 'premature' ageing: 'It is in my family that the upper eyelids loosen', as Sylvi explained. Surgeons believe that 'heavy' foreheads together with 'sagging' upper eyelids are typical for Finns and make many Finns seem older than they really are. Therefore, both 'problems' are seen as inevitable targets of surgery. One surgeon who considered recommending procedures for me commented on my upper eyelids, that their 'structure' is not typical for Finns but the eyebrows typically droop and eyes are deep-set (causing a heavy forehead). Cosmetic surgery clinics use the national gene discourse in marketing, too:

> The Finnish eyes are typically deep-set and the upper eyelid crinkle is set low ... often causing a sense of weight in the eyes.[10]

The gene discourse which contains the 'truth' of the typical racial and ethnic problems of appearance compared to the white race has spread all over the world. Since the war years cosmetic surgery has been used to guarantee 'ethnic anonymity' in the US and Europe (Haiken 1999: 186–94, Kaw 1998). In many Asian countries, eyelids and noses, for example, are moulded to appear 'whiter'. Generalised surgical procedures have actually changed the concept of the normal body in many societies. In South Korea, for example, 'double-eyelid' surgery has been established as a normal rite of passage to adulthood (e.g. Kim 2003), or becoming a normative member of a Jewish family implies a nose job in some Jewish societies in the US (Blum 2003: 123–6). In capitalist societies, breast enlargement has, according to some scholars, become an initiation rite into womanhood to an extent which is comparable to the way in which circumcisions are perceived in some other cultures (e.g. Wilson 2002). If the rise of cosmetic surgery continues, it is possible that a forehead lift and upper eyelid tightening, for example, will become routine procedures of cleaning the Finnish body from its problematic ethnic features.

The talk of the typical heavy Finnish face can also be interpreted to refer metaphorically to the heavy Finnish mind. The striking forehead and sagging eyelids give an impression of melancholy, introversion and irritation, which are all associated with the Finnish national character. Together with unassuming and calm behaviour, these traits have traditionally been valued in the Finnish culture, but now the attitude is different. The new Americanised etiquette of interaction and emotional expression requires extroversion, smiling and the overall 'positive' attitude which is eagerly taught to Finns by numerous courses of positive thinking and behaving. The etiquette has been discussed especially in the context of the new working body research which has shown that a competitive body today should not only look young and fit but also sound right, perform, communicate and express itself in controlled ways (*e.g.* Witz *et al.* 2003).

It is believed that personality, emotions and health can be read from the outer body. Marks of ageing have begun to represent negative emotions and personality traits, such as anger, tiredness, depression, sadness and aggression in the emerging culture which stigmatises ageing (*cf.* Davis 1995: 71). Many interviewees described suffering from these unfavourable facial features before their surgery, and the rejuvenation procedures were used to cure the 'wrong' emotional messages of the faces. One of them was Liisa, a 56-year-old professor, who at the time of the interview described her decision to have a facelift as a 'mental aberration'. Originally, her idea had been 'only to get my neck back' and have her eyelids 'freshened'. Instead, she had decided to have a more general facelift partly because of her surgeon's persuasion. But she felt that the result was a health and aesthetic disaster and it caused a serious haematoma. Liisa regretted her decision not only because of its outcome but also because she felt that she had behaved against her values. 'As an academic woman', as she defined herself, she felt that her self-respect should not hinge on her appearance. Further, she saw many dangers in the rise of cosmetic surgery, such as the 'disappearance of personalities', and she 'felt pity' for surgery enthusiasts. Still, she saw her two eyelid surgeries and the facelift as, in some sense, inevitable:

> It was not the idea that I should look younger or prettier but that my face communicates something that I would not like to and that it would be very tiring to go around with a stupid smile on one's face (...) so I thought that a facelift would help it (...) Still, I do not like at all that the corners of my mouth hang down so that I look angry but I have tried to learn a certain kind of basic smile.

The above quotes reveal that cosmetic surgery is not necessarily used to deny ageing but to control the representations of emotions and the condition of the body equated with ageing. It is an attempt to construct an image of complacency representing not only successful ageing but the whole life: looking youthful means being happy, harmonious and loved, which are all included in the concept of beauty. I asked the study participants to describe a beautiful person. Phrases such as 'harmonious', 'content', 'inwardly beautiful' and 'self-confident' were mentioned more often in the descriptions than direct references to outward features. The American professor of bioethics and philosophy Carl Elliott (2003: 295–304) talks about the 'tyranny of happiness' as an American obsession which surfaces in the eager use of all kinds of body enhancement technologies ranging from serotonin and hormone pills to aesthetic dentistry and surgery. My data show that happiness is pursued for its representative value; that is to say, a positive aesthetic.

Resisting stereotypes of old people by being forever middle aged
The women and men I interviewed described their decision to get cosmetic surgery as one that allowed them to combat stereotypes of old people. Old people are often stereotyped

as slow, technologically illiterate and unattractive, for example. Modern medicine has equated old age with deformity, deficiency and disease (*cf.* Gilman 1998: 9); something to be avoided and removed. Thus, people who are old according to these cultural definitions cannot possibly be happy. Cosmetic surgery is marketed as a weapon to guarantee 'hygienic' ageing, as one of the surgeons that I interviewed expressed it.

Some interviewees described their lifestyle as socially, mentally and physically active. Youthful appearance was perceived as a part of or even a prerequisite for an active life and these women eagerly consumed beauty products and services besides pretty clothes. Tyyne, a 76-year-old pensioner, was one of the interviewees who did not hesitate to wear colourful clothes, youthful make-up, and to indulge in volubility and hearty laughter. Tyyne studied at night school and worked as a photo model, actress and sales agent. She admitted she felt happy among people half her age and wanted to 'look good' in her many activities. She had already had surgery on her upper and lower eyelids and planned to get a facelift and liposuction. Tyyne wondered: '*Why* should I look a hundred years old?' Besides, 'I cannot be a kind of old person (...) and never will be, sitting at home in a rocking chair and knitting socks', she explained.

Similar to other interviewees whom I call rebellious consumers, Tyyne linked the surgery with her subjective age identity which was younger than her chronological age. These women emphasised that their aim was not to hide their age but to look good for their age. One woman clarified the idea by comparing two legendary actresses, Sophia Loren and Brigitte Bardot. The first one (presumably operated upon) looks great, she said, but the latter one (presumably not operated upon) looks 'like [she was] punched' in the eyes. After upper and lower eyelid surgeries, a facelift and a rhinoplasty, 72-year-old Vieno talked about getting old as feeling like falling into a well, and also something against which you can fight but which has to be faced one day.

> You always compare and then give yourself extended time wondering about when I get *really* old. Ten years ago it was a bigger challenge but now, at this age, you already take it more easily. I don't say I've given up but I have got used to the idea.

Vieno, like many other interviewees, represents the cult of agelessness whose key idea is the right to a 'stretched middle age' (see Jones 2004: 527–8). One interviewee, 70-year-old Oili, actually referred to her age group as 'we middle aged'. An idea of the essential self having been actualised at the early middle age is typical for many cosmetic surgery patients. Along with ageing, the body is felt to gradually move away from the real self. Interviewees had felt 'strange', 'depressed' or 'frightened' in front of the mirror and they had just wanted to become 'themselves again' by undergoing the rejuvenation surgery. The comparison between photographs and their image in the mirror had been the typical final motive for seeking surgery. With the discovery of photography and the spread of affordable cameras among the wider public, it has been possible to scrutinise individual bodily processes in detail and compare them, for example with others' ageing (Turner 1995: 251–5). Some people feel they do well from such comparison, like Elsi, who told me about a photograph of her old schoolmates gathering together after long decades:

> I looked the freshest of all, I always have. The fact is that at this age, at last, your body starts to sag ... But you can do *a lot* by yourself.

Elsi emphasised the importance of one's own responsibility in keeping one's appearance youthful. She had undergone a facelift, an upper eyelid surgery and her breasts had been reduced and lifted. In addition, a tummy tuck had been done and a liposuction had been performed on her thighs, hips and knees. At the time of the interview, she was planning still more liposuction. Elsi was clearly proud of her hard work on her body.

However, like many other interviewees who admitted having got into a vicious circle of cosmetic surgery, Elsi moralised about those others who had gone too far with their beauty projects. The interviewees typically imagined a future apocalypse with over-tightened faces and swelled lips everywhere. Some were horrified by the idea that their own mothers, for example, would have 'denied' their ageing and undergone surgery. One's own ideal, instead, was believed to be natural, and one's own procedures were seen as well founded. Many also stated that their own choices had been voluntary while others were probably pushed by someone. Others might also expect too much from the surgery, but one's own expectations were believed to be realistic (cf. Blum 2003: 286–7). Interestingly, the same kind of attitude is typical with regard to other body enhancement technologies (see Elliot 2003: 296–7).

In sum, interview participants felt that to stay forever middle aged was morally acceptable and even admirable although exceptions exist. One woman said that as a religious person, her numerous surgeries had caused her a moral dilemma. In Finland, Lutheranism has traditionally included a moral view of beautifying as vain and sinful and cosmetic surgery is probably the ultimate form of this. Those who reject or oppose cosmetic surgery often also perceive it as unnatural or violent. Some older surgery enthusiasts, however, have adopted the opposite attitude to body modification, resembling modern primitivists, who perform extreme piercing, tattooing and other techniques, or performance artist Orlan's conception of the body as 'just an inert piece of meat, lying on the table' (see Davis 2003: 110).

A human being is not untouchable [...] Solely the spirit is sacred. But the body, this is only like *any matter*. You can mould it as much as you will if you're happy with that. (Pirkko, 57, underwent a breast augmentation and planned several new procedures.)

Yet, even some of those who, in the privacy of interviews, said that it was morally acceptable to pursue cosmetic surgery, remained secretive about their use of surgery when with friends and family.

Well-deserved compensation

Some women rationalised having had cosmetic surgery on the grounds that they believed they had aged abnormally quickly due to hard life experiences. One group consisted of women who had always borne heavy responsibilities and had experience of life changes, such as divorce. One of them was Hilja, 84, who talked about her life as if it had long been sacrificed for others. During the war years, she had served as a member of the women's auxiliary services at the front. Later, as a young wife, her marriage ended in divorce because of her husband's violence, alcoholism and infidelity. Hilja became a single parent of three children and supported them by working multiple shifts as a midwife. Those years were hard and Hilja's dream was a good night's sleep. Later, Hilja started to purposefully empower herself. At the time of her retirement she told her children that she 'would not be their bank or baby-sitter'. Instead, she decided to invest her time and money in herself, including getting two facelifts, and started to travel with her friends. Hilja explained that the third age had definitely been the 'best part' of her life and cosmetic surgery had helped so much in renewing her life that she would definitely get a third facelift, if she knew for sure that she would live to the age of 90.

Interview participants used cosmetic surgery as a means of 'starting over' after emotionally difficult experiences. Some felt that sorrow and worries were literally *cut off* from the body and had been left on the operating table. Two women, Vieno and Laila, both 56, for example, wanted to relieve their suffering by having facelifts after the deaths of their husbands. During the interview, Laila started to cry while she remembered all her sorrows:

> My husband got cancer and lost his job (…) I also lost both parents and my children moved away from home. A phase of seven years when I lost everything; my husband died and my mum died right after. During his last days I took care of my husband at home, learnt to inject the morphine myself (…) It was so tough that I thought that I must erase those years from my face.

Anja, 67, on the other hand, said that several Restylane injections in three periods and upper eyelid surgery had helped her to get on her feet again after many exhausting battles with her brother concerning their family business. Tuula, 62, had suffered from cancer for many years with varying phases. She had had two facelifts and two upper eyelid surgeries because the illness and its cure had left her face so 'sad'. Tuula's opinion was that 'the days you have left should be made the best possible, with the means you have'. At the time of the interview, Tuula was going to have her third eyelid surgery and was willing to have the third facelift too, if the cancer did not come back soon. In summary, for many women, cosmetic surgery offered an opportunity to move on from difficult life events such as abuse, divorce, sickness, and depression.

Regaining respectability

Most dramatically the compensation for tough life experiences and, simultaneously, the regaining of respectability had been sought by those women who had decided to be born again after their husbands had left them. Liisi, 57, like Elsi mentioned above, literally remodelled herself after being humiliated by her husband who 'changed her for a younger and more stupid woman'. After the divorce in her forties, Liisi became seriously depressed and abused alcohol, and could barely manage her work as an entrepreneur. After years of hard life she even considered killing her youngest child and herself. Finally, Liisi managed to seek help and started to recover little by little. She went to see a plastic surgeon and asked for a metamorphosis to include 'as much as possible in a single anaesthesia'. The breasts were lifted up with a nipple transfer and augmented, and liposuction was applied to the knees, thighs and stomach. Her upper eyelids were operated upon and implants were set in the cheeks. Gradually, Liisi's tears dried up, as she described her change. At the time of the interview Liisi was planning a new breast operation, several liposuctions and 'tightening the skin everywhere where it has loosened', she said, and added that a facelift would also be performed 'immediately the face sags'. Liisi described her motive as an 'awareness of being wanted by men' although her aim was not really to find a partner. The feeling of being accepted was enough.

Many single ageing women, however, long for an intimate relationship. Interviewees deplored the small number of dating candidates of their own age group, which forced them to 'compete' with younger women, and believed that men usually preferred women younger than themselves. In a culture where an ageing woman is asexualised (*e.g.* Dinnerstein and Weitz 1998) or her sexuality is represented as ridiculous or grotesque (Markson 2003) cosmetic surgery offers a possibility and licence to extend romantic life. Ageing women are valued more for their role in the home, but this does not save them from pressures linked with ageing. Some women become grandmothers after their working careers and seek to gain extra advantages by having cosmetic surgery. Some had ended up in cosmetic surgery because their children had passed remarks about their wrinkles or even explicitly asked them to undergo surgery. Two of my interviewees, Oili (70) and Anni (62), had timed their procedures near their children's wedding days to be as youthful looking as possible. Oili described her decision to get a Dermalive injection which, unfortunately, caused a serious rejection and had to be removed by several more operations.

> My daughter said 'please go and fix those crying wrinkles (…) so that you look a little better (…) it's so easy, just go, just a half hour thing'. [She was getting married] (…) Actually, they were not bad but a woman is vain and when her child asks, the mother wants to look a little bit better.

Jeff Hearn (1995: 101) has stated that because men are valued predominantly for their career achievements, ageing manhood is often understood as a pre-death phase. That is to say, retirement means a radical retreat from active life and respected status. Both phases of manhood are valorised by the following stories from Pentti and Pertti. In commenting on his appearance before his lower eyelid surgery, Pentti (a 61-year-old retired pilot) emphasised that his 'bulldog face' was not a problem for him but for others:

> Anybody – a child, for instance who is in a shop with her mum: 'Why does that old man look like that?' I also walk badly, I have trouble with my back, and then a bulldog face. It really attracts attention […] Downstairs there is a smart shop and the lady who is the owner was having it photographed for some advertisement. I was doddering down the street and had a windcheater on, perhaps dangling a little, and a cane […] She said to a man in the photographer's group: 'Don't shoot; wait till that old lush goes by'. Or I was in a bar with X and was going to order some beer and they said: 'We will serve the lady but not the gentleman'. I was not drunk, it was only my appearance.

Another male pilot I interviewed, 62-year-old Pertti, who was still working, also had a lower eyelid surgery. His motive had been to look 'credible' at his work because he had noticed that his eye sags had caused unfavourable attention from clients. Pertti explained that, in his job, 'tired' eyes are just impossible especially in the morning because clients may suspect lack of sleep, intoxication or hangover. For Pertti, his colleagues agreed that after the surgery he looked like a more focused worker. Thus, cosmetic surgery can be seen to help in regaining respectability at work or in romance after humiliating experiences linked with an increasingly aged appearance.

Mask of happiness?

I have argued that Finnish consumers purchase cosmetic surgery to improve their quality of life. Improving quality of life for these consumers means masking signs of ageing and of negative emotions. Informants' motives for surgery range from self-pampering and therapy to pressure from family members and a desire for social respectablity. In most cases, the interviewees felt that the surgery changed their appearance to better reflect their inner self, and helped them start again after tough life experiences. In some cases, women and men felt that surgery was inevitable. The negative social feedback given to visual signs of ageing almost demanded a surgical solution. Yet, even though men and women strategically resist ageist stereotypes and discrimination by choosing surgical procedures, they simultaneously help reinforce such beliefs by trying to reconstruct youthful bodies through surgery. This is troubling, as increased rates of cosmetic surgery can shift cultural definitions of normal ageing.

The ideological core of cosmetic surgery – and the ideal of positive ageing linked to it – is that age is a subjective attitude rather than a biological fact, and one can actively resist mental and physical ageing (*e.g.* Bytheway 2003). In fact, the subjective attitude cannot be detached from the cultural discourses of ageing. The rise of the rejuvenation surgery stems from the everyday representations of the normative body, which is young, beautiful, healthy, happy, effective, and often white. Cosmetic surgery is perhaps not used to deny the accumulation of years, but to control the visual signs of negative emotions and of the body equated with ageing. The use of cosmetic surgery is thus an attempt to construct an image of happiness and interconnectedness, representing not only successful ageing but having a good life. My informants revealed that looking youthful meant being happy, harmonious and loved, which are all included in their definitions of beauty. I have shown that cosmetic surgery involves the manipulation of emotions *both* at the lived *and* representative levels, since, in an aestheticised culture, the boundary between the lived bodily experiences, such as emotions, and representations of the body have become blurred (*cf.* Ferguson 1997, Shusterman 1997). On the other hand, lived emotions sometimes change by moulding the body's surface. The association of youth with happiness is so strong that feelings of oppression and depression not directly caused by ageing are cured by surgical procedures which lessen the marks of ageing, as some of the above cases have shown.

This analysis also adds to the understanding of the local contexts in which cosmetic surgery is pursued. In a country that values the sturdy woman and views cosmetic surgery negatively, cosmetic surgery rates are growing, revealing hierarchies of whiteness and appearance. Finns are thought to have heavy foreheads, sagging eyelids and potato noses in comparison with the ideal white, 'Caucasian' face. Through cosmetic surgeries, the traditionally melancholic and reserved Finnish body is moulded to represent positiveness and openness; that is to say, that surgery is used to imitate American outgoingness and constant cheer (*e.g.* Martin 2007).

Although 90 per cent of all cosmetic surgery consumers in Finland are women, the same as, for example, in the US, this should not lead to an expectation that ageing men would not stress the importance of their appearance. Several studies indicate that ageing seems to threaten men's experiences of masculinity (*e.g.* Rosenfeld and Faircloth 2006, Oberg 2003: 120), and the cases discussed here offer some examples of that perceived threat. Further research is needed to fully understand the social meanings attached to this gendered phenomenon worldwide.

Acknowledgements

I thank the two anonymous reviewers and editors of the monograph for their invaluable help in revising this chapter to its final form.

Notes

1 The research was funded by the Finnish Academy. The research material regarding patients consisted of a survey and/or interviews of 142 Finnish respondents: 126 women and 16 men between 19–84 years of age who had undergone 2 cosmetic surgery procedures on average. They were sought through cosmetic surgery clinics and a newspaper announcement. The surgeons were contacted personally by phone or e-mail. Depending on the interviewee's choice, the interview was conducted in a cafeteria, restaurant, workplace, or the interviewee's or my home. Each interview lasted on average 1.5 hours. The research aimed to get an overview of this minimally studied phenomenon in Finland, and to gather heterogeneous material. The participants were encouraged by paying each of them a 50-euro honorarium for an interview, with a raffle of six 150-euro gift tokens among them. The surgeons were offered an analysis of the 'Customer satisfaction' part of the patient survey in cases where the participants were gathered through their clinic.
2 Ten of the surgeons were men and two were women. One of them was an Estonian whose patients are predominantly Finns, and the rest of the surgeons interviewed were Finnish.
3 Rejuvenation surgery was not restricted only to the oldest age group. The youngest individuals in this study who had undergone anti-wrinkle injections or eyelid or face surgeries were in their late thirties.
4 Phenomenological research is directed at individuals' experiences as a form of reality when the language is understood to reflect authentic sentiments and lived experiences. However, I noticed in the research how easily public discourses infiltrate bodily experiences and the words by which the experiences are described, although something is, of course, 'left outside' the shared discourses. In addition, when the interviewees talk about events which may have taken place years before, the descriptions typically organise themselves into narratives, which are always discursive constructions. Therefore, I do not categorise my viewpoint concerning the theory of the body or my methodology as either realist or constructionist, since they are seen to be intertwined.
5 Http://www.aidonkauneudenpuolesta.fi/uploadedfiles/FI_/Totuus_kauneudesta.pdf.
6 Mari Manninen: 'Kureliiveistä silikoniehostukseen' *Helsingin Sanomat*, Sunnuntai 17.12.2000, D7; *Ilta-Sanomat*, Viihde 28.11.2000, 34–35; Helena Liikanen: 'Onko silikonirintainen typerys?' *Ilta-Sanomat*, Uutiset 20.12.2000, A8.
7 Http://www.isaps.org/uploads/news_pdf/Newletter%20sponsorship%20form.pdf, read 27.8.2007.
8 Savonia is an eastern province in Finland.
9 Http://www.iltalehti.fi/kauneus/200712056886837_ks.shtml.
10 Http://www.siluetti.fi/fin/Plastiikkakirurgia/ylaluomileikkaus_pitka.shtml.

References

Balsamo, A. (1996) On the cutting edge: cosmetic surgery and new imaging technologies. In Balsamo, A. (ed.) *Technologies of the Gendered Body. Reading Cyborg Women*. Durham and London: Duke University Press.
Blum, V.L. (2003) *Flesh Wounds – the Culture of Cosmetic Surgery*. Berkeley: University of California Press.
Bordo, Susan (1993) *Unbearable Weight – Feminism, Western Culture, and the Body*. Berkeley, CA: University of California Press.
Botelho, L. and Thane, P. (eds) (2001) *Women and Ageing in British Society since 1500*. Harlow: Longman.
Brooks, A. (2004) 'Under the knife and proud of it': an analysis of the normalization of cosmetic surgery, *Critical Sociology*, 30, 2, 207–39.
Bytheway, B. (2003) Visual representations of later life. In Faircloth, C.A. (ed.) *Aging Bodies – Images and Everyday Experience*. Walnut Creek: AltaMira Press.

Davis, K. (1995) *Reshaping the Female Body: the Dilemma of Cosmetic Surgery*. New York: Routledge.

Davis, K. (2002) A dubious equality: men, women and cosmetic surgery, *Body and Society*, 8, 1, 49–65.

Davis, K. (2003) 'My body is my art'. In Davis, K. *Dubious Equalities and Embodied Differences. Cultural Studies of Cosmetic Surgery*. Lanham: Rowman and Littlefield Publishers.

Dinnerstein, M. and Weitz, R. (1998) Jane Fonda, Barbara Bush, and other aging bodies. In Weitz, R. (ed.) *The Politics of Women's Bodies – Sexuality, Appearance, and the Behavior*. New York: Oxford University Press.

Elliott, C. (2003) *Better than Well – American Medicine Meets the American Dream*. New York: W.W. Norton and Co.

Featherstone, M. (1987) Leisure, symbolic power and the life course. In Horne, J., Jary, D. and Tomlinson, A. (eds) *Sport, Leisure and Social Relations*. London: Routledge and Kegan Paul.

Featherstone, M. and Hepworth, A. (1995) Images of positive ageing – a case study of Retirement Choice Magazine. In Featherstone, M. and Wernick, A. (eds) *Images of Ageing – Cultural Representations of Later Life*. London and New York: Routledge.

Ferguson, H. (1997) Me and my shadows: on the accumulation of body images in Western society Part Two – the corporeal forms of modernity, *Body and Society*, 3, 4, 1–31.

Frank, A.W. (1991) For a sociology of the body: an analytical review. In Featherstone, M., Hepworth, M. and Turner, B.S. (eds) *The Body – Social Process and Cultural Theory*. London: Sage.

Fraser, S. (2003) *Cosmetic Surgery, Gender and Culture*. Houndmills (UK): Palgrave Macmillan.

Gagne, P. and McGaughey, D. (2002) Designing women – cultural hegemony and the exercise of power among women who have undergone elective mammoplasty, *Gender and Society*, 16, 6, 814–38.

Gilman, S.L. (1998) *Creating Beauty to Cure the Soul – Race and Psychology in the Shaping of Aesthetic Surgery*. London: Duke University Press.

Gimlin, D. (2000) Cosmetic surgery: beauty as commodity, *Qualitative Sociology*, 23, 1, 77–99.

Haiken, E. (1999) *Venus Envy – a History of Cosmetic Surgery*. Baltimore: The Johns Hopkins University Press.

Halonen, U. (2004) Villejä ja hillittyjä ruumiita. In Jokinen, E., Kaskisaari, M. and Husso, M. (eds) *Ruumis töihin! Käsite ja käytäntö*. Tampere: Vastapaino.

Hearn, J. (1995) Imaging the ageing of men. In Featherstone, M. and Wernick, A. (eds) *Images of Ageing – Cultural Representations of Later Life*. London: Routledge.

Holliday, R. and Sanchez Taylor, J. (2006) Aesthetic surgery as false beauty, *Feminist Theory*, 7, 2, 179–95.

Jones, M. (2004) Mutton cut up as lamb: mothers, daughters and cosmetic surgery, *Continuum: Journal of Media and Cultural Studies*, 18, 4, 525–39.

Kaw, E. (1998) Medicalization of racial features – Asian-American women and cosmetic surgery. In Weitz, R. (ed.) *The Politics of Women's Bodies: Sexuality, Appearance, and Behavior*. Oxford: Oxford University Press.

Kim, T. (2003) Neo-Confucian body techniques: women's bodies in Korea's consumer society, *Body and Society*, 9, 2, 97–113.

Kinnunen, T. (2008) Carving the female flesh by breast augmentation. In Hearn, J. and Burr, V. (eds) *Sex, Violence and the Body: The Erotics of Wounding*. London: Palgrave Macmillan.

Markson, E.W. (2003) The female aging body through film. In Faircloth, C.A. (ed.) *Aging Bodies – Images and Everyday Experience*. Walnut Creek: AltaMira Press.

Martin, E. (2007) *Bipolar Expeditions: Mania and Expression in American Culture*. Princeton, NJ: Princeton University Press.

Morgan, K.P. (1998) Women and the knife – cosmetic surgery and the colonization of women's bodies. In Weitz, R. (ed.) *The Politics of Women's Bodies: Sexuality, Appearance, and Behavior*. Oxford and New York: Oxford University Press.

Moustakas, C.E. (1994) *Phenomenological Research Methods*. Thousand Oaks, CA: Sage.

Negrin, L. (2000) Cosmetics and the Female Body. A critical appraisal of poststructuralist theories of masquerade, *European Journal of Cultural Studies*, 3, 1, 83–101.

Oberg, P. (2003) Images versus experience of the aging body. In Faircloth, C.A. (ed.) *Aging Bodies – Images and Everyday Experience*. Walnut Creek: AltaMira Press.

Palomäki, S-L. (2004) *Suhde vanhenemiseen – iäkkäät naiset elämänsä kertojina ja rakentajina.* Jyväskylä: University of Jyväskylä.

Rosenfeld, D. and Faircloth, C.A. (eds) (2006) *Medicalised Masculinities.* Philadelphia: Temple University Press.

Saukko, P. (2002) Studying the self: from the subjective and the social to personal and political dialogues, *Qualitative Research*, 2, 2, 244–83.

Shusterman, R. (1997) Somaesthetics and the body/media issue, *Body and Society*, 3, 3, 33–49.

Sleven, K. (2007) The embodied experiences of old lesbians. In Calasanti, T. and Slevin, K. (eds) *Age Matters: Realigning Feminist Thinking.* London: Routledge.

Taylor, C. (1987) Interpretation and the sciences of man. In Rabinow, P. and Sullivan, W.M. (eds) *Interpretive Social Science. A Second Look.* Berkeley: University of California Press.

Tervo, M. (2002) Sports, 'race' and the Finnish national identity in Helsingit Sanomat in the early twentieth century, *Nations and Nationalism*, 8, 3, 335–56.

Turner, B.S. (1995) Aging and Identity – Some reflections on the somatization of the self. In Featherstone, M. and Wernick, A. (eds) *Images of Ageing – Cultural Representations of Later Life.* London and New York: Routledge.

Vakimo, S. (1999) Maaseutu naisen ikääntymisympäristönä. In Kangas, I. and Nikander, P. (eds) *Naiset ja ikääntyminen.* Helsinki: Gaudeamus.

Van Maanen, M. (1990) *Researching Lived Experience: Human Science for an Action Sensitive Pedagogy.* New York: The State University of New York.

Wilson, T.D. (2002) Pharaonic circumcision under patriarchy and breast augmentation under phallocentric capitalism, *Violence Against Women*, 8, 4, 495–521.

Witz, A., Warhurst, C. and Nickson, D. (2003) The labour of aesthetics and the aesthetics of organization, *Organization*, 10, 1, 33–54.

8

Ageing in place and technologies of place: the lived experience of people with dementia in changing social, physical and technological environments

Katherine Brittain, Lynne Corner, Louise Robinson and John Bond

Background

Everyday technologies, intended for general use, are argued to have developed in a 'hyper-cognitive society' (Post 2000), where assumptions about cognitive ability are implicit. Dementia and cognitive impairment – although contested categories (Moreira and Bond 2008) – are on the increase (Department of Health 2009, Knapp *et al.* 2007). Currently one in six people are estimated to live with cognitive impairment, and these individuals negotiate their everyday lives and interact with everyday technologies in and outside the home space. Little is known about how those who do not fit into the normative values that underpin these cognitively able technologies interact with them, experience and understand them. Furthermore, technologies are complex, and becoming more so. It is therefore important to understand or highlight the lived experiences of those, like older people, who are often marginalised from its design and development. Older people are commonly assigned to the role of object rather than subject in the development of technology. Stereotypes of ageing and older people drive people's preconceptions about older people's needs and capabilities in that they become embedded within technology aimed at older people (Östlund 2004). Despite older people's experience as 'technocitizens', citizens that come into daily contact with technology, they are commonly represented as lacking the skills and comprehension needed to accept, negotiate and assess the risks and benefits of new technologies (Joyce and Mamo 2006). This chapter explores the varied meanings and lived experiences of older people with dementia, in relation to everyday technologies in public spaces outside of the home that both challenge and support their experience of everyday life such as road signs, buildings or mobile phones. In doing so, this chapter highlights the importance of a neglected space (Blackman *et al.* 2003), namely the outside space, in dementia research.

Technologies and control

Within social science research, 'technology and older people' is a relatively new field, with the term 'gerontechnology' being coined in the early 1990s (Östlund 2004). Gerontechnology is derived from a human to machine perspective, whereby technologies are intended to compensate for human deficiencies. Over 20 years ago, Haraway argued that humans can no longer be viewed in isolation from technology, and highlighted the impact that technologies have had for self identities (Haraway 1985). The blurring of boundaries between humans and technologies – cyborgism – represented a radical vision of what it was to be 'human' in the late 20th century (Tomas 1995). Our bodies have become increasingly reliant upon machines (Synnott 1993). More recently, it is argued that we need to 'gray the cyborg' and explore how technologies, science, gender and age intersect in our society (Joyce and Mamo 2006).

One area of particular interest has been the use of technologies in the day-to-day surveillance of the population. But, in a postmodern, global society, where technologies to aid increasing surveillance are available, we need to consider in whose interests technologies have been developed and also to consider concepts of risk and surveillance from the perspective of those being 'watched'. Certainly, there have been concerns raised about how technologies can lead to increased surveillance, which may constrain the choices of older people and undermine their decisions to take risks (Percival and Hanson 2006, Robinson *et al.* 2007). Not only are issues of power and inequalities important, but also the development of technologies needs to be critically investigated, and questions about how technologies might underpin or reinforce institutional ageism need to be asked (Joyce and Mamo 2006), particularly in relation to older people with dementia. What are the implications for older people who pursue and negotiate everyday technologies in order to support their everyday activities?

Older people, particularly those with dementia, have become surveillance targets (Kenner 2008). Kenner argues that technologies designed to support people with dementia age in place, are, in fact, reproducing and creating new forms of social control; perhaps reflecting the 'fearful' discourses about the potential dangers of older people living alone prevalent in current literature and policy debates (Kenner 2008). It may also be that what the person with dementia may see as an acceptable risk is not viewed as such by carers, with formal carers perceiving risk as the management of physical risk and older people being more concerned with their rights and risk to their personal and social identities (Ballinger and Payne 2002, Hughes 2008, Robinson *et al.* 2007). This conflict of view may be 'particularly pertinent for those with mild or moderate dementia living at home' (Percival and Hanson 2006: 898).

Technologies of place

There is no single activity that humans undertake which is not in some way technologically mediated (Ihde 1993). Drawing on Heidegger's example of the hammer, Ihde (1991) argues that through 'the-ready-to-hand' relation to our environment, technologies withdraw and become transparent. In this sense technologies act as a mediator between the person and the world, thus making the world accessible. However, if the technology is broken or missing, its 'phenomenological transparency' is changed and it can act as an opaque interference between the person and the world. Technologies can therefore be enabling and disabling, empowering and disempowering (Essén 2008, Ihde 1991, 1993).[1] Furthermore, technologies are not neutral, but rather, situated within specific contexts. People with dementia need to be situated within their social and historical context to ensure that assistive technology fits the individual rather than the individual to the technology (Wey 2004).

Furthermore, the experience of the body is influenced by the space in which it is situated; thus previously friendly spaces can become unfriendly because of changes in one's health. Access to space is tied up to a person's 'embodied relationship to physical artefacts and environments' (Freund 2001: 699). Therefore:

> The 'technisation' of the routines of daily life involve intensive and extensive use of complex and potentially dangerous technologies and spaces ... Driving at high speeds, manoeuvring traffic and even managing movement as a pedestrian through transport space become a part of everyday routines and taken for granted abilities. Yet the pervasive and intensive dependence on being able to use or relate to such technologies can be a source of stress, and can disenfranchise or put at risk those unwilling or unable to meet such demands (Freund 2001: 699).

Within this 'caffeinated, sped-up world', ageing people and bodies have the potential to remind us of the value of and threat of slowness (Joyce and Mamo 2006). Trends in the technologisation of everyday life drives the focus on technological devices that support older people to live independently at home (for example, McCreadie and Tinker 2005, Miskelly 2001, 2004). Ageing in place, the choice to remain at home is the preferred policy strategy for supporting older people who are becoming increasingly more reliant on others for care (Department of Health 2001). Within this policy agenda there is a push for the utilisation of assistive and supportive technologies to be put into people's homes in order to aid this strategy (Audit Commission 2004). However, these assistive and supportive technologies can disturb the 'established meanings and routinised activities' that encompass the experience of home (Dyck et al. 2005).

Furthermore, technologies, for some, can transform the home into an isolated and marginalised space (Brittain and Shaw 2007). With the blurring of boundaries between institutional and home space, the home has become increasingly institutionalised, thus causing ambiguities and tension for those living and working within it (Exley and Allen 2007, Milligan 2000). There are also further concerns that without human interactions working with and alongside technologies, technologies can become disabling rather than enabling (Wey 2006).

Health and place are fundamentally interrelated and mutually constitutive and in this sense the experiences of health and medicine cannot be detached from the places in which care is received (Kearns 1993). Place is a setting which is experienced and holds meaning and shapes relations between people as well as social relations and processes that make up society (Wiles 2005). Space is also important because of the way its organisation constructs bodies, it offers us both possibilities and constraints (Freund 2001). However, as with technologies, the way space is organised is not neutral, 'but rather political in the priority it gives some transport modalities and in the way "handicaps" others' (Freund 2001: 696). Therefore, when exploring the experience of public spaces and rapidly changing landscapes, attention needs to be given to the changing meaning of landscapes in which we live (Phillipson 2007).

Private and public spaces are sources of identity and therefore influence and shape our sense of self. In her work on therapeutic landscapes, Gesler (1992) moves beyond the 'static traditional landscape' and

> recognize(s) that landscapes, as well as being influenced by physical and built environments, are a product of the human mind and of material circumstance, that landscapes reflect both human intentions and actions and the constraints and structures imposed by society (Gesler 1992: 743).

When examining the question 'what makes a place a healing place?', Gesler and Kearns (2002) emphasise the importance of how different landscapes affect a person's experience of healing (Gesler and Kearns 2002). However, there has been little research that has explored everyday public spaces and thus the ordinary places that are beneficial to a person's sense of wellbeing have been neglected (Wakefield and McMullan 2005, Wilson 2003).

Technology and outdoor space
In contrast to the policy emphasis on the private space of home, Blackman et al. (2003) argue that older people's experiences in public space in the outside environment, and its role in maintaining their everyday activities, has been ignored. Rather, attention has focused on 'indoor' private space and supporting independence and autonomy within the 'home'. Blackman et al. (2003: 361) consider how people with dementia access outside environments

and argue that 'the public outdoor world is rarely conceived of as a dementia setting'. Moreover, people with behavioural symptoms associated with dementia can become further isolated because of the risk of embarrassment in public spaces (Bond and Corner 2001). It is well established how disabled people's experiences of social and economic marginalisation is compounded by the built environment in public spaces (Imrie and Kumar 1998). In common with others (Bartlett 2000, Gilliard *et al.* 2005), we argue that the social model of disability should be extended to those with cognitive impairment.

Phillipson (2007) differentiates between older people who can express their agency through 'electing' their environment and those who are 'excluded' from influencing their social and physical environment. Ogg (2005, cited in Phillipson 2007) argues that urban areas are often not adapted to the needs of older people, rather they are often the key cause of older people's social exclusion and disengagement. Phillipson (2007) raises the important issue about how different social groups experience the changing city landscape. In relation to social exclusion, notions of personhood, agency and citizenship have been increasingly applied in dementia research as a way in which people with dementia can be empowered (Baldwin 2008, Bartlett and O'Connor 2007, Blackman *et al.* 2003, Bond *et al.* 2004, Graham 2004, Kitwood 1997, Kontos 2004). However, there has been some debate as to how each concept is viewed and able to connect the private and public spaces that people with dementia inhabit.

Citizenship, a central tenet of disability studies, has been used successfully to promote the status of discriminated groups, and the extent to which people with dementia are subjected to discriminatory practices is generating increasing scrutiny (Bartlett and O'Connor 2007). Discrimination in dementia research has previously been challenged by the notion of personhood, proposed in Kitwood's work and this has effectively brought the person with dementia into focus (Kitwood 1997). Personhood, however, has also effectively promoted an individualised, apolitical, lens with which to focus on the dementia experience, neglecting social and political contexts in which the experience is played out and whereby discrimination may be overlooked. In doing so, personhood also masks the agency of people with dementia (Bartlett and O'Connor 2007).

There is a tension – evident across disciplines – between how we, as social actors, are constrained by the social structure and the extent to which we can act in an empowered way to make choices. Whether discussing landscapes or environments, the place in which the person with dementia is situated and their experiences of discrimination and empowerment are situated within debates surrounding structure and agency. In light of the push for technological support for independence, research needs to explore what is enabling and what is constraining and how people with dementia negotiate between different discourses in order to be viewed as social actors, making their own decisions. The clinical discourse surrounding dementia, which focuses on the biomedical model of illness, has individualised and medicalised the experience of dementia (Bond 1992, Bond and Corner 2001) and although recent policy has tried to redress this (Department of Health 2001, 2009), dementia is still viewed through a clinical lens. The extension of risk and surveillance is part of this 'biomedicalised' process (Clarke *et al.* 2003) and this discourse further surrounds the everyday activities of people with dementia. Thus, balancing the rights and risks of people with dementia, formal and informal carers, has been shown to be problematic, with fear of litigation taking a central stage in the management of risk for these people (Robinson *et al.* 2007).

Focusing on discourse, regulation and resistance, Foucauldian analyses of old age, have given us important critical understandings of old age in modern times. They do not, however, allow us to deal with the lived experience of being old (Tulle-Winton 2000). In order for dementia research to move forward the personal (narrative) and political (citizenship) need to be integrated (Baldwin 2008). Policy narratives, although improving, remain dominated by a biomedical focus on dementia. People with dementia are disadvantaged by their physical and social environment, prevailing discourses around risk management and the clinical emphasis on biomedical conceptions of dementia. Further research is needed, related to how people with dementia, as social actors, operate independently of and alongside social and physical environmental constraints. What choices do these actors make in the context of their lived experience of dementia? As Tulle-Winton argues:

> The task of critical gerontology and sociology therefore ought to be to imagine ways of being old that defy dominant narratives of old age and look for spaces of resistance where they are least expected (2000: 82).

This chapter examines the ordinary places that people with dementia inhabit, namely the outside public space in which they manage their everyday activities in light of constraints imposed on them by themselves and others. The chapter aims to explore how everyday technologies mediate between people with dementia and their physical and social environment. Technologies in these analyses are defined as 'universal', technologies that are intended for general use not only for specific groups (Hansson 2007), in this sense Ihde's conceptualisation of technology is also drawn upon. In doing so the data presented highlight an element of 'feeling safe' in environments that have not changed and are recognisable to the person with dementia, and how outside space can be both therapeutic and frightening.

Methods

This chapter is based on qualitative data derived from two studies concerned with examining how unfamiliar and familiar outside environments enable and disable those living with loss of memory. The research involved speaking both to people with dementia and carers of people with dementia about their views of accessing outside spaces, and their views of the benefits and risks of using technology in supporting them in achieving this. The research team recognised the need for a more participatory and inclusive approach in research involving people with dementia, as research has historically tended to exclude and silence the voice of people with dementia (Cotrell and Schulz 1993, Wilkinson 2002). Therefore, qualitative methods were seen to be the most appropriate for accessing the views of people with dementia, and focus groups were used. More detailed methods of the original research are published elsewhere (Robinson et al. 2009, 2006, 2007). Focus groups are widely used in social research, and have been used to explore a multitude of topics (Barbour and Kitzinger 1999). The strengths and weaknesses of such methods within qualitative research have also been well documented (Bloor et al. 2001, Kidd and Parshall 2000).

An inductive approach to data collection was adopted, using the constant comparative method (Glaser 1965) and deviant case analysis. In total there were four groups with 16 people with dementia and three carers (one focus group was mixed with four people with dementia and three carers whilst the others had those with dementia only). The discussions lasted approximately one hour, all were digitally recorded, transcribed verbatim and anonymised. The focus groups were held in familiar surroundings to ensure a sense of continuity and familiarity for the participants. These were facilitated by KB, LC and LR, and took place in different settings within the community (church, residential home, Alzheimer's Society). Participants were recruited from two local branches of the Alzheimer's Society in two North of England coastal towns. Thus, the participants involved formed cohesive pre-established groups. There are a number of disadvantages to using such groups, including an established pecking order on participation, and participants feeling constrained by their ongoing social relations with other members (Bamford and Bruce 2002, Bloor *et al.* 2001). There are, however, advantages to using these groups (Kitzinger 1994) and this research used familiar settings, established relations and the group dynamics in order to facilitate discussions. Carrying out participatory research with people with dementia highlights issues of recall and memory within qualitative research. However, like Plummer, we argue that all life-story research is selective work and entails issues of recall and memory; it is shaped by a person's setting, society and culture (Plummer 2001).

All recruitment strategies and interaction with participants have followed strict ethical guidelines, complying with the British Sociological Association's guidance for ethical research practice and the British Society of Gerontology's guidelines on ethical research (BSA 2002, BSG 2008). Participation was voluntary and participants were told that they could opt out at any stage of the research process.

For this chapter, we have engaged with the lived experience of people with dementia and their carers and examined how unfamiliar and familiar environments can enable and disable those living with loss of memory. The lead author began by revisiting previously coded sections of data specifically related to how everyday technologies might support people with dementia and their carers. Then, in order to explore this issue in more detail, the original transcripts were read carefully again. For this re-analysis only those focus groups held with people with memory loss are presented.

Data and discussion

Therapeutic benefits of outside space
In exploring how everyday technologies mediate between a person with dementia and their physical and social environment, we first present data related to participants' accounts of their everyday activities in the outside public space. In the initial discussions with carers and people with dementia the current levels of activity were highlighted. These included getting out walking, running, driving, everyday shopping, holidays and social gatherings. Some participants felt able and confident in carrying on with their everyday activities:

> Yes, just about, no, no problem, I just take me time, sometimes stop for a cup of tea, and I'm probably away and that for two hours, and then come back (John).

> Well she [daughter] takes me out to do my shopping, and then we have lunch, she goes home and I get the bus, two or three times a week, it's just boredom on your own (Rosie).

> Oh yes, at the sea front and I have a house up there you know. ... I often get a walk along the seafront you know and out in the countryside (David).

People with dementia have, in previous research, highlighted the enjoyment they feel when getting out into their local neighbourhood (Burton and Mitchell 2006). Similarly, for people with dementia, being able to participate in activities in the outdoor space is important, enabling them to have a sense of being 'free', as highlighted by Eileen below:

> Oh yes, I'm quite free to go out, I live by myself so you know I can go where I want. I go up to [the city] and to meetings and things you know, yes. Sometimes I think 'can I make the effort' and I think 'yes shift yourself woman' and I get up and do it (Eileen).

These activities and this enjoyment highlight people with dementia engaging and participating in a public space that they are often excluded from, by themselves or by others. Perhaps, drawing on Tulle-Winton's words, this use of our public space by those cognitively impaired, demonstrates a space of resistance where people with dementia can 'defy dominant narratives of old age'.

Outside space as a frightening space
However, not everyone felt comfortable and confident in exploring these public spaces. Although many participants talked about getting out and their enjoyment of it, some of the participants also spoke of their 'anxiety'. Everyday activities were felt to become increasingly constrained either by their own anxieties or by those around them. One participant spoke about how he used to go out but his family were anxious for him not to do so any more, and he himself, as a result of this, had become anxious. He reported missing going out immensely, and said that without the support of friends he would be confined inside more often:

> Walks, yeah. I used to walk for miles, but me family don't want us to go away far, you know, but ... Well the family really, they're frightened, you know, but I'm not, I'm not ... (Mark).

From the perspective of family and carers, not knowing where the person with dementia is, can cause some anxiety, as highlighted in Mary's concerns about her husband:

> Because I mean when they do go out you're sitting, waiting, not knowing when they're coming back. And if they're a little bit over their time from coming back from golf, you're thinking 'eee'. The first time that happened was when we had moved house ... I thought 'oh my god, he's gone back to the old house'. He hadn't, but it's not knowing. And you see it's not just us as well, it's our families isn't it? Our families are involved because if he's late back I ring a daughter and say 'has he left yours yet?', 'oh yes he should be ...', and then she panics, and so you know (Mary).

Anxiety from the family, combined with anxiety from within themselves, may act as a constraint to carrying on with what previously would have been part of their everyday practice. Anxiety and the negative impact of losing confidence in the outside environment meant that, for some, social activities were curtailed:

> It's like a fear of getting lost ... For all I want to do it, I just can't do it you know. ... Sometimes as well, which I'm not accustomed to is panic attacks, if all of a sudden there's a crowd of people, of people round me, you know if I go into a shop or somewhere I find them really busy, I just sort of draw back and I think 'oh I don't want to be here' you know? ... I just go home, because I have no ... I will just go home and I'll come back another time. ... No, I can't walk far but I have my car. I must admit my confidence has gone a bit, I used to love to go to [place], that's my favourite place in the whole world, and go up on the moors, but I haven't been for a couple of years.

Interviewer: So why's your confidence gone?

> It's just the route I think, it's not the driving, it's the route. I think I know the way but I'm not certain so I won't take the risk (*laughs*) in case I'm never seen again (Cath).

Similarly Sheila, quoted below, worried about her husband driving in unfamiliar places since they found out about his diagnosis:

> About him driving places. Because he gets rather annoyed you know, if I say to him 'we've gone the wrong way' and I think 'oh' and I sit back and then I get … I get chewed, you know, and so I think it's not worth it, not for him to get annoyed and me to get chewed, so we go to places we're used to (Sheila).

The home is a crucial site in the construction and maintenance of identity in later life (Kontos 1998). The home space can, however, become disrupted in times of ill-health with the consequence of destabilising the meaning of home and as a symbol of the vulnerable body (Dyck *et al.* 2005). Our data highlight how living with the label or diagnosis of dementia can cause public environments to become destabilised and threatening. This has implications for the person with dementia as the outside space and interactions within it are also sources of identity (Duggan *et al.* 2008).

Discussions about everyday activities in the public space for people with dementia also highlighted the uncertainty people sometimes experienced related to: their location, the route taken or the purpose of the activity:

> Because I mean last year, I mean my brother has lived in the same house for donkey's years, and last year I was going up for my tea and ended up in some … in some industrial estate, and I mean I've travelled that road … I didn't know where I was and I panicked, and I just stopped and I sat there and rang him. And he says 'where are you?' and I says 'I don't know where I am' (laughter), and he says 'well give me … tell me what you're seeing' and I said 'Well there's a sign and it says [factory] and he says 'oh you're in the next sort of village thing down' and I just thought 'I just want to get out' (*laughs*) (Cath).

> Yes I am afraid it happened just the other day. I seemed to be walking round and round in the […] area and I just couldn't put it right. … Yes, but it's the first time I have had this happen, and I think an omen perhaps of what is going to happen before much longer (Fred).

The fear of getting lost or becoming unsure has been highlighted in previous research with people with dementia. Burton and Mitchell (2006) report that the fear of getting lost provokes different feelings, for some participants fear and others embarrassment. Freund (2001) highlights our taken-for-granted abilities in a world that prioritises some technologies over others. For people with dementia, the assumptions of carrying on with everyday activities in our social and physical environments are challenged. For those living with dementia, their rights as citizens to enjoy the outside environment, may become constrained by uncertainty, both their own and that of others. This can lead them to become dislodged from places which they had previously enjoyed. However, in situations of uncertainty as to place, one participant, John, spoke about how he overcame these feelings, thus enabling him to maintain his long walks with some confidence:

> I was at the beginning, then I thought I can get past this and over this, and it … the first time that I came back. … It took us about I'd say about a year when I first came back. It took us quite a bit, the only thing … was, if you'd gone to the shop and somebody was talking to you and what [you] were going to the shop for and you forgot it, so you'd go back home and as soon as you'd get back, and then I'd remember what I want, and then come back up the road (*laughter*) And that's what

happens. ... when you're going to the shop to buy something, and somebody wants to talk to you. You've forgot what you wanted, that's what I found out, and I thought well, [sister] she's good like but she goes a bit over the top which is, well, it's not that good, but I've made me own way and I'll fight this, and I do, on the bus, anything like that (John).

Technologies of place, and the outside being an enabling space
Some of the participants spoke about how they used the physical landscape to guide them to where they wanted to go and also to give them a sense of security if they became lost. Thus, for some, physical landmarks, or everyday technologies, such as shops and signs were used as a way of mediating between themselves and the outside environment, enabling them to carry on with everyday activities:

I know the buses to get on to, and I know most of the shops in town, but I couldn't find where my hearing aid place was, but I found it in the end. ... Well I have a piece of paper with my name and address on ... and if I am not sure, I will get it out and to me, it, I'll know where to go, and where to get the bus ... And once I had been down to the hearing aid, and I came home, I wrote down where it was, because I need monthly batteries, so now I know where I am going, but I was frightened because I didn't know where I was going, but when I saw that sign, it just went back to normal (Rosie).

The sign in this instance for Rosie highlights the value of technologies of place. It enabled her to overcome her sense of fear and to carry on with her everyday activities in a public space.

We've got to use our brain box sometimes you know and you can ask questions even if we were getting lost, you can go to a couple or a single person and just say 'where's so and so and so and so'. ... Well it's independence of course and perhaps I shouldn't be saying it but I definitely always go, when I'm walking and I'm out all the time and if I see a group of people coming down, they don't come to me, I'm going to them, and it works all the time, 'how are you keeping?' and 'what have you?' 'we haven't seen you for ages', so go to the next person. I don't believe if you've got a tongue in your head, you've got a brain in your head.

Interviewer: So you're saying if you were lost or anything like that you would ask somebody?

Oh of course, no doubt about it (Tom).

Changes in the public environment, for example, changes in bus timetables or routes (both of which are technologies of place), can cause someone with cognitive impairment to curtail their outside journeys (Duggan *et al.* 2008). Tom went on to speak about his experience of his mother, who had had dementia, and, what he referred to as, her 'deliberate walks':

Well my mother, she was an advanced age but, and me father was a miner and she in the latter part of her life, she went on walks, they were deliberate walks because she was going back to where she felt comfortable. She was living on [name of road] way and she was bred and born in [place] and used to just go up and just say to me dad 'I'm just going for a little walk' and then she would get completely lost (Tom).

The theme of familiarity in physical environments was raised in a number of discussions, with some people being less concerned than others. For example, in one focus group there was a discussion about the impact of having moved house. A couple who had recently moved had found the transition quite easy and they voiced little concern about how Bob would cope in the new area, because he was already familiar with it. Their only issue was with him forgetting the name of the street in which the new house was situated:

> No because basically we're in a familiar area that we've moved to, because we moved from a three-bedroomed house into a one-bedroomed bungalow. And it's near enough relatives and we know the immediate area, so I'm not too concerned about that at present but obviously it's just when somebody asks him where he lives he can't tell them ... He has to go and ask somebody else 'what do they call my street?' (Mary).

Familiarity with a place was key for some people in enabling them to get out and carry on with their everyday activities:

> I mean I can go for miles, honestly. In areas where I know, you know, it's easy for me, but in here if I want to go to the toilet or something, you know, I can't go, I don't know where to find them, you know. It's awful, it's awful (Mark).

> Where I live I'm well known so if I open the door to go out there is always somebody 'good morning, where are you going?' and I say 'I'm just going for a little walk' and then I get further along 'good morning lovely morning', by the time I've spoken to a load of people you know (Alison).

In familiar places the person with dementia may feel safe because, as highlighted above, the familiar faces around them provide a level of security. Interacting with familiar people outdoors can be a source of identity and social inclusion (Duggan *et al.* 2008). People with dementia can experience disorientation in time and place, and familiar social and physical environments offer a way of enabling people with dementia to continue enjoying the outdoor spaces:

> I feel comfortable in [town] you know. ... I mean I can come into [town] and feel happy but going into the town I think I would be a little bit dodgy. ... No I just don't go very far really, I keep to where I live you know. ... Where I know I'll see people I know. ... I feel comfortable in [town] ... I just don't go very far really, I keep to where I live you know. I can come into [town] mind because me son lives in [town], well I just head for his house you know. ... I think you know yourself how, where to go and who you know, where to visit and things like that (Alison).

Drawing on Gesler's (1992) concept of therapeutic landscapes, it could be argued that for people with dementia, landscapes can become supportive in enabling someone who experiences memory loss to re-orientate themselves and carry on with everyday activities that they enjoy. We all use the landscape and our senses in order to carry on with everyday activities but in the case of people with mild and moderate dementia it could be argued that they are more aware of their sense of place, in that they may feel at 'risk' of becoming disorientated. Physical and social landscapes in this sense are therapeutic in that they reassure and are used as an explicit way of getting home or providing a sense of security. The use of everyday technologies (or technologies of place) in public spaces such as signs, familiar bus routes and shops can all be used as a way of mapping out where it is a person wants to go.

In a recent discussion during a feedback session with a group of people with dementia, one of the newest members of the group, Stan, spoke about how he liked looking at old photographs of where he lived because it showed him all the 'old' and established buildings that he remembered, and in doing so he could look up above the more 'modern' shops and still see the buildings he recognised and connected with in those photographs. People with dementia have shown appreciation of the nature and buildings within their local environments (Burton and Mitchell 2006). In Burton and Mitchell's research, on guided walks, some participants used trees and planting, along with buildings and landmarks such as churches and towers, as cues for wayfinding.

Furthermore, when specifically asked if they used any 'modern' technological devices to support them in outside spaces, a number of participants said that they used mobile phones. In this sense, a specific technological device, mediates between the physical and social environment and offers people with dementia a means of reassurance and a sense of security, and the ability to connect with the outside and continue their everyday activities in their social environment. This form of technology, however, is not readily accepted by everyone; one participant gave away his mobile phone because he 'likes to go where he wants to go and wants to go his own way'. Similarly, although Rosie knew her daughter wanted her to have a mobile phone to reassure her that she knew where her mother was, it was not something Rosie herself wanted to use as it made her 'hearing aid oscillate' so she was unable to hear:

> Well she asked how I felt, you know about going, I said yeah, I said it was a bit funny the first time, going on my own, but now I go every week, just to look round the shops and where things are, and she says oh that's okay, she says 'I'll buy you a phone', I said 'I don't want one', she would be phoning every five minutes, 'where are you?' (Rosie).

Rosie goes on to say that technologies, whether a mobile phone or an identity card, can take away part of her freedom to do what she wants to do; if she becomes unsure as to where she is all she has to do is stop and ask someone:

> ... it makes you feel like your freedom is taken away from you, and if somebody sees you have a card or something, they think well, I'm stupid you know. I mean if I don't know where I am, I ask somebody, I will stop them and ask, I wouldn't carry a card like that (Rosie).

Conclusions

People with dementia are often viewed in light of prevailing discourses, including a focus on biomedical aspects of dementia and risk management, and policy discourses that have served to focus on enabling autonomy within home environments. Yet, people with dementia enjoy and access outdoor spaces despite challenges from within themselves and from others. Although some participants curtailed their everyday practices in the outside environment, others used the physical and social environments to support and enable them, to continue to be social actors in outside spaces. Freund (2001) argues that the cultural significance of spatial structures and the physical features can lead a person to 'feel out of place' and thus fearful in a particular space. For people with dementia, outside places and land-scapes can be viewed as both 'therapeutic' and frightening.

This chapter demonstrates that people with mild to moderate dementia can sometimes feel out of place in outside space. But, it also shows the variety of ways people with dementia manage 'feeling out of place', with some curtailing activities and others being guided by the physical and social environments which they inhabit. Technologies can support or hinder access to these places. Familiar surroundings can provide the person with dementia with the confidence to get outdoors. The use of landscapes and environments can be enabling to those with memory loss in finding their way home when they become 'lost'. Technology develop-ments targeting people with dementia have focused primarily on the individual in terms of monitoring and surveillance. By expanding the definition of technology beyond supportive and assistive devices to include our physical landscapes this chapter highlights how people with dementia can use both their social and physical environments as a means of carrying on with their everyday activities in the outdoor space. More emphasis on how technologies of place can be used to maximise the independence of people living with dementia is needed to ensure that their perspectives and needs (not just those of carers) are included.

Acknowledgements

First, we would like to thank all the study participants for their time and valuable input; we would also like to thank the Alzheimer's Society for their help and support in recruiting participants to the research. Furthermore, we would like to acknowledge the wider team involved in the original research drawn upon in this chapter.

Note

1   For a 'typology of technologies' see Hansson (2007), he distinguishes between technologies that are more individualised, 'therapeutic and compensatory', and technologies that are more enabling, 'therapeutic' and 'universal'.

References

Audit Commission (2004) Assistive Technology: Independence and Well-being 4, Public Sector National Report. London: Audit Commission.
Baldwin, C. (2008) Narrative, citizenship and dementia: the personal and the political, *Journal of Aging Studies*, 22, 222–8.
Ballinger, C. and Payne, S. (2002) The construction of the risk of falling among and by older people, *Ageing and Society*, 22, 305–24.
Bamford, C. and Bruce, E. (2002) Success and challenges in using focus groups with older people with dementia, In Wilkinson, H. (ed.) *The Perspectives of People with Dementia: Research Methods and Motivations*. London: Jessica Kingsley Publishers.
Barbour, R.S. and Kitzinger, J. (1999) Afterword. In Barbour, R.S. and Kitzinger, J. (eds) *Developing Focus Group Research: Politics, Theory and Practice*. London: Sage.
Bartlett, R. (2000) Dementia as a disability: can we learn from disability studies and theory? *Journal of Dementia Care*, Sept/Oct, 33–39.
Bartlett, R. and O'Connor, D. (2007) From personhood to citizenship: broadening the lens for demen-tia practice and research, *Journal of Aging Studies*, 21, 107–18.

Blackman, T., Mitchell, L., Burton, E., Jenks, M., Parsons, M., Raman, S. and Williams, K. (2003) The accessibility of public spaces for people with dementia: a new priority for the 'open city', *Disability and Society*, 18, 357–71.

Bloor, M., Frankland, J., Thomas, M. and Robson, K. (2001) *Focus Groups in Social Research*. London: Sage.

Bond, J. (1992) The medicalization of dementia, *Journal of Aging Studies*, 6, 4, 397–403.

Bond, J. and Corner, L. (2001) Researching dementia: are there unique methodological challenges for health services research? *Ageing and Society*, 21, 95–116.

Bond, J., Corner, L. and Graham, R. (2004) Social science theory on dementia research: normal ageing, cultural representation and social exclusion. In Innes, A., Archibald, C. and Murphy, C. (eds) *Dementia and Social Inclusion: Marginalised Groups and Marginalised Areas of Dementia Research, Care and Practice*. London: Jessica Kingsley Publishers.

Bond, J., Corner, L., Lilley, A. and Ellwood, C. (2002) Medicalisation of insight and caregivers' response to risk in dementia, *Dementia*, 1, 3, 313–28.

Brittain, K. and Shaw, C. (2007) The social consequences of living with and dealing with incontinence – a carer's perspective, *Social Science and Medicine*, 65, 6, 1274–83.

BSA (2002) Statement of Ethical Practice for the British Sociological Association.

BSG (2008) British Society of Gerontology Guidelines on ethical research with human participants.

Burton, E. and Mitchell, L. (2006) *Inclusive Urban Design: Streets for Life*. Oxford: Architectural Press.

Clarke, A.E., Mamo, L., Fishman, J.R., Shim, J.K. and Fosket, J.R. (2003) Biomedicalization: technoscientific transformations of health, illness, and U.S. biomedicine, *American Sociological Review*, 68, 2, 161–94.

Cotrell, V. and Schulz, R. (1993) The perspective of the patient with Alzheimer's disease: a neglected dimension of dementia research, *Gerontologist*, 33, 2, 205–11.

Department of Health (2001) *National Service Framework for Older People*. London: NHS Executive.

Department of Health (2009) *Living well with Dementia: a National Dementia Strategy*. London: Department of Health.

Duggan, S., Blackman, T., Martyr, A. and van Schaik, P. (2008) The impact of early dementia on outdoor life: a shrinking World? *Dementia*, 7, 2, 191–204.

Dyck, I., Kontos, P., Angus, J. and McKeever, P. (2005) The home as a site for long-term care: the meanings and management of bodies and spaces, *Health and Place*, 11, 173–85.

Essén, A. (2008) The two facets of electronic care surveillance: an exploration of the views of older people who live with monitoring devices, *Social Science and Medicine*, 67, 128–36.

Exley, C.A.D. (2007) A critical examination of home care: end of life care as an illustrative case, *Social Science and Medicine*, 65, 11, 2317–27.

Freund, P. (2001) Bodies, disability and spaces: the social model and disabling spatial organisation, *Disability and Society*, 16, 5, 689–706.

Gesler, W.M. (1992) Therapeutic landscapes: medical issues in light of the new cultural geography, *Social Science and Medicine*, 34, 735–46.

Gesler, W.M. and Kearns, R.A. (eds) (2002) *Culture, Place, Health*. London: Routledge.

Gilliard, J., Means, R., Beattie, A. and Daker-White, G. (2005) Dementia care in England and the social model of disability: lessons and issues, *Dementia*, 4, 4, 571–86.

Glaser, B. (1965) The constant comparison: methods of qualitative analysis, *Social Problems*, 12, 436–45.

Graham, R. (2004) Cognitive citizenship: access to hip surgery for people with dementia, *Health*, 8, 3, 295–310.

Hansson, S.O. (2007) The ethics of enabling technology, *Cambridge Quarterly of Healthcare Ethics*, 16, 257–67.

Haraway, D. (1985) Manifesto for cyborgs: science, technology and socialist feminism in the 1980s, *Sociological Review*, 80, 65–108.

Hughes, R. (2008) Safer walking? Issues and ethics in the use of electronic surveillance of people with dementia, *Journal of Assertive Technologies*, 2, 1, 45–8.

Ihde, D. (1991) *Instrumental Reaslism: the Interface between Philosophy of Science and Philosophy of Technology*. Bloomington: Indiana University Press.

Ihde, D. (1993) *Philosophy of Technology – an Introduction*. New York: Paragon House.

Imrie, R. and Kumar, M. (1998) Focusing on disability and access in the built environment, *Disability and Society*, 13, 3, 357–74.

Joyce, K. and Mamo, L. (2006) Graying the cyborg: new directions in feminist analyses of aging, science and technology. In Calasanti, T.M. and Slevin, K.F. (eds) *Age Matters: Realigning Feminist Thinking*. New York: Routledge.

Kearns, R.A. (1993) Place and health: towards a reformed medical geography, *Professional Geographer*, 46, 67–72.

Kenner, A. (2008) Securing the elderly body: dementia, surveillance, and the politics of 'Aging in Place', *Surveillance and Society*, 5, 3, 252–69.

Kidd, P.S. and Parshall, M.B. (2000) Getting the focus and the group: enhancing analytical rigor in focus group research, *Qualitative Health Research*, 10, 3, 293–308.

Kitwood, T. (1997) *Dementia Reconsidered: the Person Comes First*. Buckingham: Open University Press.

Kitzinger, J. (1994) The methodology of focus groups: the importance of interaction between research participants, *Sociology of Health and Illness*, 16, 1, 103–21.

Knapp, M., Prince, M., Albanese, E., Banerjee, S., Dhanasiri, S., Fernandez, J.-L., Ferri, C., McCrone, P., Snell, T. and Stewart, R. (2007) *Dementia UK: the Full Report*. London: Alzheimer's Society.

Kontos, P. (1998) Resisting institutionalization: constructing old age and negotiating home, *Journal of Aging Studies*, 12, 2, 167–84.

Kontos, P. (2004) Embodied selfhood: redefining agency in Alzheimer's Disease. In Tulle, E. (ed.) *Old Age and Agency*. New York: Nova Science Publishers Inc.

McCreadie, C. and Tinker, A. (2005) The acceptability of assistive technology to older people, *Ageing and Society*, 25, 91–110.

Milligan, C. (2000) 'Bearing the burden': towards a restructured geography of caring, *Area*, 32, 1, 49–58.

Miskelly, F. (2001) Assistive technology in elderly care, *Age and Ageing*, 30, 455–58.

Miskelly, F. (2004) A novel system of electronic tagging in patients with dementia and wandering, *Age and Ageing*, 33, 304–06.

Moreira, T. and Bond, J. (2008) Does the prevention of brain ageing constitute anti-ageing medicine? Outline of a new space of representation for Alzheimer's Disease, *Journal of Aging Studies*, 22, 356–65.

Ogg, J. (2005) *Heat Wave*. London: The Young Foundation.

Östlund, B. (2004) Social science research on technology and the elderly – does it exist? *Science Studies*, 17, 2, 44–62.

Percival, J. and Hanson, J. (2006) Big brother or brave new world? Telecare and its implications for older people's independence and social inclusion, *Critical Social Policy*, 26, 4, 888–909.

Phillipson, C. (2007) The 'elected' and the 'excluded': sociological perspectives on the experiences of place and community in old age, *Ageing and Society*, 27, 321–42.

Plummer, K. (2001) *Documents of Life 2*, London: Sage.

Post, S. (2000), The concept of Alzheimer Disease in a hypercognitive society. In Whitehouse, P.J., Maurer, K. and Ballenger, J.F. (eds) *Concepts of Alzheimers Disease*. Baltimore: JHU Press.

Robinson, L., Brittain, K., Lindsay, S., Jackson, D. and Olivier, P. (2009) Keeping in Touch Everyday (KITE) project: developing assistive technologies with people with dementia and their carers to promote independence, *International Psychogeriatrics*, 21, 3, 494–502.

Robinson, L., Hutchings, D., Corner, L., Beyer, F., Dickinson, H., Vanoli, A., Finch, T., Hughes, J.C., Ballard, C., May, C. and Bond, J. (2006) Wandering in dementia: a systematic literature review of the effectiveness of non-pharmacological interventions to prevent wandering in dementia and evaluation of the ethical implications and acceptability of their use, *Health Technology Assessment*, 10, 26.

Robinson, L., Hutchings, D., Corner, L., Finch, T., Hughes, J., Brittain, K. and Bond, J. (2007) Balancing rights and risks – conflicting perspectives in the management of wandering in dementia, *Health, Risk and Society*, 94, 4, 389–406.

Synnott, A. (1993) *The Body Social – Symbolism, Self and Society*. London: Routledge.

Tomas, D. (1995) Feedback and cybernetics: reimaging the body in the age of the cyborg, *Body and Society*, 1, 3–4, 21–43.

Tulle-Winton, E. (2000) Old bodies. In *Hancock, P., Hughes, B., Jagger, E., Paterson, K., Russell, R., Tulle-Winton, E. and Tyler, M. (eds) The Body, Culture and Society*. Buckingham: Open University Press.

Wakefield, S. and McMullan, C. (2005) Healing in places of decline: (re)imagining everyday landscapes in Hamilton, Ontario, *Health and Place*, 11, 299–312.

Wey, S. (2004) One size does not fit all. In Marshall, M. (ed.) *Perspectives on Rehabilitation and Dementia*. London: Jessica Kingsley Publishers.

Wey, S. (2006) Working 'in the zone' – a social-ecological framework for dementia rehabilitation. In Woolham, J. (ed.) *Assistive Technology in Dementia Care: Developing the Role of Technology in the Care and Rehabilitation of People with Dementia – Current Trends and Perspectives*. London: Hawker Publications.

Wiles, J. (2005) Conceptualizing place in the care of older people: the contributions of geographical gerontology, *International Journal of Older People Nursing*, 14, 8b, 100–8.

Wilkinson, H. (2002), Including people with dementia in research: methods and motivations. In Wilkinson, H. (ed.) *The Perspectives of People with Dementia*. London: JKP.

Wilson, K. (2003) Therapeutic landscapes and first nations peoples: an exploration of culture, health and place, *Health and Place*, 9, 2, 83–93.

9

Liberating the wanderers: using technology to unlock doors for those living with dementia

Johanna M. Wigg

Introduction

This chapter explores wandering behaviour in the United States and how its social construction as a high risk activity results in locked door, long-term care environments for individuals diagnosed with dementia. My empirical research compares two dementia care settings, each relying on different technologies to oversee wanderers, including locked and unlocked environments. I analyse residents' experiences engaging with a locked door versus an unlocked door, showing that individuals' encounters with each differ in terms of emotional response.

As the global population of old people continues to grow (Weinberger 2007), the number of elders diagnosed with dementia in the world and specifically in the United States is also increasing (Hebert *et al.* 2003). Cultural definitions of dementia vary throughout the world, and in some regions dementia is non-existent. Instead, societies explain cognitive change and loss as normal ageing (Herbert 2001). The diagnosis of dementia focuses on specific neuropathological changes in an individual's brain. Alzheimer's disease is the most prominent diagnosis explaining the aetiology of dementia in the Western world (Patterson and Clarfield 2003). Whatever the disease, ' "wandering" is one of the most troublesome of behavioural problems which commonly accompany dementia' (Hope *et al.* 1994: 149).

Technologies such as key coded doors are implemented in dementia care environments to protect the individual from getting lost, injured, or from death. In these environments, wandering is perceived to be a risky behaviour, requiring social controls such as locked doors. This chapter examines the impact of locked door environments on residents and compares their experiences with those of residents with dementia living in an unlocked environment. The unlocked environment uses motion detectors to monitor the wanderers and regards wandering as a necessary activity for the individual with dementia. Comparing the two environments, I challenge the medicalisation of wandering and suggest a need to redefine approaches to safe wandering that incorporate technologies that monitor but do not confine residents.

Understanding wandering

Although the aetiology of dementia is contested and unknown, the syndrome can include 'wandering'. While not every individual living with dementia displays wandering behaviours, research suggests that between 37 per cent and 60 per cent of the population diagnosed with dementia will develop wandering behaviours at some point during the disease (Ballard *et al.* 1991, UK Alzheimer's Society 2007). Research identifies wandering as a behavioural problem often requiring institutionalised interventions, such as pharmacological restraints (Oxman and Santulli 2003). Wandering is complex and ranges from exit seeking behaviour, including elopers and runaways (Lucerno 2002), to restless pacers and modellers (Oxman and Santulli 2003). Institutional and professional definitions of wandering (*i.e.* wandering as a behavioural problem or as an articulation of need) shapes the interventions chosen.

Exploring wandering behaviour from a clinical perspective identifies it as a behavioural problem requiring pharmacological and/or behavioural interventions. Research shows that both of these approaches have limited effects (Hughes and Louw 2002, Ballard and O'Brien 1999, Howard *et al.* 2001). In examining the 'root causes of behavioural symptoms in persons with dementia' (Whall and Kolanowski 2004: 106), the 'need-driven dementia-compromised behaviour model', proposed in 1996, suggests that behaviours traditionally viewed as 'problematic' require examination according to elders' needs. By responding to their needs, care providers improve the quality of life of individuals who display specific behaviours such as physical aggression and problematic vocalisations (Whall and Kolanowski 2004).

By examining several areas of dementia-related behavioural problems, including aggression (Fisher and Swingen 1997) and disruptive vocalisations (Buchanan and Fisher 2002), attention is pointed toward environmental stimuli when examining these behaviours. The 'behavioural problem' is perceived as a means of communicating needs unable to be articulated 'normally' because of cognitive decline (Whall and Kolanowski 2004, Fisher and Swingen 1997). Research suggests the significance of environmental influence, even at the most severe stage of the disease, and recognises that the least restrictive environments help modify the unusual behaviours (Fisher and Swingen 1997, Buchanan and Fisher 2002).

Some individuals with dementia wander with agendas of escape, while others move aimlessly. The need to move results from heightened levels of anxiety, stemming from physiological, neurochemical or psychological sources (Emery and Oxman 2003, Dickinson and McLain-Kark 1998, Hope *et al.* 2001). These motives to move raise important questions about how architects design care environments to support or control wanderers.

Wandering as risky

In discussions of public health issues including long-term dementia care, risk discourses are prevalent (Lupton 2005). The emphasis on risk transforms 'probabilistic thinking' into a political discourse (Douglas 1990). This transformation occurs because of the social pressure for cultural homogeneity. By identifying certain kinds of behaviour (*e.g.* wandering) as potentially dangerous, transgressions of social norms may be deterred. The rise of a risk society, that is, a society organised around documenting, imaging, and responding to risk, emerges as a way to manage the hazards and insecurities produced by modernity (Beck 1986, 2006). Science – in its many fields and disciplines – is often used to measure and manage risk. Wandering as a behaviour is medicalised, or turned into a medical problem in need of a medical solution. This legitimates social control efforts in the name of 'protecting' wanderers. Social control through the medical gaze encourages an environment of pharmacological surveillance and physical confinement (Foucault 1995). Wandering thus signals this turn towards a risk society, as well as the jurisdiction of medicine over defining and controlling behaviours labelled risky.

The assertion of riskiness requires the formation of socially designated experts who manage risk in what is claimed to be an objective fashion (Carter 1995). With regard to science and technology studies Brian Wynne notes:

A systematic examination of the 'objective' measures of danger arrived at by experts, will always remain essential, but the lingering tendency to start from this scientific vantage point and add social perceptions as qualifications to the objective physical picture must be completely reversed (Wynne 1982: 138).

Understanding the subjective nature of defining risk among those who wander, as well as identifying which professions and stakeholders define the risk, requires an explanation of the broader culture of wandering. By culture, I am referring to the home and institutional environments in which wanderers reside, as well as the interpersonal relations between residents, family, and staff. This broader cultural context normalises the pathologisation of wandering, positioning medical experts in powerful roles as gate keepers (Foucault 1995). The research in this chapter explores the cultural and interpersonal contexts of wandering.

Wandering is a reason for institutionalisation; therefore, risk discourse plays a powerful role in this decision among professionals, families and individuals with dementia. Determination of the risk (Douglas 1990) is different depending on the degree of exit-seeking or outdoor engagement. Care providers view individuals who seek to be outdoors as 'higher risk' than those who walk aimlessly. Once institutionalised, wanderers are viewed as high risk by an institution's administration, due to the potential for lawsuits (Noyes and Silva 1993, Coleman 1993, Robinson et al. 2007a). One risk for the wanderer is the ability to become lost, and due to cognitive impairment such individuals may be unable to survive in the outside world. Wandering elders with dementia, for example, have frozen to death and died because of dehydration and malnutrition (Mitchell et al. 2005, O'Connor et al. 1990, Ballard et al. 2001).

As multilayered as the ideas of risk discourse are, so too are the social and institutionalised responses to wanderers' needs. The challenge to protect those who wander while respecting their rights is a 'balancing' act (Robinson et al. 2007a). Professionals, bound by duty as healthcare providers and the Hippocratic Oath, prioritise safety at the expense of personal rights. In contrast, families often feel that quality of life and independence are more important than safety. Although the perspective of individuals diagnosed with dementia is limited, preliminary studies suggest that these individuals want to experience life at whatever cost (Robinson et al. 2007a). In Robinson and colleagues' (2007a: 397) research, for example, one respondent replied, 'Sometimes we just go out ... haven't any idea where I am going ... just enjoy the fresh air'. The manner in which risk is defined results in specific approaches to the social control of wanderers.

Restraining or guiding wanderers: two models of intervention

The assumed risk the wanderer poses to him/herself and potentially to others heavily influences the design of the care environment. For this chapter, one can separate the possible solutions to the 'problem' of wandering (i.e. the problem defined according to medical pathologisation) into two categories: medical and non-medical. Medical solutions to wandering include restraints (Capezuti et al. 1989), such as locked doors with keypads, camouflaged doors, geriatric chairs with trays to prevent standing, even cloth and leather limb restraints (Coleman 1993).

Besides physical restraints, pharmacological or chemical restraints are used to curb wandering behaviours. Using medications to sedate individuals lessens their tendency to ambulate (Zimmer et al. 1984). Medications prescribed for anxiety often lessen the wandering impulse, while also imposing side effects such as increased confusion and physical instability (Garrard *et al.* 1991). Studies suggest a direct relationship between pharmacological restraint use and falls among those with dementia (Gillespie *et al.* 2003, Tilly and Reed 2008, Rabins *et al.* 2007). As Coleman explains, 'restraints are only exchanging one set of benefits and risks for another' (Coleman 1993: 2114).

The second category of possible solutions to the 'problem' of wandering (or what I call non-medical) accepts the biochemical understandings of the body and mind but does not try to medicate or restrain this body. In this model, the physiological causes of wandering behaviour are understood as driven by neurochemical changes associated with dementia. The abnormalities in the circadian rhythm result in high levels of anxiety (Wu and Swaab 2005). The response to the anxiety increases ambulation or movement which alters an individual's body chemistry. Wandering may be the body's response to anxiety, since it offers the physiological release needed to lessen feelings of anxiousness. Thus, this approach steers away from physical and chemical barriers to the individual's ability to move, and instead tries to accommodate it. Examples of accommodations include the use of technologies such as motion detectors and micro chips tracked by satellites, as well as educating staff about the physiological and psychosocial need to move. Using microchips, or what is popularly called tagging, involves placing a surveying device on an individual who wanders, to be able to locate the person through satellite technology (Hughes and Louw 2002, Altus *et al.* 2000). The tagging devices vary, and can include watches, bracelets, and devices sewn into clothing (Miskelly 2004, Welsh *et al.* 2003, Rasquin *et al.* 2007, McShane and Hope 1994). The companies that tag lost pets and vehicles, such as LoJack, are the same companies that are entering the business of tagging people (Saletan 2009).[1] Both the United Kingdom and Australia are exploring the use of tagging to help oversee and protect the safety of wanderers (Barry 2007, Karvelas 2008, AAP News 2008).

Although some imagine tagging as the ultimate invasion of privacy, research suggests that the technique can lessen the caregiver's stress by allowing individuals to roam without supervision (Welsh *et al.* 2003). In addition, some individuals may be able to remain at home and connected to their community longer before institutionalisation (Barry 2007, Altus *et al.* 2000). In contrast, critics argue tagging is using technology to replace people as care providers for these individuals (Barry 2007, Sturdy 2005).

Moreover, a person's experience of dementia changes constantly and affects their abilities, which has an impact on what technologies are suitable. For example, an individual who wanders may be aware of safety precautions about cars and strangers, but if this awareness wanes, a chip in their watch or clothing will not protect them. Thus, technologies must be understood in context; their use can vary and have differing effects on roaming, depending on an individual's abilities and the broader environment in which they are used.

Settings and methodologies

This study compares data from two different dementia care facilities, specifically examining how wandering protections like locked doors and motion detectors impact on wanderers' quality of life. To maintain confidentiality, I gave each site a pseudonym: Pine Tree Place and Oceanside Vista. Pine Tree Place is located in a Northeastern town of the United States. The observational unit, one of three in the facility, consists of approximately thirty residents. At the time of the study, the resident population was white and included a gender ratio of one male to three females. While the age, socio-economic status, and diagnosis of each resident was confidential, most of the population ranged in age from their late sixties into their nineties; these individuals lived with a range of diseases that resulted in dementia. The degree of dementia varied; the unit provided care from middle to late stage dementia.

The design of the unit incorporated a continuous walking loop around the perimeter of the living and dining space. Because of the potential for wandering behaviours, the unit was locked. The front entrance of Pine Tree Place had a key coded lock, as did the door to each unit within the facility. Any individual entering or exiting the units had to punch in a key code and wait for the door to open. At the back of the unit there was a key coded door that led outside to a patio and garden area. Enclosed by an eight-foot high, wooden fence, the patio also had a key coded lock on the gate.

At Pine Tree Place, I collected field notes for seven months, totalling nearly four hundred hours of daytime observation. One area of concentration concerned the residents' attempted engagement with the outdoors and exits. I analysed field notes and coded the data based on resident interaction with key coded doors. Analysis of field notes was based on constructivist grounded theory and incorporated Atlas.ti, resulting in line by line coding, the generation of memos, and theme development (Glaser and Strauss 1967, Coffey *et al.* 1996, Charmaz 2000).

I collected a second set of data over 10 years of participant observation at a smaller facility (Oceanside Vista) specialising in dementia care, with a maximum capacity of eight residents. I was employed by this facility for ten years and received permission from the administration to conduct fieldwork. The resident population was white, with ages ranging from 63 to 95, and a male/female ratio ranging from 1:2 to 1:1 over the 10-year period. While each facility was expensive (ranging from $3,500 to $7,000 per month), private pay residents at Pine Tree Place paid approximately one-third more than their counterparts at Oceanside Vista. I observed approximately 30 residents at Oceanside Vista over 10 years. Of this population, approximately one-third wandered in a manner that displayed exiting behaviour.

The facility's design included bedrooms on the perimeter and a dining and living space in the middle of the house. The outdoors was accessible through a front door leading onto a deck. Located in a rural setting, Oceanside Vista maintained walking areas which led to the ocean and up a wooded lane. Oceanside Vista did not incorporate locked doors or keypads. While wandering was a concern and reality for the facility, a motion detector alerted staff when someone entered/exited the front deck space by emitting a buzzing sound when engaged.

Like Pine Tree Place, the data collection at Oceanside Vista included fieldwork. I generated field notes during or following wandering incidents. In addition, I analysed video data of wandering. Oceanside Vista collected the data with the consent of the people granted Power of Attorney by the residents. I entered the video data and field notes into Atlas.ti for coding, memo generation and theme development. Observations at Oceanside Vista occurred during all shifts. I retrospectively analysed additional data for Oceanside Vista, integrating informal interviews with staff and discussions of wandering at staff meetings.

While employed at the facility, daily interactions with residents provided opportunity for observations of residents' wandering behaviours. My position as both participant and observer offered insight into the complexity and subtleties of wandering behaviour, and the impact of alternative technologies on the residents at Oceanside Vista. Full disclosure was made to families before admission about the research conducted at Oceanside Vista. Residents did not appear to be affected positively or negatively by the research, neither by the observation nor the video recording.

Technological interventions: locked doors or motion detectors?

In this study, I compare two different sites designed to provide for residents' safety: Pine Tree Place and Oceanside Vista. Each site had different understandings of wandering and developed technological interventions that corresponded to these definitions.

The design and structure of Pine Tree Place emphasised the need to restrain wandering through key coded entryways and patio doors, as well as regular use of geriatric chairs with locked trays. Such restriction often increased residents' anxiety. In my fieldwork, I observed incidents where concerned residents expressed a desire to leave the facility, often stating that they needed to go home, but were either unable to find the exit door, or when they found the door, they were unable to open it.

> In one situation, a resident by the name of Pauline asks Lloyd, a staff member, 'Can I get out here? Can I get out this door?' She points to the door next to us. Lloyd says, 'Um, hum'. Pauline continues, 'Well, there must be a door somewhere for relatives to come in. I want to go home; can I get out this door?' Lloyd tries to ignore her.

> In another situation, Paula sees Naomi, a nurse on the site, and smiles and walks to her. Paula asks Naomi, 'Where do I go to get out? I just want to go home'. Naomi says, 'Well, I don't know.' Paula asks again, 'Where is the door to get out?' Naomi points toward the area she just left, 'Over there, go over there and there are people around the corner'.

Pine Tree Place tried to support the idea of wandering by including large picture windows in the living room for residents to watch the outdoors. Although this strategy recognises the desire to be outdoors, it still emphasises the overall goal of restraint. Individuals can look outside; they cannot roam outdoors.

> Beatrice is working with the physical therapist. The therapist follows her with the wheelchair and tells her how to sit safely in the chair. Beatrice gets to the outside door and says, 'Can't I sit outside?' The therapist explains that it is damp and cold.

There was a door which offered access to the patio space. The door, however, was controlled by the key code.

> Leanne is in the kitchen milling about. She asked if it was warm enough to go out. The cleaning person said, 'Sure'. Leanne went over to the door, but it was locked. She said, 'Oh damn'. Another staff person said, 'The snow isn't even melting yet. It is cold out there'.

Similar to the thwarted desire to go home, the residents' inability to enter the patio or go outdoors increased their anxiety.

> After pacing the hallways for some time, and trying several exit doors, Lester says, 'Gee, I'd like to get out of this place. I don't like it. We're just caught right in here.'

Both by imagining there would be no exit, or by physically trying to open a door and finding it locked, residents' needs could not be met and their behaviours suggested increasing anxiety levels. Residents often became panicked or angry and verbally expressed their frustrations at not being able to leave the building. The following quote illustrates this finding:

A resident named Alice walks by with her jacket on. Her friend Beatrice says, 'Where are you going?' Alice says softly, so no one can hear her, 'I am getting the heck out of here'. Beatrice says, 'How long, for how long?' Alice looks at her puzzled. Beatrice says, 'When will you be back, tonight? I'll wait for you.' Alice and Beatrice start pushing on the door next to me. It is locked and they comment on how it is stuck. Alice asserts, 'I'll get out of one of them'.

Many residents sat in their wheelchairs or milled about near the entrance door. When an individual entered or exited the unit, individuals near the door took notice of who was passing through. The observational data signalled that some residents who occupied the space near the front door might be seeking to exit through the door when it opened. It was not unusual to watch a staff or family member cautiously close the door behind them to prevent a resident from following. Some residents were more difficult to redirect and the person leaving would wait until the resident was not near the door. In my fieldnotes I wrote:

Lester finishes his meal and makes his way toward the door. The staff are going in and out of the door. They make sure that he is distracted when they pass through the door.

In my fieldwork, I observed how residents became upset when a door closed in one's face and residents were not able to open it. In one instance I watched a physical therapist take a resident outside:

Rosie, another resident, asks if she can go out with them. She is told she can; however, Lester is quickly approaching and the door is shut. The original resident and therapist exit, but Rosie is left inside, with Lester who is trying to open the door.

During my fieldwork, I saw many examples of residents, both ambulatory and in wheel-chairs, pulling with all their might to open the locked door to the outside. Sometimes when residents yanked on the doors, staff would be alerted by the noise and try to redirect the individual away from the door. For example, in one case:

Alice wheels over to the door to the garden. She pulls on it very hard, shaking it back and forth. She gets a very distressed look on her face. A young man who works on the unit walks by and she says, 'I tried to get the door open'. He says, 'The door you want is over there' (pointing across the unit). Alice puts her head down and shakes it, slowly wheeling away.

The staff offered many explanations for the locked door, including stating there was no staff person available to supervise them while they were outside.

Janice tries the door but can't open it. She turns to Linda, Barry's wife, and says, 'How come I can't get out of here?' Barry's wife explains. Janice replies, 'All these people in here and I have to have a nurse to go out!' Janice walks over to Alice to tell her about not being able to get out. Alice says, 'You know how things are. You can't do anything you want to be able to do.'

When the weather was warm and dry and staff were available, residents were able to enter the patio area.

Unlike Pine Tree Place, Oceanside Vista serves a maximum of eight residents. The design is homelike, incorporating residents' pets and personal belongings, and children of staff. In addition, the staff/resident ratio of one to four potentially provided residents with more attention and support than Pine Tree Place, where the ratio was typically one to eight. This ratio does not include other Pine Tree Place staff, most of whom appeared well versed in dementia care techniques, such as cueing (prompting residents to continue with a task) and redirecting. I witnessed repeated examples of maintenance, housekeeping and administrative staff engaging with residents in appropriate ways. While these additional staff played a significant role in improving the direct care of residents, their engagement was fleeting and unpredictable. They stopped when they had a minute to spare and moved on quickly to their other responsibilities.

In contrast to Pine Tree Place, Oceanside Vista outlined, in their mission statement and literature, a philosophical commitment to not locking doors on residents. Administrative staff counselled families on Oceanside Vista's alternative approach to dealing with wandering, including incorporation of exercise and the use of motion detectors. Wandering was redefined as a necessary means of exercise for those living with anxiety because of illness. Oceanside Vista did not view wandering as a 'problem' that required social controls, but rather addressed it as a therapy that deserved recognition and support. Staff orientations, in-service training and meetings addressed scheduling walks for wanderers. In addition, staff worked together to accommodate a resident's need to exit the building and wander. For example, the facility trained staff in techniques for exchanging responsibilities to manage the wanderers' need to exit.

The structure of the facility was a necessary ingredient in redefining wandering beyond locking doors. To allow elders with dementia to wander, staff members were alerted when a resident left the building. The motion detector sounded a noise when an individual crossed in front of it. To ensure the wanderer's safety and return, staff observed and/or joined the resident on their excursion. Most of the time, the favourable staff/resident ratio of one to four allowed staff to join individuals who wanted to wander. Rare incidents occurred when staff were unable to accommodate the needs of wanderers, such as during inclement weather. Obvious signs of heightened anxiety and mood changes typically resulted, which the researcher noted. My fieldwork showed, however, that even in poor weather, efforts to dress appropriately (rain gear, snow gear) and proceed with wandering occurred. In addition, arrangements were made for residents who repeatedly exited, requiring staff to exchange duties with co-workers to accommodate the wandering. Staff meetings devoted time to discussing how to grant the needs of multiple wanderers. If two or three residents exited at the same time, the staff expressed stress at helping multiple wanderers with varying abilities. If a wanderer needed extended time, staff members used cell phones to notify a co-worker of the situation.

A regular walking routine was incorporated at the facility, supporting the concept that exercise, especially walking/wandering, is therapeutic for anxiety levels among elders with dementia. Throughout the day, staff joined residents on outdoor walks. The data showed patterns for wandering among certain residents. For example, during the afternoon and early evening hours (when the sun began to set), many residents experienced 'sundowning' effects such as increased levels of anxiety and agitation. Sundowning is a clinical term used to describe a common set of behaviours associated with the syndrome, which can manifest themselves as restlessness and wandering (Sharer 2008). Accommodating these wanderers was less difficult since the behaviour was consistent and able to be scheduled. In line with observations made at Pine Tree Place, residents in Oceanside View believed they must get home to family, such as spouses and children to make supper. Individuals sometimes packed belongings into bags and left the facility.

During the middle of supper, Arnold stood up from the table and stated that he needed to get home. He went into a bedroom and carefully folded various items (including some slippers, magazines, and a stuffed animal) into a blanket. He tied the tips of the blanket so that items inside would be secured and tossed it over his shoulder. As Arnold headed for the front door he yelled, 'Goodnight! I'm going home.'

As Arnold left the front terrace, the motion detector sounded, alerting staff that he was leaving the home. Staff responded by following him up the hill, which was roughly a quarter mile and then redirecting him to the house. When the staff needed to encourage him to turn around, his anxiety was typically lessened.

Whatever their agenda, the need to leave and feel purposeful in their process was present for all observed wanderers.

Donald walked up the lane every morning to get the newspaper. Donald explained, 'I love the fresh air. It clears my head. I also enjoy reading the sports section.'

Periodically, Donald would be unable to get the paper because of changes in the schedule and he became irritable and frustrated over his inability to leave. As soon as Donald was able to get out, his mood improved dramatically and he was able to move on with his day. By being able to walk out the front door to the outside, Donald avoided the potential for conflict and anxiety inherent in trying to open a locked door.

Other exiting or wandering patterns included individuals who merely walked out of the front door onto the terrace and then back into the house.

Patrice spent the morning going onto the front terrace and pruning the flowers in the plant pots. She would open the exit door and walk onto the terrace, pull a few dead flowers from the plants in the window boxes and return into the house. This process of walking outside and returning to the inside of the house occupied much of her morning. Patrice's daughter confirmed that she had been a gardener for much of her life and loved to 'get her hands into the earth'.

Once again, this individual's need appeared to be the simple ability to walk into the outdoors. The unlocked exit door surprised certain residents who had resided in locked door facilities before living at Oceanside Vista. Penny spent her first few days at Oceanside Vista opening and closing the front door. When encouraged to sit outside on the terrace, Penny replied, 'Really? Are you sure it's all right?'

While working, I observed dramatic reductions in anxiety before wandering compared with anxiety levels post walking. Most wanderers, who were unable to eat or sit because of anxiety, engaged in these activities after wandering. Individuals who had moved from locked-door facilities were often able to have anxiety medication levels reduced or discontinued. There appeared to be less need for the medications within the Oceanside Vista design. While data were not analysed on these observations, this area of research (the relationship between pharmacological restraints and 'unlocked' environments for wanderers) deserves further investigation.

Pine Tree Place and Oceanside Vista offered different models of long-term dementia care, as well as different perspectives on wandering. While each model defined wandering differently, the reasons given by residents for needing to wander were similar, including the desire to go home or to tend to their loved ones. At Pine Tree Place, pathologising wandering behaviour resulted in the perception of the behaviour as 'high risk' and the presence of locked doors on all the units. Although the facility tried to accommodate residents' desire to be outside by providing large picture windows, one of the institution's primary agendas (which was explicitly stated in the facility's multiple day orientation) is to prevent cognitively impaired individuals from leaving the building.

During my observation period, I witnessed a few incidents where residents managed to violate the locked environment. In one situation, a resident who was not allowed outside in the garden area without staff followed another resident and their family outside. The family notified staff of the situation and they quickly redirected the resident into the locked environment. In another instance, residents congregated around the entrance door to the unit when emergency medical staff arrived to tend to a sick resident. The door was open while the crew and stretcher moved in and out of the unit. In all the commotion, two mobile residents sped through the unlocked door and out to the lobby where they were intercepted and returned to the unit by administrative staff. These occurrences were stressful for staff, heightening people's anxiety and causing staff to confer with one another. Staff debriefed immediately following the incident, discussing how the incident could have happened and how to prevent it from happening again. Perhaps part of the need to prevent individuals from leaving the building related to a fear of legal action, a concern recognised and justified in the literature (Noyes and Silva 1993, Coleman 1993, Robinson *et al.* 2007a).

Because of the design of Pine Tree Place, the staff/resident ratio was wide enough potentially to create the chances for individuals to escape from the property. Even more significant, however, was the impact on each individual's life. By not having enough staff available to cater to the needs of the residents, the redirection of residents and inability to engage with the outside world occurred regularly. Robinson and colleagues' data support this finding in a response from a nursing staff member about risk management and resident access to the outside:

> The gardens are there but you can't go out because it's too wet or too cold or we can't spare the staff because you might fall (2007b: 398).

The medical model supports the focus on the behaviour as a product of the disease, rather than implications and needs of the individual. The psychological impact on the individuals appeared potentially harmful. Through observations of residents encountering locked doors, I witnessed multiple instances of increased problematic behaviours such as yelling and expressions of rage, or depressive behaviours of withdrawal.

Oceanside Vista defined wandering as a necessary ingredient of quality care for individuals with dementia. The design of the facility and the programming focused on integrating the need for movement and wandering. The scheduled walking programme promoted physical activity throughout the day and the open-door policy allowed residents to exit the facility at their discretion. Motion detectors acted to promote staff awareness of the need to observe and/or escort the individual in the wandering. The ability to move and exercise often lessened the anxiety levels at specific times of the day, such as in the late afternoon. The need for pharmacological intervention for anxiety was often reduced or discontinued.

The many faces of surveillance

At Pine Tree Place, the pathologisation of wandering established a legitimisation for locked doors. 'There is no doubt that the gaze, first described by Foucault, is being transformed into a virtual gaze, rooted in both technology and biomedical contexts' (Sinha 2000: 304).

Constant surveillance and control of space is viewed as essential to avoid potentially 'high risk' wandering. The nurses' station at Pine Tree Place was strategically situated facing the entrance/exit of the unit. Foucauldian concepts of surveillance and Bentham's panopticon (Foucault 1995) were visible throughout the facility. For example, residents at Pine Tree Place congregated near the entrance/exit. In doing so, those who were observers (medical professionals) and the observed (residents) shared in surveillance behaviours. It was typical to witness residents surveying the whereabouts of other residents with respect to the entrance/exit. My observations suggested that residents, staff and even family experienced the effects of the Benthamian panoptic principle, whereby the observer and the observed were all prisoners behind the locked door of the unit (Foucault 1995, Holmes 2001).

Motion detectors at Oceanside Vista also use surveillance but to a different end. Inherent in the presence of motion detectors is the understanding that wandering is not safe alone and requires support. An individual engages in wandering when the motion detector is triggered. The ability of the individual to leave and enter the outdoors recognises the potential human need to move beyond confines of enclosed space, not locked behind doors, nor struggling to open a locked door. The individual's physical and psychological transition to heightened levels of anxiety and panic is challenging to witness. While the examples in the data depicted elders who did lose control when they could not exit, the wanderer, who was able to move out of the setting into the outdoors and move without restraint, regularly appeared less psychologically traumatised.

Motion detectors allow for a redefinition of 'risk' as it applies to the wanderer. The accommodation requires surveillance or observation, but from a less hierarchical and constraining presence, reducing pathologisation. Through a combination of human and technological support, a partnership can form between wanderer and care provider. While the wanderer can benefit from exiting, so too can the care provider, in terms of exercise, an equalised relationship, and interpersonal interaction. Wanderer and care provider often engage in conversation and build relationships during the wandering. The developing relationship and engagement between wanderer and care provider potentially works to lessen the pathologisation of the behaviour. Rather than observer and observed being locked into buildings, the wanderer and care provider are liberated.

Conclusions

Instead of pathologising wandering as a component of the biomedicalisation of dementia, redefining wandering as purposeful and therapeutic in long-term dementia care may create more elder-friendly environments of care that focus on the needs of the individuals who wander. This chapter shows that creating 'unlocked' facilities is possible through incorporating technologies, such as motion detectors and cell phones; however, changes in staff/resident ratios must also accommodate the need for staff to wander with residents. While some facilities may be unable to acquire additional staff, perhaps staff employed for housekeeping or maintenance might be able to support the wandering by spending time with residents out of doors. Being outdoors and exercising does not simply support residents: it is an added benefit for staff as well. To understand the full impact of the different effects of technologies, further research is needed on similar environments (specific to size and staff/resident ratio).

By comparing the technologies of locked doors and motion detectors in context, this chapter shows that distinctions exist between surveillance technologies that chiefly engage in social control and surveillance technologies that encourage greater independence and interpersonal interaction between staff and resident. Instead of stigmatising, medicating, or creating physical barriers to wandering, facilities can find ways to support roving in safe, healthy ways. Such practices, though, require more investment in staff and maintaining a better staff to resident ratio.

While less institutionalised long-term care environments are being developed for elders who are cognitively competent within the United States (Thomas 2004), developing new environments for cognitively impaired elders is more limited. Moving away from large-scale, locked door, institutional models of long-term care, which encourage restraint forms of surveillance and heightened anxiety for staff and residents, to facilities with motion detectors and staff guides, may offer care that addresses wanderers' desires (as well as their caregivers' or staff's needs). Redefining the concepts of dementia care, wandering, and risk management beyond pathologisation requires a rehumanisation of the wanderer. Allowing the wanderer to wander (with the help of motion detectors and staff guides) may empower a person who has been dehumanised through the pathologisation of dementia and its associated (wandering) behaviours. Researchers and facility designers should explore the complex selfhood as embodied by those living with dementia. Such moves go beyond the biomedical model to 'treat' dementia and offer the possibility of what Kitwood (1997: 133) calls the rehumanising process of 'personalisation'.

Throughout Kitwood's work (1997), the call for a cultural transformation encourages recognition and engagement of individuals with dementia. This chapter shows that wandering is another area that can be redefined and promoted (with the support of technology) in an attempt to further this cultural transformation. Further research should be conducted to address the options available to larger facilities with fewer staff. Programmme development within such facilities is a starting point from which to change the culture of wandering. The staff's perception of wandering is critical for how it is addressed within the facility. It involves redefining wandering as necessary and vital to the health of the resident, rather than a problem behaviour which must be controlled. Providing an unlocked environment in which the resident and staff can wander together is also essential to deconstructing the pathology of wandering and encouraging supportive relations between staff and wanderers.

Acknowledgements

I wish to thank Susan Bell and Peter Conrad for their encouragement and the anonymous referees for their insightful critiques and suggestions.

Note

1   Currently in the United States, tagging dementia residents in long-term care settings is limited, such as Oatfield Estates in Oregon (Shapiro 2006). The Indiana legislature is conducting feasibility studies of GPS tracking for community dwelling dementia patients (Weidenbener 2009). Twenty residents living with dementia in the Thames Valley and Somerset areas of England are participating in a two-year effectiveness study of GPS tracking (BBC News 2009).

References

AAP News (2008) *FED: Alzheimer's tags set alarming precedent: civil libertarians.* AAP News, Financial Times Information Limited – Asia Africa Intelligence Wire.

Altus, D.E., Mathews, R.M., Xaverius, P.K., Engelman, K.K.. and Nolan, B.A.D. (2000) Evaluating an electronic monitoring system for people who wander, *American Journal of Alzheimer's Disease and Other Dementias*, 15, 2, 21–125.

Ballard, C.G., Mohan, R.N.C., Bannister, C., *et al.* (1991) Wandering in dementia sufferers, *International Journal of Geriatric Psychiatry*, 6, 611–14.

Ballard, C.G. and O'Brien, J. (1999) Treating behavioral and psychological signs in Alzheimer's disease: the evidence for current pharmacological treatments is not strong, *British Medical Journal*, 319, 138–9.

Ballard, C., O'Brien, J., James, I. and Swann, A. (2001) *Dementia: Management of Behavioral and Psychological Symptoms*. Oxford: Oxford University Press.

Barry, N. (2007) *Controversial tagging may offer dementia sufferers the freedom to roam.* The Press and Journal, Aberdeen (UK): Northcliffe Electronic Publishing.

BBC News. (2009) Tracking dementia patients with GPS, (http://news.bbc.co.uk/2/hi/health/7946767. stm).

Beck, U. (1986) *Risk Society: Towards a New Modernity*. London: Sage.

Beck, U. (2006) Living in a world risk society, *Economy and Society*, 35, 3, 329–45.

Bond, J. (1992) The medicalization of dementia, *Journal of Aging Studies*, 6, 4, 397–403.

Buchanan, J.A. and Fisher, J.E. (2002) Functional assessment and noncontingent reinforcement in the treatment of disruptive vocalization in elderly dementia patients, *Journal of Applied Behavior Analysis*, 35, 99–103.

Capezuti, E., Evans, L., Strumpf, N. and Maislin, G. (1989) Physical restraint use and falls in nursing home residents, *Journal of the American Geriatrics Society*, 44, 6, 627–33.

Carter, S. (1995) Boundaries of danger and uncertainty: an analysis of technological culture of risk assessment. In J. Gabe (ed.) *Medicine, Health and Risk: Sociological Approaches*. Oxford: Blackwell Publishers Limited.

Charmaz, K. (2000) Grounded Theory: Objectivist and Constructivist Methods. In Denzin, N.K. and Lincoln, Y.S. (eds), *Handbook of Qualitative Research*, 2nd Edition. Thousand Oaks: Sage.

Coffey, A., Holbrook, B. and Atkinson, P. (1996) Qualitative data analysis: technologies and representations, *Sociological Research Online*, 1, 1, http://www.socresonline.org.uk/socresonline/1/1/4. html.

Coleman, E.A. (1993) Physical Restraint Use in Nursing Home Patients with Dementia, *Journal of the American Medical Association*, 270, 17, 2114–15.

Conrad, P. (1992) Medicalization and social control, *Annual Review of Sociology*, 18, 209–32.

Dickinson, J.I. and McLain-Kark, J. (1998) Wandering behavior and attempted exits among residents diagnosed with dementia-related illnesses: a qualitative approach, *Journal of Women and Aging*, 10, 2, 23–34.

Douglas, M. (1990) Risk as a forensic resource: from 'chance' to 'danger', *Daedalus*, 119, 4, 1–16.

Emery, V. Olga, B. and Oxman, Thomas E. (eds) (2003) *Dementia: Presentations, Differential Diagnosis, and Nosology*. Baltimore: The Johns Hopkins University Press.

Estes, C. and Binney, E. (1989) The biomedicaliszation of aging, *The Gerontologist*, 29, 5, 587–96.

Fisher, J.E. and Swingen, D.N. (1997) Contextual factors in the assessment and management of aggression in dementia patients, *Cognitive and Behavioral Practice*, 4, 171–90.

Foucault, M. (1995) *Discipline and Punish*. New York: Vintage Books.

Garrard, J., Makris, L., Dunham, T., Heston, L.L., Cooper, S., Ratner, E.R., Zelterman, D. and Kane, R.L. (1991) Evaluation of neuroleptic use by nursing home elderly under proposed medicare and medicaid regulations, *Journal of the American Medical Association*, 265, 463–67.

Gillespie, L.D., Gillespie, W.J., Robertson, M.C., *et al.* (2003) Interventions for preventing falls in elderly people, *Cochrane Database Systematic Review*, 4, CD000340.

Glaser, B.G. and Strauss, A.L. (1967) *The Discovery of Grounded Theory: Strategies for Qualitative Research*. New York: Aldine de Gruyter.

Hebert, L.E., Scherr, P.A., Bienias, J.L, Bennett, D.A. and Evans, D.A. (2003) Alzheimer's disease in the U.S. population: prevalence estimates using the 2000 census, *Archives of Neurology*, 60, 1119–22.

Herbert, C.P. (2001) Cultural aspects of dementia, *Canadian Journal of Neurological Sciences*, 28, Supplement 1, S77–82.

Holmes, D. (2001) From iron gaze to nursing care: mental health nursing in the era of panopticism, *Journal of Psychiatric and Mental Health Nursing*, 8, 7–15.

Hope, T., Tilling, K.M., Gedling, K., Keene, J., Cooper, S.D. and Fairburn, C.G. (1994) The structure of wandering in dementia, *International Journal of Geriatric Psyhcology*, 9, 149–55.

Hope, T., Keene, J., McShane, R.H., Fairburn, C.G., Gedling, K. and Jacoby, R. (2001) Wandering in dementia: a longitudinal study, *International Psychogeriatrics*, 13, 2, 137–47.

Howard, R., Ballard, C., O'Brien, J. and Burns, A., on behalf of the UK and Ireland Group for Optimization of Management in Dementia. (2001) Guidelines for the management of agitation in dementia, *International Journal of Geriatric Psychiatry*, 16(7), 714–17.

Hughes, J.C. and Louw, S.J. (2002) Electronic tagging of people with dementia who wander, *British Medical Journal*, 325, 847–8.

Karvelas, P. (2008) *Safety plan to tag dementia patients*, The Australian, Nationwide News Pty Limited.

Kitwood, T. (1997) *Dementia Reconsidered: the Person Comes First*. Buckingham: Open University Press.

Lucerno, M. (2002) Intervention strategies for exit-seeking wandering behavior in dementia residents, *American Journal of Alzheimer's Disease and Other Dementias*, 53, 277–80.

Lupton, D. (2005) Risk as moral danger: the social and political functions of risk discourse in public health. In Conrad, P. (ed.) *The Sociology of Health and Illness: Clinical Perspectives*. New York: Worth Publishers.

Lyman, K. (1989) Bringing the social back in: a critique of the biomedicalization of dementia, *The Gerontologist*, 29, 5, 597–605.

McShane, R. and Hope, T. (1994) Tracking patients who wander: ethics and technology, *Lancet*, 343, 8908. 1274.

Miskelly, F. (2004) A novel system of electronic tagging in patients with dementia and wandering, *Age and Ageing*, 33, 3, 304–06.

Mitchell, S.L., Teno, J.M., Miller, S.C. and Mor, V. (2005) A national study of the location of death for older persons with dementia, *Journal of the American Geriatrics Society*, 53, 299–305.

Moss, R.J. and LaPuma, J. (1991) The ethics of mechanical restraints, *Hastings Center Report*, 21, 22–5.

Noyes, L.E. and Silva, M.C. (1993) The ethics of locked special care units for persons with Alzheimer's disease, *American Journal of Alzheimer's Disease and Other Dementias*, 8, 4, 12–15.

O'Connor, D.W., Pollitt, P.A., Roth, M., *et al.* (1990) Problems reported by relatives in a community study of dementia, *British Journal of Psychiatry*, 156, 835–41.

Oxman, T.E. and Santulli, Robert B. (2003) Approaches to the Treatment of Dementing Illness. In Emery, V. Olga B. and Oxman, T.E. (eds) *Dementia: Presentations, Differential Diagnosis, and Nosology*. Baltimore: The Johns Hopkins University Press.

Patterson, C.J. and Clarfield, A.M. (2003) Diagnostic Procedures for dementia. In Emery, V., Olga, B. and Oxman, T.E. (eds) *Dementia: Presentations, Differential Diagnosis, and Nosology*. Baltimore: The Johns Hopkins University Press.

Rabins, P., Blacker, D., Bland, W., *et al.* (2007) *Practice Guideline for the Treatment of Patients with Alzheimer's Disease and Other Dementia*, 2nd Edition, (http://www.psychiatryonline.com/pracGuide/loadGuidelinePdf.aspx?file=AlzPG101007).

Rasquin, S.M.C., Willems, C., de Vlieger, S., Geers, R.P.J. and Soede, M. (2007) The use of technical devices to support outdoor mobility of dementia patients, *Technology and Disability*, 19, 113–20.

Robinson, L., Hutchings, D., Corner, L., Finch, T., Hughes, J., Brittain, K. and Bond, J. (2007a) Balancing rights and risks: conflicting perspectives in the management of wandering in dementia, *Health, Risk and Society*, 9, 4, 389–406.

Robinson, L., Hutchings, D., Dickinson, H.O., Corner, L., Beyer, F., Finch, T., Hughes, J., Vanoli, A., Ballard, C. and Bond, J. (2007b) Effectiveness and acceptability of non-pharmacological interventions to reduce wandering in dementia: a systematic review, *International Journal of Geriatric Psychiatry*, 22, 9–22.

Saletan, W. (2009) Lojack for people, *Human Nature: Science, Technology and Life*, http://www.slate.com/blogs/blogs/humannature/archive/2009/02/11/lojack-for-people.aspx.

Sharer, J. (2008) Tackling sundowning in a patient with Alzheimer's Disease, *MEDSURG Nursing*, 17, 1, 27–9.

Sinha, A. (2000) An overview of telemedicine: the virtual gaze of health care in the next century, *Medical Anthropology Quarterly*, 14, 3, 291–309.

Shapiro, J. (2006) Home for seniors trades privacy for security, NPR (http://www.npr.org/s.php?sId=5443317&m=1).

Sturdy, D. (2005) Electronic support for 21st century care, *Age and Ageing*, 34, 421–22.

Thomas, W.H. (2004) *What are Old People for? How Elders Will Save the World*. Acton: VanderWyk and Burnham.

Tilly, J. and Reed, P. (2008) Falls, wandering, and physical restraints: a review of interventions for individuals with dementia in assisted living and nursing homes, *Alzheimer's Care Today*, 9, 1, 45–50.

UK Alzheimer's Society (2007) Electronic tagging – enabling or disabling people with dementia? 27 December http://www.alzheimers.org.uk/site/scripts/news_article.php?newsID=239.

Weidenbener, L.S. (2009) Indiana lawmakers study GPS tracking for dementia patients, *Courier-Journal*, 18 August, (http://www.courier-journal.com/article/20090818/NEWS02/908180360/Indiana + lawmakers + study + GPS + tracking + for + dementia + patients).

Weinberger, M.B. (2007) Population aging: a global overview. In Robinson, M., Novelli, W., Pearson, C. and Norris, L. (eds) *Global Health and Global Aging*. San Francisco: Jossey-Bass.

Welsh, S., Hassiotis, A., O'Mahoney, G. and Deahl, M. (2003) Big brother is watching you: the ethical implications of electronic surveillance measures in the elderly with dementia and in adults with learning difficulties, *Aging and Mental Health*, 7, 5, 372–75.

Whall, A.L. and Kolanowski, A.M. (2004) Editorial: The need-driven dementia-compromised behavior model – a framework for understanding the behavioral symptoms of dementia, *Aging and Mental Health*, 8, 2, 106–08.

Wigg, J.M. (2007) *A Culture of Dementia: Examining Interpersonal Relationships between Elders with Dementia*. PhD diss, Brandeis University.

Wu, Y. and Swaab, D.F. (2005) The human pineal gland and melatonin in aging and Alzheimer's disease, *Journal of Pineal Research*, 38, 3, 145–52.

Wynne, B. (1982) Institutional mythologies and dual societies in the management of risk. In Kunreuther, H. and Ley, E. (eds) *The Risk Analysis Controversy: an Institutional Perspective*. Berlin: Springer-Verlag.

Zimmer, J.A., Watson, N. and Treat, A. (1984) Behavioral problems among patients in skilled nursing facilities, *American Journal of Public Health*, 74, 1118–21.

10

Output that counts: pedometers, sociability and the contested terrain of older adult fitness walking

Denise A. Copelton

Introduction

In this chapter I examine a hospital-sponsored walking group for older adults, noting how group norms of sociability, convivial conversation, and lack of competition precluded the adoption of pedometer-measured step goals as originally envisaged by hospital organisers. I draw on social studies of science and technology and research on sociability in leisure pursuits to understand how women walkers, in particular, constructed personal and group identities that were incompatible with pedometer use, demonstrating how non-users of technology are embedded in and influenced by micro-level interactional norms. In contrast to biomedical models of health, which focus predominantly on exercise outputs like step counts, these findings suggest that sociability is an important component of health maintenance leisure activities for older adults.

US health guidelines recommend that adults engage in 30 minutes of moderate-intensity activity most days of the week (USDHHS 1996, 2000). Walking is a low-impact, moderate-intensity activity that most can pursue throughout the lifecourse (Simonsick *et al.* 2005, Takamine 2001). Its non-competitive nature, lack of formal rules, and the fact that few skills are necessary to participate led health promoters to herald walking as an ideal fitness activity for older adults, inactive persons, and those with negative attitudes toward or hesitant to begin physical activity (Hultquist 2005, Simonsick *et al.* 2005, Takamine 2001).

Regular walking has many documented health benefits including a reduced risk of diabetes (Gregg *et al.* 2003), heart disease (Iwane *et al.* 2000, Manson *et al.* 2002), osteoporosis (Greendale *et al.* 1995), and all-cause mortality (Gregg *et al.* 2003). It lowers blood pressure (Albright and Thompson 2006, Iwane *et al.* 2000, Moreau *et al.* 2001), improves cognitive functioning (Weuve *et al.* 2004) and body image (Tucker and Mortell 1993), and maintains functional ability in older adults (Brach *et al.* 2003, Hamdorf and Penhall 1999, Simonsick *et al.* 2005).

Medical professional organisations and federal initiatives including the *Surgeon General's Report on Physical Activity and Health* and *Healthy People 2010* endorse walking as a health promoting activity, while employers encourage walking in an attempt to lower healthcare costs. No initiative has been more influential in promoting walking as a fitness activity than 10,000 steps programmes. Yet, a majority of the population still does not meet current physical activity recommendations (CDC 2003, Hughes *et al.* 2005). Thus, organised fitness activities and outreach efforts continue to be important conduits for increasing exercise adherence.

Pedometers and the quantification of walking

As walking has been redefined as a physical fitness activity, health promoters have placed greater emphasis on quantifying it. A pedometer is a small electronic device worn on the waistband that counts the wearer's steps. Although popularised in the US in the 1990s, pedometer technology is not new. Thomas Jefferson invented an early pedometer between 1785–89 and sent the device to James Madison with these instructions:

> Cut a little hole in the bottom of your left watch pocket, pass the hook and tape through it, and down between the breeches and drawers and fix the hook on the edge of your knee band, an inch from the knee buckle; then hook the instrument itself by a small hook on the upper edge of the watch pocket. Your tape being well adjusted in length, your double steps will be exactly counted by the instrument (Fouts 1922: 319).

Measuring hip movement, contemporary pedometers employ the same principles as Jefferson's early version, but use a spring-mounted arm in place of Jefferson's attached tape and digital counters instead of mechanical ones (Berlin *et al.* 2006). Despite design improvements, the accuracy of step counts is highly variable and depends on the sensitivity of the model used, walking speed, and user characteristics. Accuracy improves with speed (Bassett *et al.* 1996, Crouter *et al.* 2003, Schneider *et al.* 2004), but even the best pedometers are less reliable when used by persons with impaired gait or slower speed, characteristics more common among older walkers (Cyarto *et al.* 2004).

For health and fitness educators, pedometers are a convenient, low-cost, user-friendly technology that offers immediate feedback on accumulated activity levels (Croteau 2004, Croteau and Richeson 2005, Tudor-Locke 2002). Heralded as motivational tools that promote exercise adherence, pedometers have been incorporated into health promotion programmes nationwide. Most common among these are 10,000 steps programmes, which encourage individuals to walk 10,000 steps a day to maintain health. Ten thousand steps programmes originated in Japan and were imported to the US through health maintenance organisations like HealthPartners, whose trademarked '10,000 Steps' has been adopted widely and earned a 2004 Innovation in Prevention Award from the US Department of Health and Human Services (Schnirring 2001). In 2005, Excellus BlueCross/BlueShield earned accolades for its walking programme (PCPFS 2005), signifying the high esteem granted to walking programmes among health promotion efforts. Mainstream news articles also encourage Americans to walk for health and use pedometers to measure progress toward step-specific goals (deSa 2001, Hellmich 2005, 2007). These programmes have widespread appeal and demonstrated success in increasing participants' activity levels and lowering health risk factors (Croteau 2004, Croteau and Richeson 2005, Heesch *et al.* 2005, Hultquist 2005, Rooney *et al.* 2003, Schneider *et al.* 2006).

Pedometer-assisted walking programmes employ traditional behaviour modification techniques, including goal setting and monitoring (Dinger *et al.* 2005). In these programmes, step counts are the output that counts. Critics argue that a universal step goal, such as 10,000 per day, may be too low for some groups (children and active adults) and too high for others (older adults and those with sedentary lifestyles), and question the validity of programmes that promote a single target (Berlin *et al.* 2006, Le Masurier *et al.* 2003, Schneider *et al.* 2006, Tudor-Locke and Bassett 2004). Permitting users to set personal goals is just as effective in promoting physical activity as establishing a universal goal of 10,000 steps (Sidman *et al.* 2004). Since pedometers do not measure activity intensity, frequency, or duration, step counts alone cannot adequately assess whether current physical activity guidelines are being achieved (Berlin *et al.* 2006, Le Masurier *et al.* 2003). Nevertheless, pedometer-based fitness interventions remain popular even as researchers debate their utility.

Pedometer-based walking programmes' exclusive focus on quantity of steps walked also overrides concerns about the *quality* of walks, especially their social quality. Do pedometers change the social experience of walking? How do walkers respond to pedometer technology in organised walking programmes? In the following sections I review relevant research in science and technology studies and sociability in leisure pursuits, and describe the ethnographic methods used.

The social construction of pedometer technology

Because step programmes require pedometers, they reconfigure walking as a technologically-mediated activity. The Social Construction of Technology (SCOT) approach emphasises how different social groups imbue technologies with diverse meanings (Oudshoorn and Pinch 2005, Pinch and Bijker 1984). Different groups use pedometers for particular ends and designers and consumers may view pedometers differently (Wyatt 2005). Health and fitness evaluation researchers interested in furthering evidence-based fitness programmes have an instrumental relationship to pedometers, viewing them as tools (like pulse monitors or stop watches) that provide standardised outputs to which other health indicators are correlated.

Little research has examined pedometers from the user's perspective. A study of men's responses to a 10,000 steps programme in Australia found that while some viewed pedometers as motivational tools, others saw them as 'novelty trinkets' that they would not use regularly (Burton et al. 2008). Because men and women often have different relationships to technology (Cowan 1983, Livingstone 1992, Sandelowski 1994), it is important to examine if user and non-user constructions of pedometers are gendered. For example, women are more likely to view technology as facilitating social interaction, whereas men view technology as an acceptable substitute for it (Livingstone 1992). Very little is known about women's constructions and use of pedometers.

Other scholars have examined the domestication of technology (Lie and Sorenson 1996, Silverstone et al. 1992, Sorenson 2006, Sorenson et al. 2000). According to Sorenson et al. (2000: 240), 'To domesticate an artifact is to negotiate its meaning and practice in a dynamic, interactive manner. This negotiation implies that technology as well as social relations are transformed'. Whether and how a technology is domesticated depends on the economy of meanings shared by the group. This moral economy, including norms and values, both affects and is affected by the domestication of technology (Silverstone et al. 1992, Silverstone 2006).

Domestication entails four inter-related processes: appropriation, objectification, incorporation and conversion (Oudshoorn and Pinch 2005, Silverstone et al. 1992, Sorenson et al. 2000). Appropriation involves the acquisition of technology, while objectification concerns its display. The display of technology objectifies the values of its users and others who identify with the technology (Silverstone et al. 1992: 22–3). Incorporation entails the technology's use and integration into a set of daily practices. Finally, conversion refers to how a technology configures relationships between users and others, typically, through 'status claims' and 'expressing a specific lifestyle' (Oudshoorn and Pinch 2005: 15). Domestication thus involves both practical and symbolic work, including the symbolic meanings users and non-users ascribe to an object, and the consequences of these meanings for individual and group identities and for the technology's long-term use (Oudshoorn and Pinch 2005, Wyatt 2005). It also entails a cognitive dimension, including the 'intellectual appropriation of new knowledge' (Sorenson et al. 2000: 240). Sociologists must attend to the symbolic meanings and practical consequences of pedometers, and to how users appropriate the new knowledge pedometers create (step counts).

Health, sociability, and older adults

Though health concerns are a typical motivation for exercise (Duncan *et al.* 1994, Takamine 2001), walking also offers opportunities for sociability, which serves as an incentive for continued participation (Glover *et al.* 2005, Stebbins 2002). I rely on Simmel's (1950) formulation of sociability, a form of social interaction marked by a playful spirit, convivial conversation, and an egalitarian ethos to which hierarchy and competition are antithetical.

Institutions like hospitals can facilitate sociability, even when they are organised for other purposes (Cheang 2002, Hope and Havir 2002, Oldenburg 1989, Stebbins 2002). The need for safe, secure public settings is common in studies of leisure and sociability among older adults, with casinos, restaurants and clubs supplying such a context (Cheang 2002, Duncan *et al.* 1994, 1995, Hope and Havir 2002, Stalp *et al.* 2008, Yarnal 2006). Casino gambling offers older adults 'something to do' that is fun and entertaining, and seniors value gambling's social rewards more highly than its financial ones (Hope and Havir 2002: 184). Older adult regulars at fast-food restaurants share food, stories and jokes, fostering a sense of community (Cheang 2002: 314). Eschewing fund raising, volunteering, and the creation of sociability *for others* characteristic of women's organisations (Daniels 1985), the Red Hat Society (RHS) allows older women to enjoy sociable relations and to initiate fun for themselves (Stalp *et al.* 2008, Yarnal 2006).

Conversation adds a significant social element that provides positive reinforcement over and above walking's health benefits, leads to greater enjoyment, and promotes exercise adherence (Tucker and Mortell 1993). Women are especially likely to report lack of walking companions as a deterrent to walking (Ball *et al.* 2001). Duncan *et al.* (1994) found that mall walking facilitated new social contacts, fostered a sense of community, and reduced the social isolation that sometimes follows retirement. Given that social contacts are beneficial for overall health (House *et al.* 1988, Klinenberg 2001, 2002), it is surprising that few studies examine the social aspects of organised walking for older adults. Most research focuses exclusively on walking's health benefits (Hultquist 2005, Manson *et al.* 2002, Tucker and Mortell 1993). Walking is conspicuously absent in sociological studies of sociability (but see Ortiz 1992, Schact and Unnithan 1991), and most sociological research on walking focuses narrowly on mall walking (Duncan *et al.* 1994, 1995, Ortiz 1992, Schacht and Unnithan 1991).

Research methods

I conducted participant observation of a hospital-sponsored walking group for adults aged 50 and over, attending weekly walks of approximately 90 minutes each from late August through to mid-December 2004 for a total of 14 separate observations. I participated in all group activities and conversed informally with members. Given the setting and activity involved, namely physical exercise, I did not take detailed notes in the field. Instead, I recorded jotted notes (Lofland and Lofland 1995) in the field and audio-notes immediately after meetings. I transcribed and expanded both sets of notes to create complete field notes for each observation. This process facilitated detailed note-taking, without it becoming obtrusive in the field.

At the time of the study, the club consisted of approximately 30 adults, with 8–15 walkers participating in any given week. Walkers' ages ranged from 50–79 years, with a majority of women. A core of five 'regulars' attended weekly, including one man. Throughout my five months of participant observation, only two other men attended once each. One had been a regular member previously, but stopped attending when his wife began cancer treatment.

I conducted key informant interviews (Gilchrist and Williams 1999) with four 'regulars' to uncover the social and personal meanings they attached to walking with the group, and with the walking club co-ordinator and Wellness Center Director about the club, its history, and overall importance among wellness initiatives. Interviews were tape-recorded and transcribed and occurred at the health campus and members' homes.

Pedometers and the reconfiguration of the Walkie Talkies

The Walkie Talkies began in 1998 as part of a 'Senior Product Line' targeting older adults at a large, non-profit community hospital. The line was terminated concurrent with the opening of a Geriatric Treatment Center, and the Walkie Talkies is the only remaining programme. Tammy, the walking club co-ordinator, explained the philosophy behind the group:

> The idea was to start a [walking] club for seniors. We wanted to emphasise that fitness was important for them. We tried to emphasise overall fitness so they don't think the only thing they have to do is walk. They also need aerobic exercise, they need to be strong, and need to do strength training to be strong (Tammy).

The walking club manual explains the importance of physical fitness for older adults, while cool-down exercises incorporate strength training.

The Walkie Talkies originally met three days a week, alternating mornings and afternoons. Low attendance led group leaders to restrict meetings to Thursday mornings two years prior to my field research. Initially, the group was structured like many popular walking initiatives. Members received a free pedometer, t-shirt, walking club manual, activity log, and resistance band (a large rubber band that can be stretched with the legs or arms for strength training). Members were encouraged to adopt personal fitness goals and chart progress with pedometers. Small prizes and social recognition were offered to those achieving their goals. However, the club underwent significant changes after inception, and when I began field research in August 2004, the emphasis on fitness goals was non-existent. Only Tammy wore a pedometer, and during my five months of participant observation she distributed only resistance bands to new walkers. Given the focus on pedometers and fitness goals common in walking programmes and initially incorporated into this one, I was surprised to find such a focus absent.

The revised format began with walkers assembling outside the main entrance of the hospital out-patient campus just prior to 10:00 AM. As walkers arrive, greetings are exchanged and conversations begun. Warm-up consists of stretching, but is also a time for introductions and announcements. The standard walking route consists of walking the perimeter of the buildings on paved sidewalks and parking lots. Participants walk at their own pace and maintain lively conversations. Walkers reassemble at the main entrance around 11:00 AM for cool-down. Walkers return at different times and more conversations are shared as walkers arrive. Cool-down consists of more conversation, stretching, and working with resistance bands, alternating weekly between legs and arms. Finally, cool-down is followed by 'story time,' when Tammy, the nurse-coordinator, shares a funny joke or story while leading balancing exercises, either standing on one foot or tip-toes. Walkers typically disperse immediately following story time.

Tammy explained that pedometers, step counts, and goal setting were dropped in favour of this structure:

[Monitoring goals and step counts] didn't make any difference and seemed to turn people off more than anything...Ideally if something met more often it would make more sense to do those things (Tammy).

According to Tammy, monitoring step counts via pedometers was both a 'turn off' for walkers and ineffective for increasing activity levels. Nevertheless, she relies heavily on meeting frequency in her explanation for the shifting group focus and rejection of pedometers. In the following sections, I describe the moral economy of the Walkie Talkies, the group norms and values that predominated. I then discuss how this moral economy precluded the domestication of pedometers within the group.

Walking for health and camaraderie

Most walkers joined Walkie Talkies for health reasons, emphasising an age-specific need for regular exercise. Ruth explained: 'I should be doing exercise at my age. It's good for me'. Helen underscored the ease of walking: 'I thought I should walk, and I *can* walk'. Despite walking for health, walkers had modest expectations that did not include specific fitness goals, making pedometer use unlikely. Florence was typical: 'I don't think I have any other expectations except getting myself back into a routine of doing something'. Joining a walking group appealed to members precisely because it required a commitment to regular exercise. Helen explained, 'I just thought if I joined a group I'd be more apt to do it more often, more regularly'.

Although initially joining for health reasons, members cited the social aspects of the group as their primary reason for returning week after week. Though walkers' social outlets were numerous and varied (*e.g.* bowling, cards and pinochle, volunteering) walkers repeatedly emphasised the positive opportunities for sociability the walking group afforded through common references to group 'camaraderie'. Miriam explained, 'I look forward to the camaraderie. I like the people. They're very nice, interesting, and fun to be with'. When asked what he felt was the most beneficial aspect of the club, Gary replied, 'the main thing is the camaraderie'. According to walkers, conversation facilitated camaraderie, while competition detracted from it.

The importance of conversation

Conversations were an important, if not *the* most important, component of group walks. Miriam underscored the significance of talk: 'It's probably more fun to walk with the group because you have someone to talk with'. Talking introduced an element of fun, helped pass the time, and gave walkers something to focus on besides exercise. Doris remarked, 'When you walk with a group it's easier. You can walk and talk and before you know it you've walked for an hour'.

Sociability was facilitated by the related practices of walking in pairs and talking. Walkers spontaneously pair up according to who is standing next to whom in warm-up, although a few walkers occasionally seek out particular partners:

It always changes, seems to anyway. And like a lot of times you do want to talk with someone specific or sometimes…they just kind of pair off. So you don't walk with the same person usually (Helen).

Spontaneous pairing promoted variety in walking partners, creating broad social ties, as Gary notes: 'I've walked with just about everyone in the group at one time or another and it's always good. It always turns out to be a positive experience'.

Conversations provide a rationale for returning week after week, to keep up to date on the activities of group members, reinforcing group cohesion. Ruth explained:

As you meet people, walk with them especially, you find out more about them. Rather than just doing your exercises and going home, you walk with them, you find out more about them, so you want to know what's happening with them. I think sometimes I come just to see what's going on (Ruth).

Knowing what is happening in other members' lives helped walkers feel connected and facilitated exercise adherence. Though they joined Walkie Talkies for health reasons, members adhered to the walking regimen for social reasons.

Topics of conversation included knitting, cooking, vacations, television, and sporting and community events, all *safe* topics unlikely to offend. Miriam explained, 'A lot of times [we talk about] my travels because everybody wants to know about them…[or] getting ready for a holiday, or sometimes you talk about current events. Nothing too deep, you know. No animosity'. Not wanting to create animosity was probably the main reason politics were discussed so infrequently, despite the fact that the research occurred in a battleground state concurrent with the hotly contested 2004 US presidential election. Discussing politics or other serious matters might disrupt group harmony and sociability, thereby violating group norms.

During formal interviews, walkers highlighted the jovial nature of the group. 'We always have a lot of laughs,' explained Miriam. During field work, I observed several running jokes, including two concerning resistance bands. During cool-down, Tammy led exercises with the band, alternating weekly between arms and legs. Leg exercises were particularly challenging and walkers regularly attempted to convince Tammy that the week's focus was arms. In response to Tammy's query, 'What are we doing this week?' walkers regularly shouted 'Arms!' Tammy laughed and corrected them, and good-natured groans followed.

When work with the resistance band is complete, walkers roll it up and secure it with a string or rubber band to keep it from unravelling. It takes Fran twice as long to roll her band because she is so meticulous about rolling it tightly and uniformly. This often results in Tammy moving to other stretches before Fran has finished. 'Oh, Fran is still rolling!' and 'Better hurry up Fran!' are common jocular comments and Fran often plays along by taking extra long to finish, or by laughingly pointing out to Tammy that she is still rolling. Such good-natured joking, especially when done at the expense of another, exemplifies the camaraderie and sociability within the group. Fran never appeared hurt by jokes at her expense, and willingly participated in the jovial exchanges.

Group activities, including warm-up, walking, cool-down, and story time were ripe for the creation of good times. Lively conversation and good-natured joking were interwoven throughout these activities, highlighting the prominent position of sociability within the moral economy of the group. In fact, sociability trumped physical activity and the goal of walking for health. Walking merely provided a context or excuse for enjoying sociable relations and pedometers seemed out of place in such a context.

Competition and hierarchy as threats to sociability

Walkers overwhelmingly emphasised the non-competitive and non-hierarchical nature of the group, which had direct implications for pedometer use. Concern with step counts, walking greater distances, or walking faster might put unnecessary pressure on members, create hierarchies, and challenge group norms and values. Miriam highlights the group's pressure-free atmosphere as an attractive characteristic: 'You can just come and do your own thing and enjoy it without being pressured. I think that's one reason it's successful'. Doris explained, 'There are no demands or restrictions or pressures to do anything, and no one says walk faster ... And everybody's strictly on their own as to setting their pace'. Helen explained that stopping and resting was perfectly acceptable:

> Sometimes some of the girls won't walk the whole hour. They'll do part of it and then sit down, which is fine. I mean, that's why I like it because if you're not feeling like walking an hour you can rest a bit...It's not a negative thing if you want to stop (Helen).

One morning Ruth and Ethel, who had been walking a few yards in front of me, stopped and sat on a bench near the sidewalk. Thinking one of them might be injured, I asked, 'Is everything OK?' 'Oh, we just stopped to talk,' Ethel replied, 'We're OK'.

'Doing their own thing' aligned with many walkers' non-competitive sense of self. Helen explained, 'I've never been competitive ... if I'm doing something, I will do it well, but I don't need to outdo somebody'. According to walkers, the club's success derived from its non-competitive structure, which prevented the formation of hierarchies based on who could 'outdo' whom. Helen continued,

> They don't expect you to do some of the exercises if you don't feel like you are able to. It's not like you must do what the group does, like you see some of these groups. I couldn't do that. No, I don't want to do that either (Helen).

Monitoring step counts appears counter to the preservation of this non-competitive, non-hierarchical culture.

Many walkers perceived aerobics and other classes at local gyms as inherently competitive and thus culturally distinct from the moral economy prevalent within the Walkie Talkies. Only one walker, Gary (also the only regular male participant), actually belonged to a gym. Women walkers, in particular, were acutely aware of how they might be judged negatively at gyms, in terms of their physical abilities, age, and physique. Unlike mall walking and gyms, which are open to persons of any age, the age-restricted environment of the Walkie Talkies limits the extent to which women members would be judged negatively in comparison to younger persons:

> I like to swim, and I haven't found a place yet I feel I can comfortably swim. I don't look too great in a bathing suit anymore and I'm trying to find places that have just my age group (Fran).

> I don't have to wear cute little outfits to get here, you know (laughs)...I would be uncomfortable if I had to wear certain things, whereas here we can just come as we are...And I wouldn't be comfortable with you know a 35-year-old trotting around (Helen).

Age-restricted fitness activities such as the Walkie Talkies may be especially appealing to older women who desire to limit competition and hierarchy based on age, ability, body size, and appearance. In particular, the Walkie Talkies provides older women with a safe space unfettered by the ageist assumptions of worth and value that equate goodness with youth, youth with feminine beauty, and that permeate the moral economy of many contemporary social spaces, including fitness centres.

The club's non-competitive nature was also reflected in regulars' responses to my question concerning what information would be important for newcomers. Gary stressed, 'I think it's important to realise…that you should only do what your body allows you to do. Don't try to overdo it or compete with anybody else in the club, because that's not what it's all about. We're here to just enjoy ourselves and to get some physical activity'. Gary's statement is revealing in that he places social enjoyment before physical activity. Like other walkers, despite joining the group for health reasons, the social enjoyment of walking became more paramount over time. In fact, Gary emphasised repeatedly that the health benefits were secondary to the social aspects of the club: 'I still enjoy the walking, but I would probably continue to come even if I didn't need the walking'. Clearly, for members, walking is not merely about health maintenance. While health promoters typically treat walking as an instrumental health-directed activity, for walkers themselves, it was a sociable activity pursued principally for enjoyment and secondarily for health.

The moral economy and the failure to domesticate pedometers

Having detailed the norms and values prevalent within the Walkie Talkies, I explore how this moral economy prevented the domestication of pedometers. The emphasis on sociable interactions, already well established when my field research began, was probably the main reason walkers rejected pedometers, but embraced resistance bands. Wearing a pedometer, logging steps, and measuring progress toward fitness goals would put pressure on group members to walk faster and for greater distances, and create hierarchies among them. Women, in particular, were especially uninterested in anything that might introduce disharmony into the group. Technology that was not associated with these negative qualities was domesticated, and resistance bands continued to be used collectively, as part of the cool-down ritual regimen. Even though pedometers count less accurately the steps of slower walkers, and the models distributed were less sophisticated than those recommended in fitness research, none (including Tammy) mentioned pedometer inadequacy as a reason for non-use. Pedometers were so insignificant that, despite prompting in conversations and interviews, most walkers either could not or would not expand beyond short explanations. The following excerpt from Dorothy's interview is typical:

DC: Did you receive a pedometer when you joined the group?
D: Yes.
DC: Have you ever used it?
D: No, no I haven't.
DC: Tell me why not.
D: I don't know, I just never did.
DC: Is there a particular reason?
D: No, I just never did.

Clearly, pedometers are not a high priority of the Walkie Talkies, and even when asked directly about them, participants had little, if anything, to say. Thus, the discussion that follows relies less on walkers' self-reports, and instead draws heavily from my interpretation of how the observed moral economy of the group impacted on the domestication process.

Because they were no longer being distributed, walkers who had been members of the group longer were more likely to have received a pedometer when they joined. For some, the appropriation of the technology occurred at the point they joined. For the relative newcomers, joining the walking group and acquiring a pedometer constitute separate acts, and none that I spoke with elected to purchase one or considered doing so.

Among those who received free pedometers, none but Tammy, the nurse-coordinator, brought them to walks. Thus, members failed to objectify or display pedometers within the group, which also meant none used or incorporated pedometers into the walking routine. For Tammy, her status as leader was sufficient to explain her alignment with pedometers. When Tammy was absent, another nurse filled in. Not as familiar with warm-up and cool-down exercises, she did fewer stretches and less resistance band work, which some attributed to her inability to complete the exercises physically. Miriam explained, 'She doesn't know [the exercises] and I don't think she's physically up to doing some of them'. By contrast, members viewed Tammy as physically fit and readily capable of completing all exercises, which they considered necessary attributes in a co-ordinator. Her pedometer use was therefore interpreted in light of her co-ordinator position and fitness level, which prevented others from perceiving her as overly competitive. Importantly, physical fitness and the ability to complete all exercises were not necessary attributes of walkers themselves.

Because women walkers saw themselves as non-competitive, wearing a pedometer and monitoring step counts within the group might be perceived as attempting to outperform others. Not only would this violate group norms, it would also conflict with walkers' own identity construction. Unlike basketballs, tennis rackets or resistance bands, pedometers are not just 'used'; they are also *worn*. Incorporating the device onto one's person (part of its objectification), is simultaneously a very intimate and social act that contributes to one's symbolic presentation of self. At the very least, wearing a pedometer indicates to others that the user is monitoring walking activity via step counts. Because women walkers construed competition negatively, they may have been especially unwilling to wear a pedometer for fear that others would assume they were more concerned with 'out-stepping' others than with maintaining sociable relations. Pedometer *non-use* was how members expressed life-styles and claimed statuses consistent with the moral economy of the group.

Pedometers symbolise competition and a potential for hierarchy that is contrary to both sociable group relations and women walkers' sense of self. This symbolic dimension had the practical implication of preventing widespread adoption of pedometers. On a cognitive level, since most walkers were unaware of their step counts, there was no opportunity to reflect on this knowledge. Only Gary used his pedometer 'occasion[ally],' mostly because he found it 'interesting' to know how many steps he took in various activities. Gary's response is consistent with prior research indicating that men treat pedometers as 'trinkets' and step counts as interesting, but inconsequential, data (Burton *et al.* 2008). Significantly, Gary never wore his pedometer at group walks, further underscoring how the moral economy of the group precluded pedometer domestication within it.

In regard to pedometers then, group members conformed to a culture of non-use. Yet group norms did not prohibit domesticating all technology, as walkers did use resistance bands during cool-down exercises. While one technology is more 'low tech' than the other, walkers' resistance to the relatively 'higher tech' pedometer and acceptance of the comparatively 'lower tech' resistance band should not be ascribed to simplistic and ageist explanations like technophobia among older adults. Field research and interviews in walkers' homes revealed that walkers domesticated a variety of technologies in their personal lives, including household technology (*i.e.* microwaves, answering machines) and other fitness technologies (*i.e.* stair climbers, exercise bikes).

Unlike pedometers, whose use was no longer overtly encouraged by Tammy, resistance bands were, and if a walker forgot his or her band, Tammy would loan them one. Importantly, walkers did not construe the band negatively, only particular uses of it. Walkers only resisted using the bands for leg work, as evidenced by members' weekly attempts to convince Tammy to lead arm instead of leg exercises. Significantly, while one *could* count stretches manually, no one did, and, unlike pedometers, successfully using a resistance band does not require it. Walkers did as many repetitions as they were able during the two to three minutes allotted for each stretch, and Tammy never counted aloud as she performed stretches in an attempt to co-ordinate or quantify walkers' movements. As with walking, stretches were completed at walkers' own pace, with some pausing to rest, especially during the more difficult leg exercises. Despite their association with physically challenging stretches, walkers did not imbue resistance bands with the same negative associations they attributed to pedometers. Bands did not promote quantifying exercise outputs, foster competition, or create hierarchies. Instead, by making resistance bands the focus of regular jokes, they became a means for furthering sociability within the group. The disparate symbolic meanings of the two technologies point to the significance of micro-interactional norms for the domestication of technology within a given group.

Conclusion

Most contemporary walking programmes quantify walking with pedometers, set target step counts, and monitor progress towards that target. However, Walkie Talkies members expressed little interest in pedometers, step counts, and fitness targets. This case study reveals the central function of the club for most walkers was less about health promotion and more about building and maintaining social capital. For group leaders and fitness promoters, walking and steps are what count, but for walkers, talking and sociability count more. These differing priorities highlight the contested terrain of older adult fitness walking.

Organised walking was meaningful to participants because it facilitated pleasurable interactions that most referred to as camaraderie. Though walkers were motivated to join the club by health concerns, it was the sociability of the group that mattered for continued participation. The non-competitive nature of the club precluded the formation of hierarchies based on speed or step counts, and the 'come as you are' ethos reassured women walkers, in particular, that status distinctions common in other fitness activities would not arise in the Walkie Talkies. Time and again, walkers disparaged the perceived competitiveness of health clubs, aerobics classes, and gyms. Within this moral economy, pedometers, which quantify walking, permit hierarchies based on step counts and symbolise competition, appeared antithetical to group norms.

Although based on a small qualitative study, these findings suggest that health campaigns that structure walking as a *social* activity may find a more receptive audience among older adults, especially older women. While medical sociologists have documented that social connections contribute to health maintenance (House *et al.* 1988, Klinenberg 2001, 2002), my research goes one step further by demonstrating the importance of *sociability* in leisure pursuits for exercise adherence and health maintenance. Similar to casino gambling, Red Hat Society membership, and frequenting fast-food restaurants, exercise, for the older adult participants in this study, was really about having fun in an environment free of ageism, hierarchy and competition. If the non-competitive nature of walking is what attracts older adults to it, especially older women, then 10,000 steps programmes, with their exclusive focus on step counts, may be counterproductive. Instead of focusing on quantifiable exercise outputs, health and fitness researchers should pay greater attention to the social process of exercise. Outreach efforts that highlight the positive opportunities for sociability found through organised fitness activities such as group walking, may be more effective for recruiting older adults to these and similar programmes.

Acknowledgements

An earlier version of this chapter was presented at the 2006 meeting of the Eastern Sociological Society. I would like to thank the two anonymous reviewers, and Joan Spade, Marybeth Stalp and Gayle Sulik for their insightful and constructive feedback on this chapter.

References

Albright, C. and Thompson, D. (2006) The effectiveness of walking in preventing cardiovascular disease in women: a review of the current literature, *Journal of Women's Health*, 15, 3, 271–80.

Ball, K., Bauman, A., Leslie, E. and Owen, N. (2001) Perceived environmental aesthetics and convenience and company are associated with walking for exercise among Australian adults, *Preventive Medicine*, 33, 434–40.

Bassett, D., Ainsworth, B., Leggett, S., Mathien, C., Main, J., Hunter, D. and Duncan, G. (1996) Accuracy of five electronic pedometers for measuring distance walked, *Medicine and Science in Sports and Exercise*, 28, 1071–7.

Berlin, J.E., Storti, K.L. and Brach, J.S. (2006) Using activity monitors to measure physical activity in free living conditions, *Physical Therapy*, 86, 1137–45.

Brach, J., FitzGerald, S., Newman, A., Kelsey, S., Kuller, L., VanSwearingen, J. and Krishka, A. (2003) Physical activity and functional status in community-dwelling older women, *Archives of Internal Medicine*, 163, 2565–71.

Burton, N., Walsh, A. and Brown, W. (2008) It just doesn't speak to me: mid-aged men's reactions to '10,000 Steps a Day', *Health Promotion Journal of Australia*, 10, 52–9.

Centers for Disease Control and Prevention (2003) Prevalence of physical activity, including lifestyle activities, among adults: United States, 2000–2001, *Morbidity and Mortality Weekly Report*, 52, 764–69.

Cheang, M. (2002) Older adults' frequent visits to a fast-food restaurant: nonobligatory social interaction and the significance of play in a 'third place', *Journal of Aging Studies*, 16, 303–21.

Cowan, R. (1983) *More Work for Mother: the Ironies of Household Technology from the Open Hearth to the Microwave*. NY: Basic.

Croteau, K. (2004) A preliminary study on the impact of a pedometer-based intervention on daily steps, *American Journal of Health Promotion*, 18, 217–20.

Croteau, K. and Richeson, N. (2005) A matter of health: using pedometers to increase the physical activity of older adults, Activities, *Adaptation and Aging*, 30, 37–47.

Crouter, S., Schneider, P., Karabulut, M. and Bassett, D. (2003) Validity of 10 electronic pedometers for measuring steps, distance and energy cost, *Medicine and Science in Sports and Exercise*, 35, 1455–60.

Cyarto, E., Myers, A. and Tudor-Locke, C. (2004) Pedometer accuracy in nursing home and community-dwelling older adults, *Medicine and Science in Sports and Exercise*, 36, 205–9.

Daniels, A.K. (1985) Good times and good works: the place of sociability in the work of women volunteers, *Social Problems*, 32, 363–74.

DeSa, P. (2001) Easy steps to shape up and slim down, *Prevention* 53, 7. Retrieved 8 June 2007, *Academic Search Premier.*

Dinger, M., Heesch, K. and McClary, K. (2005) Feasibility of a minimal contact intervention to promote walking among insufficiently active women, *American Journal of Health Promotion*, 20, 2–6.

Duncan, H., Travis, S. and McAuley, W. (1994) The meaning of and motivation for mall walking among older adults, Activities, *Adaptation, and Aging*, 19, 37–53.

Duncan, H., Travis, S. and McAuley, W. (1995) An emergent theoretical model for interventions encouraging physical activity (mall walking) among older adults, *Journal of Applied Gerontology*, 14, 64–77.

Fouts, L. (1922) Jefferson the inventor, and his relation to the patent system, *Journal of the Patent Office Society*, 4, 316–31.

Gilchrist, V. and Williams, R. (1999) Key informant interviews. In *Crabtree*, B. and Miller, W. (eds) *Doing Qualitative Research*, 2nd Edition. Thousand Oaks, CA: Sage.

Glover, T., Shinew, K. and Parry, D. (2005) Association, sociability and civic culture: the democratic effect of community gardening, *Leisure Sciences*, 27, 75–92.

Greendale, G., Barrett-Conner, E., Edelstein, S., Ingles, S. and Haile, R. (1995) Lifetime leisure exercise and osteoporosis: the Rancho Bernardo study, *American Journal of Epidemiology*, 141, 10, 951–9.

Gregg, E., Gerzoff, R., Caspersen, C., Williamson, D. and Narayan, K.M.V. (2003) Relationship of walking to mortality among US adults with diabetes, *Archives of Internal Medicine*, 163, 1440–7.

Hamdorf, P.A. and Penhall, R.K. (1999) Walking with its training effects on the fitness and activity patterns of 79–91 year old females, *Australian and New Zealand Journal of Medicine*, 29, 22–8.

Heesch, K., Dinger, M., McClary, K. and Rice, K. (2005) Experiences of women in a minimal contact pedometer-based intervention: a qualitative study, *Women and Health*, 41, 2, 97–116.

Hellmich, N. (2005) A 30-minute walk is good, but a 10,000-step walk is better, *USA Today*, 6 April, 7D.

Hellmich, N. (2007) Find your stride for exercise, *USA Today*, 20 August, 4D.

Hope, J. and Havir, L. (2002) You bet they're having fun! Older Americans and casino gambling, *Journal of Aging Studies*, 16, 177–97.

House, J., Landis, K. and Umberson, D. (1988) Social relationships and health, *Science*, 241, 540–5.

Hughes, S., Prohaska, T., Rimmer, J. and Heller, T. (2005) Promoting physical activity among older people, *Generations*, 29, 2, 54–9.

Hultquist, C. (2005) Comparison of walking recommendations on previously inactive women, *Medicine and Science in Sports and Exercise*, 37, 4, 676–83.

Iwane, M., Arita, M., Tomimoto, S., Satani, O., Matsumoto, M., Miyashita, K. and Nishio, I. (2000) Walking 10,000 steps/day or more reduces blood pressure and sympathetic nerve activity in mild essential hypertension, *Hypertensive Research*, 23, 573–80.

Klinenberg, E. (2001) Dying alone: the social production of urban isolation, *Ethnography*, 2, 499–529.

Klinenberg, E. (2002) *Heat Wave: a Social Autopsy of Disaster in Chicago*. Chicago: University of Chicago Press.

Le Masurier, G., Sidman, C. and Corbin, C. (2003) Accumulating 10,000 steps: does this meet current physical activity guidelines? *Research Quarterly for Exercise and Sport*, 74, 4, 389–94.

Lie, M. and Sorenson, H.K. (1996) *Making Technology our Own? Domesticating Technology into Everyday Life*. Oslo: Scandinavian University Press.

Livingstone, S. (1992) The meaning of domestic technologies: a personal construct analysis of familial gender relations. In Silverstone, R. and Hirsch, E. (eds) *Consuming Technologies*. NY: Routledge.

Lofland, J. and Lofland, L. (1995) *Analyzing Social Settings*. 3rd edition. NY: Wadsworth.

Manson, J.E., Greenland, P., LaCroix, A.Z., Stefanick, M.L., Mouton, C.P., Oberman, A., Perri, M.G., Sheps, D.S., Pettinger, M.B. and Siscovick, D.S. (2002) Walking compared with vigorous exercise for the prevention of cardiovascular events in women, *New England Journal of Medicine*, 347, 10, 716–25.

Moreau, K.L., Degarmo, R., Langley, J., Mcmahon, C., Howley, E.T., Bassett, D.R. and Thompson, D.L. (2001) Increasing daily walking lowers blood pressure in postmenopausal women, *Medicine and Science in Sports and Exercise*, 33, 1825–31.

Oldenburg, R. (1989) *The Great Good Place: Cafes, Coffee Shops, Bookstores, Bars, Hair Salons, and Other Hangouts at the Heart of a Community*. NY: Marlowe and Co.

Ortis, S.M. (1994) Shopping for sociability in the mall, *Research in Community Sociology*, Supplement 1, 183–99.

Oudshoorn, N. and Pinch, T. (2005) Introduction: How users and non-users matter. In Oudshoorn, N. and Pinch, T. (eds) *How Users Matter: the Co-construction of Users and Technology*. Cambridge, MA: MIT Press.

Pinch, T. and Bijker, W. (1984) The social construction of facts and artifacts: or how the sociology of science and the sociology of technology might benefit each other, *Social Studies of Science*, 14, 399–431.

President's Council on Physical Fitness and Sports (2005) Programs leading the way to change, PCPFS E-Newsletter, Fall. Available: http://www.fitness.gov/enewsletter/Fall05_preventionawards.htm.

Rooney, B., Smalley, K., Larson, J. and Havens, S. (2003) Is knowing enough? Increasing physical activity by wearing a pedometer, *Wisconsin Medical Journal*, 102, 31–6.

Sandelowski, M. (1994) Separate, but less unequal: fetal ultrasonography and the transformation of expectant mother/fatherhood, *Gender and Society*, 8, 230–45.

Schacht, S. and Unnithan, N.P. (1991) Mall walking and urban sociability, *Sociological Spectrum*, 11, 351–67.

Schneider, P., Crouter, S. and Bassett, D. (2004) Pedometer measures of free-living physical activity: Comparison of 13 models, *Medicine and Science in Sports and Exercise*, 36, 331–5.

Schneider, P., Bassett, D., Thompson, D., Pronk, N. and Bielak, K. (2006) Effects of a 10,000 steps per day goal in overweight adults, *American Journal of Health Promotion*, 21, 85–9.

Schnirring, L. (2001) Can exercise gadgets motivate patients? *Physician and Sportsmedicine* 29. Retrieved 7 June, 2007 from *Academic Search Premier*.

Sidman, C., Corbin, C. and Le Masurier, G. (2004) Promoting physical activity among sedentary women using pedometers, *Research Quarterly for Exercise and Sport*, 75, 122–9.

Silverstone, R. (2006) Domesticating domestication. Reflections on the life of a concept. In Berker, T., Hartmann, M., Punie, Y. and Ward, K. (eds) *Domestication of Media and Technology*. NY: Open University Press.

Silverstone, R., Hirsch, E. and Morley, D. (1992) Information and communication technologies and the moral economy of the household. In Silverstone, R. and Hirsch, E. (eds) *Consuming Technologies*. NY: Routledge.

Simmel, G. (1950) Sociability, an example of pure, or formal, sociology. In Wolff, H. (ed.) *The Sociology of Georg Simmel*. NY: Free Press.

Simonsick, E.M., Guralnik, J.M., Volpato, S., Balfour, J. and Fried, L.P. (2005) Just get out the door! Importance of walking outside the home for maintaining mobility: Findings from the Women's Health and Aging Study, *Journal of the American Geriatrics Society*, 53, 2, 198–203.

Sorenson, K. (2006) Domestication: the enactment of technology. In Berker, T., Hartmann, M., Punie, Y. and Ward, K. (eds) *Domestication of Media and Technology*. NY: Open University Press.

Sorenson, K., Aune, M. and Hatling, M. (2000) Against linearity: on the cultural appropriation of science and technology. In Dierkes, M. and von Grote, C. (eds) *Between Understanding and Trust*. Amsterdam: Harwood.

Stalp, M.C., Radina, M.E. and Lynch, A. (2008) We do it cuz it's fun: creating women's leisure space through Red Hat Society membership, *Sociological Perspectives*, 512, 325–48.

Stebbins, R. (2002) *The Organizational Basis of Leisure Participation*. State College, PA: Venture.

Takamine, O. (2001) Differences in characteristics between Japanese walkers and sport participants, *International Review for the Sociology of Sport*, 35, 4, 379–91.

Tucker, L. and Mortell, R. (1993) Comparison of the effects of walking and weight training programs on body image in middle-aged women: an experimental study, *American Journal of Health Promotion*, 8, 34–42.

Tudor-Locke, C. (2002) Taking steps toward increased physical activity: Using pedometers to measure and motivate, *President's Council on Physical Fitness and Sports: Research Digest*, 17.

Tudor-Locke, C. and Bassett, D. (2004) How many steps/day are enough? Preliminary pedometer indices for public health, *Sports Medicine*, 34, 1–8.

U.S. Department of Health and Human Services (1996) *Physical Activity and Health: A Report of the Surgeon General*. Atlanta, GA.

U.S. Department of Health and Human Services (2000) *Healthy People 2010: Understanding and Improving Health* (2nd Edition). Washington, DC: U.S. Government Printing Office.

Weuve, J., Kang, J. H., Manson, J.E., Breteler, M.M.B., Ware, J.H. and Grodstein, F. (2004) Physical activity, including walking, and cognitive function in older women, *Journal of the American Medical Association*, 292, 1454–61.

Wyatt, S. (2005) Non-users also matter: the construction of users and non-users of the internet. In Oudshoorn, N. and Pinch, T. (eds) *How Users Matter: the Co-construction of Users and Technology*. Cambridge, MA: MIT Press.

Yarnal, C.M. (2006) The Red Hat Society: exploring the role of play, liminality, and communitas in older women's lives, *Journal of Women and Aging*, 18, 3, 51–73.

11

Doing it my way: old women, technology and wellbeing
Meika Loe

Introduction

Understanding how old women create support for themselves near the end of life is an important topic, and particularly pressing as the population ages, becomes feminised, and remains largely home-centred. In 2000, 4.2 million people in the United States were aged 85 and older; this number is projected to increase to almost 10 million by 2030 and to 21 million by 2050. The ratio of women to men in this category is roughly 2:1 (US Census Bureau 2005).

Currently 83 per cent of Americans aged 65 and over own their own homes, in comparison with four per cent who reside in long-term care facilities (Mann 2003). Given the growing population of elders likely to 'age in place' – or in their homes – in future generations, scholars of ageing (as well as commercial entities) have focused on the role of assistive technologies and design in home care. While ageing scholarship increasingly focuses on elders as technology users, a significant proportion of ageing scholarship also emphasises what is done *for* elders: how elders are cared for, how assistive technology and universal design products are made to assist elders, and caregivers, etc. (*e.g.* Charness and Schaie 2003). Scholarship emphasising the 'impact' of technology can reinforce ageist notions of elders as dependent passive receivers of care; this framing can miss how elders can be agents, and how 'technologies can be used [by elders] as weapons to fight to remain independent and in maintaining contact with the outside world' (Gutman 2003: 260). In other words, elders can be technology experts and negotiators. For example, while we know that household technologies such as telephones and eyeglasses are crucial to day-to-day lives (Mann 2003), we do not have a sense of how elders creatively utilise, reject, and make sense of a wide array of old and new technologies in their lives.

This chapter focuses on women in their nineties (nonagenarians) who are ageing in place in upstate New York. I analyse these old women's use of everyday technological tools to care for themselves in old age and construct meaning. I argue that despite what we may expect, nonagenarian women can be and are technogenarians in their active use of everyday technologies to create meaningful lives and maintain health. Specifically, old women use and negotiate old and new technologies in the context of gendered repertoires to achieve goals such as self-efficacy, wellbeing, and connectedness.

This chapter explores how old women take responsibility for their own health and care through adapting everyday technologies – from slow cookers to gardening tools to televisions – to fit their needs and to age comfortably (Cruikshank 2003). I argue that health for elders includes being able to maintain social networks, intellectual growth and participation, and physical wellbeing; much of this is accomplished with the help of everyday technologies. Policy makers must take this into account, and address the cost of monthly telephone, television, and internet bills in ageing initiatives.

An emphasis on the everyday lives and meaning-making of elders reveals how (1) old women are agentic, actively identifying, adjusting and rejecting a range of technologies to enable self-care, (2) successful ageing for nonagenarians means ageing comfortably, and (3) everyday household technologies *are* assistive ageing technologies or health technologies; in other words, the line between health and non-health technologies, as well as low and high tech, are blurred when elders are put at the centre of analysis.

This research takes place in New York state, where ageing in place – or ageing at home – is a key policy initiative as well as the most common way to age. In upstate New York, roughly 80 per cent are already doing so (Humphreys 2007), and a significant proportion of these are women living alone, practising self-care and playing the role of 'solo problem solvers' with the help of technology (Charness 2003: 16). Ageing in place ideally demands a certain degree of wellbeing, and elders' use of technologies can be crucial in maintaining their sense of cognitive, emotional, and physical abilities.

Ageing in place

As population numbers and healthcare costs grow, 'ageing in place' has become a buzzword for a variety of stakeholders in the United States. State and federal entities as well as health management corporations are invested in reducing costly institutional care for elders. Increasingly, Medicare funding subsidises home-based healthcare in the United States. Medical research teams in Canada and the US are currently exploring and assessing costs and health outcomes associated with 'home hospitalisation' in relation to traditional inpatient hospital care.[1] In this changing medico-political context, Gitlin (2003) points out that 'home is quickly becoming the context for a widening array of health and human services' with expanded Medicare coverage for care at home, decreased hospital stays and increases in outpatient services. Particularly for the physically frail, the boundaries of hospital and home have blended (2003: 190).

Given the blurring of home and healthcare, elders themselves state a preference for ageing at home. Forty years of national survey research, including that of the American Association of Retired Persons (AARP), reveals that the vast majority of elders prefer to age at home. Elders cite normalcy, continuity in self-identity, autonomy, and control as reasons for this preference (Gitlin 2003: 198). Many prefer to die in their own homes. However, critics argue that ageing at home can be extremely isolating, and that home-based healthcare and transport can be expensive and difficult to access. Importantly, informal caregivers like family members still provide 80 per cent of care to dependent old persons living at home (Binstock and Chuff 2000, Burke 2009).

Given this context, elders and state entities may attach different meanings to ageing in place. Many elders associate ageing in place with staying at home and in being in control of their day-to-day lives; avoiding institutionalisation can help to preserve autonomy and dignity. State entities support these initiatives primarily as a cost-saving measure; to cut back on healthcare and hospitalisation costs.

Technology plays a key role in ageing in place initiatives and in the day-to-day support of elders. While most technologies are not devised with an elder user in mind, many research centres and private businesses are now emerging to fill this niche (Joyce *et al.* 2007). For example, an increasing number of US housing developers are integrating universal design by creating living environments that are accessible and effective for all ages and abilities, including ramps instead of stairs, kitchen counters at a variety of heights and cabinets with pull-out shelves. And Japan's private sector leads the way in communications technology innovations for an ageing populace (Joyce *et al.* 2007).[2]

Elder tech users

This chapter attempts to bridge several bodies of work: science and technology literature on technology users; feminist research on gender and technology; and social gerontology research on place, ageing and technology. Most centrally, this work contributes to a growing body of literature on users and technology (*e.g.* Cowan 1983, Woolgar 1991, Kline and Pinch 1996, Oudshoorn and Pinch 2005). This literature focuses on technology and users as mutually constructed (Oudshoorn and Pinch 2005), both embedded and made meaningful in their social worlds where each reciprocally acts upon and influences the other. This body of work has not fully explored tech users across the age spectrum, and how ageing and technology use intersect. This 'context of use' is crucial when analysing 'gerontechnologies' and how these are utilised and appropriated in everyday lives.

Feminist scholars remind us that technology means different things to differently situated people. Users inscribe technologies with their own scripts for appropriate use (Akrich 1992), and these scripts can be gender and age based. Cowan (1983) brought the fields of history of technology and women's history together, emphasising women as users of technology, and how their social position in gendered (domestic) worlds contributes to the meanings they attach to technologies. The discussion of gender and technology is a robust field, but discussion of elders is relatively absent (*e.g.* Moore 2007, Wajcman 1991).

Over the past several decades a growing body of work emphasises young and middle-aged women's active role in appropriating technology, from reproductive technologies, to household technologies, to computer technologies, and women's resistance to exclusion in this and other technological arenas. However, very few scholars are exploring how contemporary elders utilise and ascribe meaning to technologies into their day-to-day lives.[3] This is particularly true in the gerontology literature which tends to be more evaluative than ethnographic, emphasising, for example, how technology may be used to accomplish goals, rather than exploring the meanings elders attach to technology in their everyday lives.

This chapter begins from the premise that technology structures women's lives and at the same time is utilised in the expression of womanhood, even in old age. Lifelong gender roles and expectations – including housework, care work, appearance work, relationship work, and health work – continue to organise elders' lives and technology use in old age. Women learn to use technology to meet this range of gendered work expectations throughout their lives. Thus, to borrow a key theoretical device from gender studies, it follows that in the process of 'doing gender' (West and Zimmerman 1987), women display expertise in technology modification, creation, and use, across the lifecourse.

This work responds to a call for scholarship (Joyce and Mamo 2006) that merges feminist ageing studies with science and technology studies, and in the process, work that reclaims old men and women as technologically literate, rather than as victims of technology and design. Specifically, this chapter examines how old women actively and creatively appropriate a wide range of technologies to achieve specific ends.

Methods

Gubrium and Holstein (2000) argue that knowledge of old age should come from the aged themselves. This research was conducted with this in mind, using in-depth interviews coupled with both lifecourse and symbolic interactionist approaches. A lifecourse approach emphasises common themes, continuity and change across one's lifespan, and how these biographical aspects can shape contemporary realities, such as technology use. A symbolic interactionist framework focuses on how individuals actively participate in their environments and create social realities and meanings through these interactions. My focus here is to use both of these approaches to understand how biography, place, and social context shape elders' active technology use and concurrent meaning making.

Because all informants for this study were born before 1930, their gendered scripts as well as approaches to ageing, health and technology probably differ from those women born in later birth cohorts (Hardy 2003). For example, many nonagenarians have learned to live in moderation, and to appreciate and use technologies as they became available, including radios, sewing machines, kettles and slow cookers. Today, few own or regularly use microwaves, dishwashers, or computers. Some are ambivalent about new biotechnologies like prescription drugs and medical devices (especially those not utilised by their parents), but may also defer to their doctors when it comes to unfamiliar health issues. While there may be notable exceptions, this cohort effect is a crucial part of understanding their common social contexts and familiarity with particular technologies.

Data were collected through interviews and participant observation with 10 women aged 90–96 who are actively ageing in place in upstate New York. Initial contacts were made through connections with senior services centres, senior activities programs, social clubs, and local newspaper coverage. The majority of women interviewed are also participating in the author's longitudinal research project on ageing in New York, and have taken part in a series of interviews from 2006 to 2009. Interviews took place in their homes (apartment, condo or house), located in two counties in upstate New York, one rural and one an urban and suburban mix. All took part in at least one in-depth semi-structured digitally-recorded interview during this period. Interviews included open-ended questions across the lifecourse, focusing on each woman's family, educational and work backgrounds as well as current daily routines and approaches to ageing and self-care. All interviews were taped, transcribed, and coded thematically.

In addition, I employed ethnographic methods to collect data about lived day-to-day experiences. Beyond regular visits to homes, between 2006 and 2009 I participated in informants' lives and daily routines outside their homes, including intermittent doctor visits, grocery shopping trips, social club meetings, exercise classes, neighbourhood meals, funeral services and religious rituals. In addition, I logged approximately 150 hours observing a combination of regional ageing-related meetings and conferences, touring institutions dedicated to elder care, and conducting interviews with professionals in elder support and care.

The sample of ten women is largely representative of the national population in the 85 and over age group. According to the US Census (2005) category of the 'oldest old' (85+), 70 per cent lived in non-family one-person households and 79 per cent of the women in this category were widows. In terms of racial demographics, over 90 per cent of those over 85 years of age were White; six per cent were Black. Likewise, this sample includes eight widows and two married couples. Nine identify as White (with Polish, Danish, Irish, Italian, or Jewish ethnic backgrounds) and one as Black. Of the ten nonagenarians, eight live independently and two live with and care for spouses. In terms of housing, two rent apartments, two own condos, and six own houses.

These old women co-ordinate their own care in the context of a normal range of ageing-related sensory, cognitive, and physical difficulties. At the same time, most experience ageing-related strengths including domain-specific knowledge and daily task management skills (Morrow 2003). Notably, none of the women in the sample are wheelchair-bound; all are ambulatory in some way and this dramatically shapes their self-care regimens. Two women, Florence and Lillian, employ a home healthcare aid for a few hours each day. The rest of the sample depends on informal caregivers. Four have family members living within a 20-mile radius of their homes who help with transport and care on an intermittent basis.[4] In general, most nonagenarians in this sample *prefer* to be totally independent, or to go beyond family assistance to utilise social networks, formal transport services (including paid drivers and public transport), or delivery services for day-to-day needs. The question, then, is how do nonagenarians independently manage self-care and daily routines?

Gutman (2003) states that there still exists 'a dearth of research that explores elders' experiences with built environment and everyday task accomplishment'. The following sections aim to fill in these gaps, exploring how, for old women, constructing a self-care routine is technology work. In addition, caring for home and self is gendered work; women generally are socialised to co-ordinate their own care throughout their adult lives, as well as to construct and design home spaces that help them to meet their needs as well as that of their family. For old women who are their own primary caretakers, everyday mundane technologies can be significant in designing an ever-changing self-care repertoire to enable self-sufficiency, as well as control, independence and health.[5]

From tea bags to automobiles: nonagenarians get moving

Mobility is a central component of creating and maintaining wellbeing (Carp 1998). The spectrum of technologies that enable mobility for elders is much broader than walking sticks, walkers, wheelchairs and stair lifts – typically classified as 'assistive devices' – and can include everything from automobiles, to public transport, to rock salt, security systems, special shoes, clothing, medication, heaters, and caffeinated beverages. Some elders prefer to be sedentary or home bound, and technologies like reclining chairs and walkers (used mostly as tables) can be used to support this goal as well. Most importantly, nonagenarians creatively utilise a broad range of mobility tools (not always as designers imagine they would be used) to achieve a variety of goals.

For example, Ruth has a self-designed mobility system that includes a variety of technologies, including walkers, a scooter, countertops, rock salt, and a home security system, each with a particular purpose. Her electric scooter is for use outside on the sidewalks, in nice weather. However, Ruth needs someone to bring it outside (down a few stairs) for her to use it, so it typically sits in her dark sitting room, covered. Her indoor walker moves with her, but not everywhere. Because she inhabits a compact area on the ground floor of her home, she relies on counters and walls for leverage when navigating halls and the kitchen. However, when she needs to leave the house, she must walk a distance to the back door, and relies on walker #1 to get there. She leaves one walker at the top of the back staircase, and at the bottom stands her walker #2, waiting for her. Walker #2 goes with Ruth when she must leave the house for doctor's appointments. In the winter, Ruth keeps a bucket of rock salt near her back door and scatters the salt on the icy concrete before stepping outside. A few steps (on the salt) with the help of the walker and she can reach the door of the car waiting to drive her to her appointment. Together her walkers are 'absolutely necessary' as 'another pair of legs' without which Ruth believes she would fall. Finally, Ruth says she would never leave the house without operating her home security system, including a variety of locks and a security alarm; these assuage her fears and assure her that everything will be the same when she returns.

Walkers can serve a variety of purposes. After losing her balance while walking in her neighbourhood this past year, Alice relies on her walker to navigate her home and beyond. She calls her red walker her 'saviour' because it allows her to continue to 'get out and around'. This device is primarily used for mobility assurance, balance and movement, but it also doubles as a key piece of furniture and storage space. Whether the walker is being actively used or not, it is always nearby and Alice's purse is always draped over the side. Florence is even better prepared, storing her flashlight, a chequebook, and pocketbook on the walker shelf. She also hangs her life support remote health monitoring device over the side. Since Florence spends most of the day in her recliner resting her sore back with the walker at her side, the walker is more table space than mobility device. In this way the walker ironically enables Florence to (primarily) avoid ambulatory discomfort, and support her sedentary lifestyle.

Mary lives with her husband on the second floor of a 'walkup' (an apartment building with no elevator) downtown. They use walking canes to steady themselves on the outside stairs and then once inside, her husband uses a stair lift to get up to the floor they inhabit. Together these assistive devices enable them to continue to live downtown, in the same building where Mary's husband housed his dental practice 40 years ago. Mary says she dislikes anything that makes her dependent, but she uses a walking cane to prevent falls. 'It gives me the feeling that maybe I'll be okay.' Likewise, she says she uses the stair lift when she has morning stiffness and when she has to carry groceries up, but prefers to walk most of the time. Mary is able to approach these mobility technologies as an option for comfort, security, and health. Interestingly, when grandchildren and neighbours visit, these technologies take on new meanings: the stair lift becomes a fun ride for all ages and the cane becomes a toy walking stick.

Mary, Shana, and Julia drive their own cars, mostly during the day and on short familiar routes. For Julia the car is a crucial component in her life that allows her to remain engaged in activities; a way to 'get with people' at church, with her book group, and over meals. It is a way to access the social networks that sustain her. However, she fears driving at night, admitting that she gets scared, and lost, and 'driveways get confused with streets'. Shana, a committed gardener, says she must continue to drive her station wagon to pick up new plants at the nursery. Alice, who does not drive, keeps her 1970s era car in the garage, available to anyone who will drive it, including a driver she hires to take her shopping, on picnics, and to medical appointments. She holds out hope that someday, when her vision improves, she will be back driving. For her and Mary access to a car symbolises years of independence and self-sufficiency. This can still be achieved, in part, with a hired driver who operates the women's cars on their terms.

Anna and Dorothy depend on walking to get to most places they need to visit. Each highly values her active lifestyle, and depends on various technologies to stay consistent with her exercise routines. Neither is interested in elder-specific mobility devices, nor do they need them. Instead, they depend on transport options, hot beverages, and special fabrics and materials to stay warm, comfortable, and confident. Taking the bus and then walking to the community swimming pool enables Anna to 'see sides of my city I have never seen before'. Anna then relies on her swimsuit and shower cap for regular exercise in the indoor pool (in all seasons). Similarly, Dorothy swears by her 'beloved Yaktrax', special shoes that grip the ice, as well as a full-length insulated coat, to feel secure on a winter day's walk.

Several nonagenarians mentioned the importance of heaters, medication and hot caffeinated beverages to help them to get moving and participate in healthy activities. For Anna, a hot cup of coffee warms and energises her before her pool exercise class. Similarly, Ruth depends on a routine that combines strong hot tea, over-the-counter pain relievers, and a heated bathroom to loosen her joints and get moving in the mornings. These technologies then facilitate their mobility as they intend it.

Many of these elders' daily routines might be summed up as 'preventative medicine' using a medicalisation model. However, while some technologies associated with these routines may have been prescribed by medical professionals, the context and meanings surrounding their use are much broader. These routines are extensions of lifelong self-care approaches that have less to do with a medical model, and much more to do with lifelong patterns of 'doing gender' in combination with self-soothing rituals and social networks, to promote wellbeing, comfort, and confidence.

Tools like the telephone, discussed in more detail in the next section, can also be seen as accessories to doing gender *and* mobility, as they enable elders to stay connected and co-ordinate rides and driving services. In sum, the list of mobility technologies that nonagenarians utilise goes beyond the expected to include a number of tools that can extend comfort zones beyond elders' homes and enhance comfort, confidence, mobility and ambulatory control.

'My collection of handy gadgets': staying in touch, feeling alive
The telephone is the top technology that elders rely on, particularly women who are taught to value social connection (Mann 2003). However, few scholars have explored how elders use the telephone and communications technologies as tools for health and self-care, further blurring the boundaries between home and hospital.

For the nonagenarians with whom I spoke, the telephone holds instrumental and symbolic meanings associated with mortality, overcoming loneliness, co-ordinating care, and staying in touch with family and friends. Everyone agrees about the importance of this technology. Nonagenarians talked about the telephone being a primary tool in case of a personal emergency; yet they also referred to it as a reminder of one's own mortality as well as that of one's friends and loved ones. Many associate a ringing phone with the possibility of news of another friend or family member who is gone. All of these women come from an era when telephone use was rare; it was utilised primarily to convey important news. After receiving a call about the death of a dear friend, Alice commented that when it comes to her 'collection of handy gadgets', including calculators, timers, a CD-player, a walker, a television, and a computer, '[T]he telephone … is probably the most important thing because it means life and death'.

At the same time, elders actively use the telephone as a tool for staying connected, to feel part of something larger than oneself, to feel needed, and to maintain friendships particularly in the context of limited mobility. Without the ability to interact with others, all these women would experience isolation in their own homes in magnified ways. Alice points out that social relationships and health motivations tend to underlie technology use. She says, 'The only real necessity beyond food, drink and shelter is friendship, and if technology can enable this, it can be important'. She goes on to say that many of her friends are either deceased or unable to leave their homes. Staying in touch with friends who are housebound requires regular use of the telephone.

Alice and others find that cordless phones can be crucial for maintaining social networks as well as for co-ordinating self-care. Having a telephone nearby provides assurance that emergency service providers can be reached. Doctors' offices, pharmacies, care providers, and drivers can be reached by phone. Alice jokes that if the phone rings a long time, this means she has left it in the bathroom again. Dorothy has a strategy to avoid this; she never lets her cordless telephone leave her side. Dorothy has a special purse for her telephone that she carries with her throughout the day. She developed this strategy after she learned the hard way, having fallen during the night far from the telephone.

Communications technologies are a key tool for those ageing in place, serving as medical assistive technology as well as a familiar communication tool. Old women's uses of technologies are in part informed by fears of being injured and left helpless. In addition to phones, remote communication tools may be purchased by elders, and these can be associated with very different social meanings. Alice tells of how she begins and ends her day by pressing the button on her Lifeline communication device 'to let them know I'm OK'. This detached health monitoring is perfect for Alice, who prefers to keep most medical technology at bay, but also feels reassured that if she needed help, this device would dispatch it. The machine also helps to order her day. However, this technology can become intrusive. When Alice had to leave town unexpectedly, she left a note on her door explaining the situation in case anyone checked on her. When she returned she realised that an emergency unit had been dispatched, and had ransacked her home in the process of trying to locate her.

While Alice and Florence pay for a phone-based health monitoring program called Lifeline Medical Alert[6] in their urban area, the majority of nonagenarians create their own grassroots health monitoring networks and avoid the monthly bills associated with remote monitoring. For example, every morning several neighbours in a rural village check in on one another. Joanne calls Carol at 8am. Carol then calls Dorothy. If for some reason someone does not answer, the next step is to make a visit. Dorothy admits that this calling network has saved her life several times. Recently, a friend helped her to install an amplified phone ringer to ensure that she hears the phone. Rose relies on an evening phone check-in with a friend who always asks if she needs anything. For Ruth, who is almost completely home-bound (with many days spent in bed), a ringing telephone is a reminder that she is alive. When a friend calls, she frequently tells him or her, 'Your call reminds me that I am alive, that I am not forgotten'.

Phone communication offers a sense of continuity across the lifecourse for women like Ruth and Rose for whom friendship and motherhood have become synonymous with quality of life, and even life itself. Regular telephone calls offer countless benefits beyond this: a reminder that someone cares; a routine that helps to order a day; a sense of participation in the outside world; and a feeling of security. Most importantly, perhaps, communication technologies including amplifiers, cordless phones and lifeline devices, in combination with nonagenarians' creative approaches to monitoring and staying in touch (*e.g.* phone trees and phone purses) have enabled ageing in place for most study participants.

'Have you seen my apparatus?' Using machines to foster intellectual growth
While the telephone is crucial for health, elders incorporate a range of other communications technologies, including computers, televisions, and radios, into self-care routines and meaning making. These tools not only help them stay connected and in control, but also help to foster intellectual growth and by association, the health benefits that scientists now associate with brain stimulation.

Despite her daily reliance on the telephone, Dorothy says the computer is the one machine she could not live without. She uses the computer not only for email correspondence, but also for typing and storing her memoirs, engaging in translation work (as a favour to academic friends), and for monitoring her finances. She explains:

> I even write my checks on the computer. Nobody else in the village does this, I don't think. They may not know about it. I think it is wonderful. It helps me because sometimes I don't know if 2 and 2 is 4 or 22! So this way I can see what I'm working with (Dorothy).

Not only does the computer provide Dorothy with a steady hand and a clear budget, but it also reinforces her reputation as a technogenarian in her community, a reputation of which she is proud.

Ruth stares at a screen every day, but it is not a computer. Because her eyes are poor, she relies on a machine that helps her read. It magnifies the text of each book page and projects it onto a large screen, from which she reads. Ruth explains that she has been reading since age five, but now she cannot read normally. She lost a retina in the concentration camp, and so she has only one good eye. 'Have you seen my apparatus?' she asks. She walks me into her reading room, pointing out a small television-like machine on a desk. She points to the power cord, plugged into the wall, then carefully turns on the monitor and the mouse-like 'reader' and moves it on the page of a Jewish community newsletter to show me how she reads with the help of the machine. Nearby on the twin bed is a stack of reading material, including holiday cards, business cards, newspapers and hardbound books. Ruth's reading machine helps her to be both involved in her community and in control of her life, as well as to escape. She uses this technology to keep up with a broad range of personal business. At the same time, she uses the machine to enable her to escape from her immediate life and pain, into her favourite fiction books. 'I would be dead without the apparatus,' she says.

All the nonagenarians in my sample incorporate televisions and radios into their lives in various ways. For many, watching or listening to the news is a way to feel connected to community and history; many associate this technology with family tradition. Some emphasised particular programming that they choose to consume. Alice never misses listening to the city mayor discuss local issues on a weekly radio program. Ruth has always listened to music to lighten her mood. Others watch the local news to stay in touch with the world around them.

For Lillian and her husband, television (movie) time represents something they can look forward to in the evenings. Lillian associates this time and technology with romance and companionship. She says:

> I am so in love with this man ... Every night Bernie picks out something for us to watch. So we see a movie or something else – we have full cable. So that is great fun. We like the romances, they are so wonderful (Lillian).

Alice and Shana utilise public television programming to learn new things. This passive learning sometimes spurred active learning for each of them. Alice commented, 'I saw the poet laureate on Charlie Rose [interview show] so I got this book out to get more information on her. Very interesting poetry!' Similarly, Shana recalled, 'I watched Julia Child on public television – she lived to age 93! She reinforced my love of cooking'. In these examples, we see how technology creates a sense of social engagement, ranging from a romantic evening to exposure to new written works or ways of ageing.

Similarly, Anna is always looking for a new project and television helps her with this. Because she has a particular interest in successful women in society, Anna has incorporated the evening news with Katie Couric into her routine:

> I'm following the career of Katie Couric. She got the interview with the pilot, I saw. You know, the Hudson River landing – just a few weeks ago. A big triumph for Katie! And I appreciate her salary – five million a year. That's a sizeable salary (Anna).

Florence's recliner faces the television and a flashing photo frame with family pictures. She says she is content to watch television to pass the time. But she has grown tired of the repetition both on television and in her photo frame, commenting 'I've seen it all on TV. They are all repeats. And the pictures, I've memorised them all.' In contrast to the others, the imaging technologies that Florence depends upon for stimulation have failed to deliver what she desires. In nonagenarians' daily lives, communications technologies can provide a respite from loneliness and boredom, and/or or intensify these emotions. They can symbolise mortality and life, stimulation or stasis, isolation or connection, and continuity and change. Elders like Ruth, Dorothy, Anna, Alice, and Lillian use technologies like the radio, the computer, the reading machine, and the television to maintain lifelong continuity, control and connectedness, mental health and wellbeing. As with the telephone, each uses these devices to extend their participation with the outside world, particularly in the context of compromised health and mobility.

Fun with sauté pans and slow cookers: creatively nourishing oneself
For many nonagenarians, kitchen technologies such as kettles, slow cookers, stoves and ovens are key instruments for self-care. They are also tools that can elicit creativity, connection, expression, health and even exciting new challenges. Such tools, many of which existed in the kitchens they inhabited as children or newlyweds, provide continuity over the course of a day and a life.

Shana, who was deboning a chicken just as I arrived for an interview, pointed to her kitchen as one of her favourite spaces in her home, and the place in which she starts her day. Ruth also begins her day in the kitchen, and described how turning the kettle on in the morning helps to 'psych [herself] up' and face the day. She explains, 'First thing I do is turn on the kettle and get two tea bags – I need a hot strong tea to start the day. Then I go and wash myself.' For both of these women, preparing food and drink was akin to preparing oneself for what lay ahead. Kitchens and kitchen technologies can be extensions of self, family, and lifelong routines.

For Anna, a self-described 'diet freak' in response to being 'robust' as a child, a specific food preparation routine (involving a slow cooker) allows her to maintain her weight and figure. Dorothy, someone who is always looking for a new challenge, has recently discovered that stovetop food preparation can be a creative process that can be novel, suspenseful and rewarding:

> Cooking is a completely creative thing. With fresh vegetables and chicken and fish, and there's so much you can do with those things! In the summer I go to the farmers market and in the winter I go on Fridays with a friend to the store. And I always get too much! But it is the process, the fun, and looking forward to eating it. Sometimes [what I sauté in the pan] it turns out great, sometimes not (Dorothy).

Julia describes how kitchen technologies enable her and a homeless friend to eat together; each warming up frozen or canned foods in the microwave for dinner:

> She brings food – she's one of those who goes to the dumpster – you know that grocery stores have to throw out out-of-date things, so she gets good quality frozen meals and brings that with her. She eats with me and offers it, but I don't take it. I just warm up canned soup or something. But I enjoy her company! (Julia).

Several nonagenarians mentioned the electric slow-cooker as their favourite kitchen technology, perhaps because of its ease of use; it is difficult to burn a meal or make a mistake using this technology. When I first met Alice she talked about the importance of her slow cooker in terms of ease when it comes to making hot healthy meals for herself. She had just replaced her 'tired' 35-year-old model with a new 'beautiful' one. With changes in economic markets as well as her energy level and eyesight, Alice now attaches slightly different meanings to this technology:

My new fun project is to create meals that are as cheap as possible, and healthy. Like rice and beans. I'd like to make large portions that I can freeze for the future as well. That way I can save money and time and work on other things, like taxes (Alice).

This section reveals how lifelong gender roles and expectations continue to organise elders' lives and technology use in old age. Social scripts that nonagenarians attach to kitchen technologies go well beyond health and food preparation. Kitchen technologies are used here to aid in achieving a wide range of goals including saving money, building connections, achieving a particular diet, waking up, carrying on family traditions, and expressing and nourishing oneself. This list of daily goals conveys the multidimensionality of self-care and health in old age. Ironically, while kitchen, mobility, and communication technologies are central to daily meaning making for women nonagenarians focused on health and autonomy, medical technologies rarely enter into discussions about self-care.

'Newfangled medical things': monitoring one's body and opting out

Pharmaceuticals and over-the-counter medications are generally associated with health and wellbeing. However, paying attention to the meanings nonagenarians attach to medical use and non-use can illuminate how these biotechnologies are positioned as an array of techniques elders use to practice self-care. When asked about their medications, nonagenarians tend to say very little, suggesting that biotechnology has limited symbolic importance in their daily routines. Lillian remarked on the sheer number of pills that she takes on a daily basis. Julia commented on the pretty colours, saying, 'I take a mass of pills. eight pills a day. I have four in the morning and they are yellow, white, blue and pink. So pretty! And I take the ones that make me lightheaded at night. I guess I have a bad heart'. Others were not aware of exactly how many pills they took in a typical day, and what they were for.

Ruth and Lillian spoke of medications that are meaningful to them in large part because they are tied to their own history or family tradition. They spoke of these biomedical technologies as a way to neutralise the body, to balance things out. Interestingly, both utilised biomedical products that were widely available (over the counter and by prescription) with long histories of use in the United States:

In the morning, to get going I take two tea bags – very hot strong tea ... I take my daily laxative – I have a weak stomach from the war, we all do, from not eating. And I take my extra strength Tylenol. I use this [Velcro wrist support] so that I will not move my wrist. I did not want the surgery. So I use these instead (Ruth).

Nitro ... it is such a nothing pill, and I've been taking it forever. But [when I asked for it in the hospital] the doctor didn't give it to me, and that's when I had my heart attack. Why wouldn't he do this? My grandmother took this. I still remember her sticking it under her tongue, and I'd ask what it was and she gave me the sign with her finger like 'wait' and then tell me, 'That's Nitroglycerin'. It makes me feel better. I always keep it by my bed at night (Lillian).

Pharmaceutical technologies that are linked to family and personal history, like Ruth's laxatives, which she has taken since leaving the concentration camp at the end of WWII, and Lillian's nitroglycerin tablets, which she witnessed being taken by her grandmother, can be added to the list of tools that help to provide continuity across the lifecourse. However, aspects of medical technology that are unfamiliar can be unwelcome. Lillian, Alice and Mary spoke critically about the medical profession and over-use of medical technologies in their own lives:

I talk with [a friend] about old age and what they do to old people – medically I mean – these newfangled medical things. She told me she saw someone in the hospital, 83, and she was in pain, and they were giving her something so she could live five months. We both agree, we don't want any part of that. We'd rather be comfortable. To me, the eye [injections] are worth doing. I can try that again, and see if it works. So far not. But that other stuff – I won't take it. It is for the doctors, not for us. Their pride. That's why I'm not going to a nursing home. I need to be in control – that's the big thing (Alice).

Recently I have been having TIAs [transient ischemic attacks] … they come on quickly and then disappear. Even though I feel fine afterwards, I go to the emergency room to be checked. Each time I am subjected to a full day of tests, and sometimes they keep me overnight to observe. This is frustrating, because I know I am fine and really I just want to be home. Then last week my gynecologist suggested a precautionary measure – a biopsy – to make sure I didn't have ovarian cancer. Was this really necessary? I don't know. I didn't really want to go, but [my daughter] wouldn't let me pass on it. Afterwards I was very uncomfortable and had heavy bleeding for weeks. It reminded me of the surgery I had – that created more stress on my body, in new places. I just don't know about all of this (Mary).

In this section, nonagenarians are negotiating medicine in their daily lives, making decisions about both use and *non-use* of medical technology, revealing a spectrum of meaning making around biotechnology. For these women it comes down to self-determination and control – are they able to make decisions about their own care, or is their care determined by others? For Alice, having a choice about a medical procedure for her eyes fits with her self-care ethic. In contrast, being 'subjected' to medical surveillance and care can be akin to being in a nursing home where a patient retains very little self-determination, a fate Alice and Mary both describe as 'worse than death'.

Conclusion

This study contributes to research that explores how old women creatively utilise and adapt everyday technologies to construct meaningful lives. Nonagenarians can teach us how everyday technologies can become technologies of ageing; instruments of continuity, control and health; or just the opposite. As we have seen, creative use of technology underscores self-determination and nonagenarians' ability to do self-care mostly on their own, even as some are thwarted by techno-solutions.

This research contributes to our understanding of health, ageing, and gender as agentic; as actively 'done' in day-to-day life (West and Zimmerman 1987) in combination with technology use. When Alice is engaged in her daily slow-cooker food preparation routine, she is accomplishing womanhood and wellbeing in her active use of technology, and in the context of a life of women's work nourishing others (DeVault 1991). Nonagenarians in this sample push on scholarship in gender studies and science and technology studies to reveal how the active accomplishment of gender is technology-based just as it is age- and health-focused.

Years of care work involving technology may translate as a cumulative advantage for women at the end of the lifecourse (O'Rand 2002). Conversely, elders hoping to age in place may be disadvantaged if their life skills do not 'fit' with self-care (Moore and Stratton 2002). Many women nonagenarians have developed creative approaches to technology use and self-care, and utilise these daily in their final years of life. These techniques include designing purses for phones, staging walkers at key places, using reading machines to connect and escape, creating telephone monitoring networks among friends, sewing items to enable comfort at home, using computers to keep track of household finances, and utilising simple kitchen technologies to create affordable healthy meals. In these ways, nonagenerians further their lifelong expertise in using technologies that assist with care work and the co-ordination of routine mundane tasks. This expertise, now taken for granted after years of practice, comes in handy when it comes to food preparation, health monitoring, connecting with others, and creating and maintaining a home over many years. Such domain-specific knowledge can be a key advantage and safety net in the context of ageing, allowing elders the ability to prove self-efficacy and remain at home and healthy, late in life. However, there is a downside, as most women do not have the option to retire from this gendered work.

As communities include more individuals ageing in place, all elders must be able to meet their own health needs through access to care *and* technology. While much political rhetoric focuses on access to care issues, key technologies like telephone and television services, as well as other communications technologies, kitchen technologies, and mobility technologies can be 'the difference between life and death'. And they can also be costly. Age-based technology discounts and coverage are crucial to ensuring access to these 'health' technologies. Policies aimed at assisting elders as they pursue health, community, and changing forms of independence need to address the escalating costs of communication technologies in the home.

These old women's lives reveal that perhaps the answer to the question about an ageing populace, home support and health is not simply new biotechnologies, assistive technologies or design strategies, but a renewed emphasis on elder agency and an awareness of existing technology repertoires and daily strategies to emphasise continuity and autonomy. After all, despite all the emphasis on successful ageing, elders in this project ultimately aim to achieve something more akin to comfortable ageing that emphasises ease (Cruikshank 2003).

For these nonagenarians, a self-care ethic is about accomplishing and maintaining a broad sense of health that involves comfort, confidence, continuity, autonomy *and* social capital in the context of old age. The real power of technology, as many of these nonage-narian women reveal, is in the implicit social relationships and other manifestations of humanity that underlie our use of tools and devices. As we have seen, self-efficacy and ageing in place are realistic goals when technology can be used to reveal and reinforce social networks, ensure continuity across the lifecourse (when it comes to everyday routines and roles), and enable intellectual participation and physical wellbeing.

Acknowledgements

I am indebted to Jennifer Reich and Kelly Joyce for support and feedback on this chapter.

Notes

1   For a discussion of the hospitalisation at home movement in long-term care, see, for example, *The American Journal of Managed Care* 2009 Jan; 15 (1) 49–56, and *Canadian Medical Association Journal*. 2009 January: 180 (2).

2   For example, US universities have started ageing centres to develop new technologies such as Cornell's environmental geriatrics program, Georgia Institute for Technology's Center for Research and Education on Ageing and Technology, and MIT's age lab. Companies such as Life

Solutions Plus sell products aimed to ensure independent living. For more on this, see Joyce *et al.*, (2007).

3   In my research on the Viagra phenomenon (2004), I explore how women and men across the age spectrum configure and inscribe this biomedical product with a wide range of gendered meanings, social norms and values.

4   While this chapter focuses on elder self-care, it should be noted that most of these women are not necessarily *always* alone when it comes to problem-solving and personal care. Most are also cared for in a variety of ways by other women; this is the care work that family members, friends, housecleaners, nursing aides, healthcare workers, and others perform. These support players are primarily younger women, and in health and domestic work fields, these are increasingly women of colour, poor women, and women from developing countries. This group of caregivers is crucial to the success of ageing in place initiatives. Even the two married couples in this sample who proudly take care of each other when it comes to health monitoring and emotional support, depend on regular assistance from a driver as well as neighbours and family; one couple also depends on a daily nursing aid to prepare meals and perform housekeeping tasks.

5   I have found in my broader study on ageing in place that those who are unable to master self-care repertoires late in life may risk losing control over the living environment and care. For example, a male informant in his late eighties told me that his discomfort with communication technologies (such as the telephone) may be a problem when it comes to overall health and wellbeing. Another explained that after his wife died, he fell apart. He could not manage to take care of himself, and lost a great deal of weight. His 'saving grace' was moving to an assisted living environment where meals and cleaning are taken care of.

6   The Lifeline Medical Alert website says '[the program] costs little more than a dollar a day, but the specific amount may vary slightly depending on which Lifeline program is nearest to you and which equipment and services you choose'. A phone call to the centre estimates a monthly bill of $38 with a one-time installation fee of $55. In this case, the cost is not the only barrier to use for elders like Dorothy. The independent ethic that comes with living in a remote rural location also contributes to this decision, as well as longtime, hard-earned trust in friendship networks that may not be granted to unknown service providers.

References

Akrich, M. (1992) The de-scription of technical objects. In Bijker, W. and Law, J. (eds) *Shaping Technology/Building Society: Studies in Sociotechnical Change*. Cambridge, MA: MIT Press.

Binstock, R.E. and Chuff, L.E. (2000) *Home Care Advances: Essential Research and Policy Issues*. New York: Springer.

Burke, C. (2009) Observations on health care reform: thinking long-term, Nelson A. Rockefeller Institute of Government Report. http://www.rockinst.org/observations/burkec/2009-03health_care_reform_thinking_long_term.aspx.

Calasanti, T. and Slevin, K. (2006) *Age Matters: Realigning Feminist Thinking*. New York: Routledge.

Charness, N. and Schaie, K.W. (eds) *Impact of Technology on Successful Aging*. New York: Springer Publishing Company.

Charness, N. (2003) Commentary: access, motivation, ability, design and training: necessary conditions for older adult success with technology. In Charness, N. and Schaie, K.W. (eds) *Impact of Technology on Successful Aging*. New York: Springer Publishing Company.

Cowan, R.S. (1983) *More Work for Mother: the Ironies of Household Technology from the Open Hearth to the Microwave*. New York: Basic Books.

Cruikshank, M. (2003) *Learning to Be Old: Gender, Culture and Aging*. New York: Roman and Littlefield.

DeVault, M.L. (1991) *Feeding the Family, the Social Organisation of Caring as Gendered Work*. Chicago: University of Chicago Press.

Gubrium, J.F. and Holstein, J.A. (2000) *Introduction, Aging and Everyday Life*. New York: Blackwell.

Gitlin, L.N. (2003) Commentary: next steps in home modification and assistive technology research. In Charness, N. and Schaie, K.W. (eds) *Impact of Technology on Successful Aging*, New York: Springer Publishing Company.

Gutman, G.M. (2003) Commentary: Gerontechnology and the home environment. In Charness, N. and Schaie, K.W. (eds) *Impact of Technology on Successful Aging*. New York: Springer Publishing Company.

Hardy, M. (2003) Is it all about aging? Technology and aging in social context. In Charness, N. and Schaie, K.W. (eds) *Impact of Technology on Successful Aging*. New York: Springer Publishing Company.

He, W., Sengupta, M., Velkoff, V.A. and DeBarros, K.A. (2005) *U.S. Census Bureau, Current Population Reports, P23–209, 65+ in the United States: 2005*, Washington, DC: US Government Printing Office.

Humphreys, J. (2007) Upstate New York Regional Review, *Federal Reserve Bank of New York*, 2, 2, 1.

Joyce, K. and Mamo, L. (2006) Graying the cyborg: new directions in feminist analyses of aging, science, and technology. In Calasanti, T. and Slevin, K. (eds) *Age Matters: Realigning Feminist Thinking*. NY: Routledge.

Joyce, K., Williamson, J. and Mamo, L. (2007) Technology, science, and ageism: an examination of three patterns of discrimination, *Indian Journal of Gerontology*, 21, 2, 110–27.

Kaufman, S.R. (1986) *The Ageless Self: Sources of Meaning in Late Life*. Madison: University of Wisconsin Press.

Kline, R. and Pinch, T. (1996) Users as agents of technological change: the social construction of the automobile in the rural United States, *Technology and Culture*, 37, 4, 763–95.

Kontos, P.K. (2000) Resisting institutionalization: constructing old age and negotiating home. In Gubrium, J.F. and Holstein, J.A. (eds) *Aging and Everyday Life*. NY: Blackwell.

Loe, M. (2004) *The Rise of Viagra: How the Little Blue Pill Changed Sex in America*. New York: New York University Press.

Lawton, M.P. (1990) Aging and performance on home tasks. *Human Factors*, 32, 527–36.

Mann, W.C. (2003) Assistive technology. In Charness, N. and Schaie, K.W. (eds) *Impact of Technology on Successful Aging*. New York: Springer Publishing Company.

Martin, M. (1991) *Hello Central? Gender, Technology and Culture in the Formation of Telephone Systems*. Montreal: Mc-Gill Queens University Press.

McGaw, J.A. (2003) Why feminine technologies matter. In Lerman, N.E., Oldenziel, R. and Mohun, A.P. (eds) *Gender and Technology: a Reader*. Baltimore: Johns Hopkins University Press.

Moore, A.J. and Stratton, D.C. (2002) *Resilient Widowers: Older Men Speak for Themselves*. New York: Springer.

Moore, L.J. (2007) *Sperm Counts: Overcome by Man's Most Precious Fluid*. New York: NewYork University Press.

Morrow, D. (2003) Commentary: technology as environmental support for older adults' daily activities. In Charness, N. and Schaie, K.W. (eds) *Impact of Technology on Successful Aging*. New York: Springer Publishing Company.

O'Rand, A.M. (2002) Cumulative advantage theory in lifecourse research, *Annual Review of Gerontology and Geriatrics*, 22, 14–20.

Oudshoorn, N. and Pinch, T. (2005). *How Users Matter: the Co-Construction of Users and Technology (Inside Technology)*. Boston: MIT Press.

United States Census Bureau (2005) 65+ in the United States, Current Population Reports.

Wahl, H. and Mollenkopf, H. (2003) Impact of everyday technology in the home environment on older adults' quality of life, In Charness, N. and Schaie, K.W. (eds) *Impact of Technology on Successful Aging*. New York: Springer Publishing Company.

Wajcman, J. (1991) *Feminists Confront Technology*. Cambridge, UK: Polity Press.

West, C. and Zimmerman, D.H. (1987) Doing gender, *Gender and Society*, 1, 2, 125–51.

Woolgar, S. (1991) The turn to technology in social studies of science, *Science, Technology and Human Values*, 16, 1, 20–50.

12

'But obviously not for me': robots, laboratories and the defiant identity of elder test users

Louis Neven

Introduction

In popular and academic discussions of robotics for elders, and arguably in discussions of other technologies for aged people as well, one can often find a specific set of claims. These claims include several related statements: populations are ageing across the world, costs of aged care and healthcare are increasing, qualified staff to care for old people is increasingly getting scarce, and old people prefer to live independently as long as possible (Sparrow and Sparrow 2006). This type of reasoning often concludes that ageing populations lead to unprecedented challenges around the world and robotic technology can solve or mitigate one or more of these challenges. The point here is not that these challenges and demographic trends are not real or problematic, nor that the proposed technologies cannot play important roles in helping to solve or mitigate these problems. In this type of discourse, however, elders are positioned as having deteriorating health and needing costly care, which in turn will drain limited healthcare resources. This is a narrow portrayal of elders in which old age is strongly related to illness, frailty, lost competences, and expense.

Given this broader cultural context, an important question arises: which images of old people underlie innovation processes? If ideas like the ones discussed above underlie innovation processes, then the resulting technologies may implicitly or explicitly position elder users as frail, ill, or in need of care. To explain the relation between common views of elders and technological design, the concept of 'user representation' (Akrich 1995) is useful. User representation refers to the explicit and implicit images of a technology's prospective user. These representations emerge in the work of designers, engineers, researchers and other professionals involved in the innovation process and explicitly or implicitly inform decision making in design processes.[1] User representations can be built into a technology, or in Akrich's (1992) and Latour's (1992) terms, 'inscripted' in the technology. These 'inscriptions' are important as, in Akrich's words, 'technical objects have political strength. They may change social relations, but they also stabilize, naturalize, depoliticize, and translate these into other media' (1992: 222).

There is an important link between user representations (and script), and studies of ageism (Calasanti and King 2005, Calasanti and Slevin 2006, Joyce and Mamo 2006, Laws 1995, Minichiello *et al.* 2000). When user representations are ageist, such ideas may be inscripted in the technology and may act in materialised form in society, while at the same time becoming nearly invisible and seemingly part of the natural order of things. Part of understanding 'the gray cyborg' (Joyce and Mamo 2006) involves becoming sensitive to and analysing potential ageist (or age) scripts. Examining how ageing users are imagined in design processes is the starting point for understanding the age scripts in technology and the subsequent socio-technical practices of elder cyborgs.

This chapter focuses on test users and designers' user representations in tests with a human-interaction robot. For the purpose of this chapter, the robot will be called iRo.[2] A Dutch firm's research department developed iRo: the firm specialises in developing health-care and wellbeing related technologies such as telemedicine and medical imaging technologies. The designers imagined iRo as a technology that could initially keep elders mentally active and preserve or enhance their cognitive health, and then later serve as an assistive technology to which a variety of applications could be added if the elder users became frail, ill, or less mobile as they aged. Various representations of elders, of their health and their ideas about technology, are present in the iRo research project. These tests thus provide an opportunity to study the ways in which elder users are represented and how these ideas of elder users and their health are being turned into material objects.

Research methodology

In order to study how researchers and test users imagined robot use and ageing, a multi-method, qualitative approach was adopted. First, semi-structured in-depth interviews were conducted. I had informal conversations – partly via e-mail – with four researchers (two psychologists and two engineers). The researchers were all in their mid-twenties to early forties. The two researchers who were particularly active in the project were interviewed in depth. I did one interview during the laboratory phase where both researchers were present and one interview after the field tests at which only one of them – 'Marjolein' – was present. Both interviews were taped and fully transcribed. In this chapter the two main researchers will be called Johan and Marjolein. Johan, a middle-aged male engineer, is a senior researcher who supervised the project. Marjolein, a young woman, is a junior researcher with a background in psychology. She conducted the laboratory tests and co-ordinated daily affairs. I was not allowed to interview participants as Johan and Marjolein were concerned that they should not be overburdened.

Secondly, I conducted fieldwork by observing people aged between 62 and 79 as they interacted with iRo and researchers in the laboratory. In total, I observed six tests which lasted about half an hour to one hour each. I also observed six interviews between Marjolein and the test users, which lasted about half an hour each and took place directly after the tests. I interviewed the researchers about six other tests and the field tests conducted at users' homes to gain information on the researchers' perspective on these tests and on the behaviour of elder participants. Interviews and fieldwork were conducted between August 2007 and January 2008.

Finally, I analysed how elder users are portrayed in documents and publications produced by the research department. These documents included technical documentation about iRo, publications from earlier research with iRo, preparatory research for these tests, consent forms, questionnaires, and a full report of test results. All data were systematically read and statements in which old people were represented in any way were copied into a data file. The data file was subsequently used to generate and check categorisations of user representations. Though the empirical basis of this research is relatively small and generalis-ability is limited, the combination of these methods provides insight in test practices, representation work, and the creation of health robot technologies.

It proved necessary to anonymise the research project and the company. Thus it is not possible to refer directly to or quote publications, though summaries will be given. As already noted, the names iRo, Marjolein and Johan are fictitious. However, quotes from interviews and observations, translated by the author from Dutch into English, are provided. All quoted statements from Johan and Marjolein stem from interviews. All quoted statements from elder participants stem from observations.

The co-development of iRo and ideas about iRo's elder user

IRo was developed by the research department of a Dutch profit-based company that operates on an international market. The company focuses mostly on developing technology in the area of health and wellbeing. Within this company, there is an increasing focus on (health-related) technologies for elder users. This increasing focus on elder users is a world wide trend, as exemplified by MIT's Age Lab, the Georgia Institute of Technology's Human Factors and Aging Laboratory, the European Ambient Assisted Living project and the creation and marketing of robots intended for, or tested with, elders, like Aibo, Ifbot, Wakamura and Paro.[3] These robots range from robotic animals (Paro) or pets (Aibo) to robotic companions and assistants (Ifbot, Wakamura). Although most robots are not designed solely with elder users in mind, companies do imagine these robots as health technologies for elders and hope they will help prevent cognitive decline, combat loneliness, or provide reminders to take medication as people age. Robot use is hoped to help individuals age at home, and thus alleviate the healthcare costs associated with the move of elders into nursing homes or hospitals.

IRo as a tool to gain knowledge about elder users
The researchers initially developed iRo to understand the ways in which users interact with socially intelligent robots. Though iRo has a polished appearance, Johan stressed that iRo was not a product and was solely intended 'as a research prototype', at least for now. However, based on the iRo research project, the researchers envisaged the future development of robots which could be sold to aged consumers as both preventative technologies that help maintain cognitive health and as assistive technologies to be used when cognitive skills or mobility decline.

Depending on iRo's programming, it can perform tasks itself but it can also serve as an interface for digital technologies. For example, in other tests iRo was used to set alarm clocks and operate audio equipment. It is easy to communicate with iRo. No commands need to be learned. Instead, a user can speak plain Dutch to iRo and iRo responds likewise. Like Kismet (an anthropomorphic robot that mimics human facial expressions)[4], iRo has the ability to blink, nod, frown, smile and grimace. The development of iRo is thus in line with trends in social robotics towards ordinary conversation and displaying and reacting to emotions (Weber 2008).

Though iRo is built out of plastics, electronics, and servomotors, iRo's most fluid component is its software. The researchers can change iRo's software, which turns it into a robot with a different application. For the tests with elder participants, the researchers programmed several cognitively challenging games and puzzles into iRo and wrote conversational software which allowed iRo to make game-related comments like: 'I'll have to think of a clever move now' or 'you have to jump'. The researchers also added a digital game board, which was connected to iRo and placed between iRo and the participant. Together, this turned iRo into a game companion for elder users. The board games and puzzles were designed to be both entertaining and cognitively stimulating in order to help maintain elders' cognitive health.

The researchers went to considerable lengths to increase their understanding of elder users. This is in line with the research department's guiding vision (which is stated in various publications and vision statements) in which technology should 'know' and adapt to the user. Adhering to this vision, the researchers' focus was directed towards understanding the elder user, which was considered integral to technical research. This is reflected in their user-centred design approach,[5] the use of scientific literature on elder users, the interdisciplinary composition of the research team, and the design of their laboratory. By making the laboratory look like a middle-class elder persons' apartment, it was hoped that participants would feel relaxed and behave naturally.

The researchers' attention to the importance of users can further be seen in their decision to conduct two week-long tests in people's homes. Concerned about methodological shortcomings of laboratory testing, Johan mentioned, 'if people come for two hours – like with Marjolein's tests now – they all like it, but what happens after longer periods of time?' Therefore, field tests – placing iRo in elders' homes – were deemed necessary. With every research project, the researchers gathered more information about user behaviour in relation to iRo, and they thus progressively built up an image of elder users. Interestingly, despite this concern for understanding users, the researchers would struggle to incorporate the participants' alternative views on iRo which emerged during the tests.

Initial ideas of elder users and their health
The researchers initially developed their views about (health) robots and elders by carrying out an exploratory literature review and organising a workshop in which ideas were generated for specific tasks or activities which iRo could perform, such as being a game companion. In both the literature review as well as the workshop, researchers imagined old people as varied; elders were imagined as having differences in preferences, needs, lifestyles, mental and physical abilities and social environments. They were thus not simply imagined as frail, lonely, or forgetful.

Based on the workshop findings, all ideas for applications were evaluated with the help of experts in the area of aged care[6] together with other experts: staff members of a nursing home. These two groups considered the application that would make iRo function as an opponent or a companion in playing games the most promising, so it was developed further. These games would be entertaining, but Johan explained that they were 'not just games for fun, which is what you would focus on with children, but [the games had] the goal of stimulating their cognitive abilities'. The game application was thus designed to support the cognitive health of iRo's elder users. The long-term view for developing iRo was also health related, in particular to a possible transition to frailty or illness in later life. Marjolein explained: 'The idea is to get an iRo into their homes as early as possible, so that they get used to it, but also so that it can be adapted to their skills. A person of 65 perhaps doesn't need anybody to keep his agenda, but five years later it may be necessary for him to check what he should do every day, or for him to be reminded that he should take his medication. Research has shown that it is better if [iRo] has a different function at the beginning and that he can adapt to the skills of people. In that case, people will be more likely to accept it than if you say at 70: here's your iRo, it will help you to remember now'.

Thus, even though the board games and puzzles would be fun and cognitively stimulating, in the future, iRo could play additional assistive roles in the maintenance of the health of elders. IRo could, for instance, remind them to measure their blood pressure or take their medication. The combination of assistive and cognitively stimulating applications illustrates the researchers' idea of health – one that includes physical, mental, and cognitive dimensions and imagines these as interrelated and changing. In addition to these ideas about health, the researchers also reflected on acceptance and rejection of (health) technologies and devised strategies to entice elders to accept a health robot in their lives.

The tests

The criteria for selecting participants were strict. Marjolein explained: 'There are a number of requirements. First, 65 years and older, to be sure they are retired and home all day, so they have time to play with it [iRo]. Secondly, living in a single-person household, to make sure that no one else can play with it'.[7] (The researchers focused on single-person households as multiple users would render their data unusable.) The age of participants was evenly spread between 62 and 79 years and the number of male and female participants was equal. The researchers screened for physical disability, colour blindness, and early signs of dementia. The focus of this test was on cognitively healthy elder users, as the researchers wanted to develop and test technologies for maintaining cognitive health. In addition, the researchers judged people with declining cognitive health less capable of completing the tests.

The researchers were mainly interested in the long-term interactions between ageing users and iRo, as they had previously only conducted short-term research projects in the laboratory. In addition, they wanted to know whether, as Marjolein put it, 'relationship building strategies, that have been shown in literature from human-human, human-robot and human-animal interaction to foster relationships' could be used to create and deepen relationships between iRo and elders. In order to answer their questions they chose to do two rounds of tests; one round in their laboratory and another more extensive round of field testing a couple of months later in which the participants would have iRo in their home for several weeks. The objectives of the first round of tests were to check whether iRo functioned well technically, whether the participants perceived iRo as appealing and easy to use, and whether they enjoyed playing games with iRo. However, as the final report mentioned, the most important objective of the laboratory test was to 'recruit participants for the field test'.

On the whole, the elder test users turned up early at the laboratory. Marjolein would welcome them and chat with them over a cup of coffee. Following completion of a consent form, a questionnaire, and a test for colour-blindness, Marjolein retreated to the 'bedroom' of the laboratory and left the participant to interact with iRo. She would only intervene if the interaction ground to a halt. This happened, for instance, when a test user inadvertently made a wrong move during a game and subsequently did not understand iRo's suggestions for correcting this. When the games were finished, Marjolein returned to interview the participant. While some participants experienced some difficulties interacting with iRo, they were generally enthusiastic about iRo. They said that they liked the games, and thought iRo looked fun. One woman said, she liked 'the way he flutters his eyelids'.

All but one of the participants who were asked decided to take part in the field test. This test comprised two periods of two weeks in which the participants would have two variations of iRo – a version with and a version without relation-building software. The test users could play as much as they liked. On average they played for about 40 minutes a day, mostly when there was a gap in their schedules. Marjolein reported that, irrespective of the version, test users enjoyed having iRo in their homes. 'They admitted that they talked to it', noted Marjolein, something she had not expected. Some participants got emotionally attached to iRo. 'Most of them said that they were going to miss it. It was a question in the interview, but a few said that without me asking the question', Marjolein explained. After two sessions of two weeks, the researchers picked up the iRos from the participants' homes. The data logged by iRo's programs were analysed along with other types of data, including test user diaries in which participants were free to write down relevant events and thoughts. Subsequently, the researchers' report concluded that interactions with iRo could be sustained for longer periods if the applications were varied and compelling. Furthermore, strategies to build relationships between users and the robot were relatively effective.

Researchers imagine elders as needing and wanting iRo

The researchers' views linked up with, but also went beyond, the discourse mentioned in the introduction. Referring to demographic data provided by the World Health Organisation and the United Nations, the researchers acknowledged that the number of old people is growing, especially in developed countries, that the cost of (health) care will increase, and that there will be a dearth of qualified staff to care for ageing people. A research department publication concluded that elders want to live independently as long as possible, but also that their quality of life is reduced when they live alone. Robots were presented as a technology that can play an assistive role in the everyday lives of elders, providing practical assistance that allowed users to stay in their homes and that could potentially function as an emotional and intellectual companion. In a preparatory document the researchers recognised that loneliness was a taboo, and the final report concluded that elders felt positive about a robotic companion if they could develop a bond with it; furthermore, it is possible for researchers to devise strategies to develop these bonds. The researchers agreed with Reeves and Nass (1996) that people tend to treat computers and robots as social actors and react emotionally to them, despite the fact that they may rationalise their behaviour afterwards. A research project leading up to the tests concluded that acceptance of technology by elders was also improved if they understood that the technology could help them live independently. The researchers had learned in another research project that the combination of entertainment and a cognitively stimulating activity benefits elders; they also feel positive about this, as they worry about their mental health, creating a need for the application which was tested with iRo.

Thus, ageing users were portrayed in a specific way. Though the researchers were employed by the company, they had a scientific approach to design; using scientific methods, fostering links with universities and publishing their results in scientific journals. The researchers methodically built an image of elders and their relation to technologies like iRo. This image consisted of two main parts. First, the researchers found that old people needed (health) robots, if not now, then certainly in the future. The second part went beyond the discourse mentioned in the introduction, stating that elders would accept (health) robots, see their benefits and even bond with them. In effect, the researchers believed that elder users not only needed such a robot but that eventually they would want it too. Despite complexities like diversity of elder users and the taboo of loneliness, this combination of societal and personal need for robotic technologies and the elder users' willingness to accept such technologies, allowed the researchers to make a strong case for developing (health) robotic technology for elders.

This 'need and want' representation was largely in place before the tests were conducted and the tests mainly reinforced it. This representation thus provides one answer to the question of how the user is represented in these tests. Leaving it there, however, as other studies have, would render invisible another group actively making their own user representations: the elder participants themselves.

Test users' representations: how not to be old and lonely

Generally, it is assumed that only researchers, designers, engineers and other professionals involved in creating technology form user representations. Test users apparently do not play an active role in this process, only passively providing input for the work of researchers, designers and engineers. However, users are seldom passive and test users have been shown to be no exception (Epstein 1995, Feenberg 1995, Oudshoorn 2003). The elder participants in the user studies of iRo were also active. They reacted to images of old people, and, as will be shown, actively created their own images of the prospective user of the technology.

During conversations with Marjolein, the test users would state that they liked iRo, liked playing games with it and thought it worked very well. However, they also repeatedly, and often without provocation, mentioned that iRo was not a robot for them. For instance, one woman said: 'I still lead too much of an active life; I've always been amongst people. I don't need an iRo, not yet anyway'. One of the men related it to his hobby: 'At home I am still very active, I really don't have spare time. I collect old army radios, you see. That takes time and I like doing it. It's creative work, so that's good as well. It keeps me busy.' Later he added: 'Maybe if I was all washed up [incapacitated], but I don't need to be kept busy. But I think there are plenty of old people sitting behind their geraniums who need to be kept busy, for them it would be good'. Another man said: 'If you were, say, old and growing demented, than I could imagine this being a good thing, but for me?' and 'You'd have to be a lonely old person, chained to your home with few contacts. I still go to my checkers club.' Another woman reported: 'I play games with people, with my friends (...). Therefore I don't have an iRo. I am not lonely, so I'm not planning on getting one of these. If people are lonely and have difficulties getting in touch with other people, they'd go out and get one, but I don't need it.'

While Marjolein mentioned that 'there was one woman who said: this is something for me, but she was very housebound', in the end, 10 out of 12 participants in the laboratory test reported that iRo was not for them. Most participants felt that the intended user was housebound, old, lonely, feeble and in need of care and attention, and they did not want to be equated with this person.

In part, this equation resulted from the participants knowing that they were selected to test this prototype on the basis of their age and the fact that they lived alone. They thus assumed that iRo was intended for older people with few social contacts. But Johan and Marjolein attributed a substantial part of this interpretation to the way in which robots for old people were portrayed in newspapers and on television: 'This positioning of iRo for only old and lonely people could have been due to the fact that iRo was in the media a bit before the test [as] a robot exclusively for elders', Marjolein said. She added: 'they had just seen on television that robots, similar to iRo, are placed in retirement homes, for some entertainment'. There was also a newspaper article about Aibo in retirement homes; thus, according to Marjolein, 'the image of a robot for lonely older people, they just got that from the newspaper'. This portrayal of robots meant that the researchers were faced with a problem. Marjolein explained, 'You've got to change that image. The fact that they saw on television that iRo is just for old people, is just an unfortunate coincidence. Otherwise, they perhaps would not have kept so stubbornly to this notion, that this is only for really old people. People who are very lonely, can't do anything and just sit at home.'

Despite the researchers' attempt to explain away the association of iRo with dependence and loneliness as a short term effect of media stories, test users felt that iRo was a signifier of old age, loneliness and needing care. The elder test users did not see themselves as such. Instead, they made it clear to the researchers that they were (still) active and independent. Furthermore, they presented themselves as possessing sound physical and cognitive health and as (still) having a wide social network. Minichiello et al. (2000) have shown that ageing people can create an image of 'old' people and actively dissociate themselves from that group. The test users did exactly that; they made the prospective user of iRo into somebody else, somebody older, lonelier and in need of care, and they actively dissociated themselves from this user.

Test users imagine themselves as helpful and not old

Interestingly, when asked at the end of the laboratory test, all but one of the test users agreed to take part in the field test. This seems counter-intuitive: why would you want a robot in your house for four weeks if it is a signifier of old age, poor health and loneliness to you, and you actively want to position yourself as not old, frail and lonesome?

A first indicator is that nearly all the elder test users, as Marjolein explained, 'had participated in prior research or were persuaded [to participate] by their children because they work here'. Thus, this particular set of test users was inclined to participate because they knew the company and perhaps because they did not want to disappoint their children. In addition to this, the elder test users mentioned that they participated in the test to help other elders. One woman said 'I think it's fun and interesting, not because I want one but to help somebody else. I like that (...) I think I am helping people with this.' One of the men told the researchers that he thought he was 'still too good' for an iRo, but he made it clear that he knew 'enough people who would benefit from one'. The elder test users positioned iRo as 'a good thing' which they wanted to associate themselves with as a test user (though not as the prospective user). The elder participants thus displayed altruistic motives for participating in the tests, which has also been observed for test users in drug testing for AIDS patients (Epstein 1996) and for male contraceptives (Oudshoorn 2003). Thus, the participants created another image – one of themselves as helpful elder test users.

Thus, they embraced the idea of 'successful aging' (Calasanti and King 2005), as they tried to position themselves as active, healthy, altruistic, helpful old people, seemingly (still) untouched by the negative consequences of ageing. This image of themselves as successfully ageing elder test users, allowed them to further widen the gap between themselves and the perceived prospective user of iRo, while simultaneously allowing them to use and enjoy iRo.

Researchers' responses to elder test users' ideas

Test users thus also created user representations, either in accordance with who they thought the prospective user of the technology was, or in accordance with what they thought a good test user should do. The researchers had to deal with these alternative images of the (test) user. On the whole, the researchers tried to remain focused on their initial research questions, in spite of the participants' additional responses. There was, for instance, no mention in the final report of how test users' distanced themselves from the perceived prospective user of iRo. In interviews, the defiant responses were acknowledged as relevant, but were simultaneously seen as a relatively small incident, caused by media attention on robots for elders and as something that could be addressed by an early introduction of iRo into the lives of people, meaning when people were in their late fifties or early sixties, and iRo would then still only be, in Johan's words, 'just for fun'. In the end, the representations made by test users added little to the researchers' understanding of potential meanings attached to the technology.

Instead of taking the participants' user representations into account, the researchers saw these responses as a side issue that presented them with some difficulties and additional work. Marjolein found that getting 'helpful' elder test users to provide the desired information could prove difficult. She mentioned that the participants gave 'please-me answers' or that they reasoned not from their own perspective, but 'tried to reason from a consumer perspective, so: "Oh, if iRo does this, then this offends the consumer, so you should maybe change this"', assuming that this perspective was most valuable to the researchers. Also, the researchers made changes to iRo between the two phases of the field test, to give the impression to the elder participants that their input was taken into account, because the researchers, as Marjolein said, 'did not want to disappoint them'. The researchers had to perform additional forms of work to cope with elder participants behaving according to what the elders thought were helpful test users.

Thus, the researchers held another user representation; an image of what old people are like *as test users* and how to work with them. According to Marjolein and Johan, working with elder test users is different from working with other age categories. Marjolein explained: 'First of all, I think you can find more test users in other target groups. It is simpler, they're more open to something like this.' Johan thought they might be 'insecure'; Marjolein added that the word research might make them 'a little scared' and she also felt that 'they might be afraid that we're going to sell them something'. The researchers reserved extra time for the elders who were willing to partake in the tests. Johan explained: 'They all show up early, sometimes even half an hour. With people aged, say, up to 50, that just doesn't happen'. He added: 'you've got to put more time in, making contact, making appointments, phoning them again. But also during the experiment, (…) the people like to talk, it's an outing for them.' Nevertheless, the researchers made sure the tests would not be too long, as they did not want to overburden the participants. Explanations for using iRo were also modified. Marjolein explained: 'you've got to do it slowly, give an example, demonstrate it first, and then let them do it'. Johan added: 'These are just people who interact less easily with technology than younger generations. You've got to take that into account' and 'people gradually forget the instructions'. Marjolein continued: 'But you can't underestimate them. They'll also see how far they can go.' She recalled one elder man who ignored the instructions to find out 'what iRo can and can't do'. Coping with these differences meant work for the researchers. The researchers had to find elder participants, schedule more time, persuade them to stick with what they were asked to do and interpret and make selections in the information put forward by the participants to stay focused on their research questions. The researchers thus also held a 'craft representation', a set of images of what old people are like *as test users* and the specific skills and changes in testing practices required to work with them. They thus created a setting in which they could negate the test users' ideas about the imagined user and their rejection of him/her.

Conclusion

This chapter focused on participants and researchers who actively tested iRo, a robot intended to enhance the health of elder users. This study has shown how age-based assumptions lay at the heart of technology design and implementation, both for technology designers and prospective users. In this case, designers expected that old people would have a need for and could benefit from robots, particularly when it came to physical, cognitive and mental health maintenance and support. Elders would see these benefits, accept robots in their lives and bond with them. Thus, elder users would need and eventually also want (health) robots. During the tests, however, the elder participants also created a representation of the prospective user of iRo. This user was old, lonely and physically or mentally frail, and the participants actively dissociated themselves from this imagined user. This was a reaction to the type of user that they felt the tests required and also to the way in which iRo and similar robots were portrayed in documentaries, news programmes and newspaper articles. However, instead of becoming defiant 'rejecters' (Wyatt 2003), the participants tapped into a repertoire of successful ageing, positioning themselves as healthy, active elders who were helping needy old people. This representation allowed the participants to distance themselves further from the supposed prospective user of iRo. The researchers took these representations into account, but virtually exclusively in a craft representation; a representation of old people as test users and the specific craft of working with them. Thus, the participants' representations had little influence on the researchers' view of elder users of (robotic) technology.

Joyce and Mamo (2006) argue that it is important to study how elders are configured or represented as technology users. They emphasise how science and technology studies (STS) 'rarely takes up aging and ageism as a central concern' (Joyce and Mamo 2006: 109). Indeed, barring a few exceptions like Hyysalo (2006), there has been little attention paid to elder technology users (and their representations) within studies of science and technology. This chapter describes the ways in which elder users were represented by the researchers, the user representations devised by the participants, and the ways in which they used these representations to dissociate themselves from old people (Minichiello *et al.* 2000). This chapter has also shown how researchers adapted their testing practices to accommodate aged participants and negate their ideas about the prospective user. This is thus in line with, and gives extra weight to, the point put forward by Mackay *et al.* (2000), that designers are not just configuring the user, but are also configured by their organisations and, as this chapter has shown, by the behaviour of test users and the portrayals of technologies in the media.

Though the researchers were employed by a company, they based their work on scientific principles and methods. They carefully and methodically built up a representation of elder users, emphasising the need for a robot like iRo, but also that elders would accept and eventually want iRo. This combination allowed them to legitimise the development of (health) robots like iRo. Nevertheless, the representation work performed by elder test users, which provided a different gloss on elder users, remains a form of invisible work (Star and Strauss 1999) if it is not taken into account in the researchers' representations. Even if technology could be beneficial to the health and wellbeing of elder users, elder users who feel that they are being positioned as old, lonely and frail may rightly refuse to be positioned as such and consequently refuse to use the technology. Recognising and taking into account user representations formed by elder users, for instance in user tests, is important as it could help prevent ageist scripts, and resistance to and non-use of technology by elder users by charting positive and negative interpretations of the supposed prospective user of a technology. This information could then serve as input for more reflexive (re)design of technologies.

The engineers, researchers and designers should, however, not be solely held accountable for the representations formed by elder users. This case also shows that the media played an important role in forming images of elder users of robotics, which in fact went against the grain of what the researchers meant to achieve. Ideally, a number of parties – for instance, journalists, but also policy makers, politicians and scientists – should share the responsibility for creating more refined, non-ageist images of elder users, which could thus lead to more refined user representations.[8]

Acknowledgements

I would like to thank two anonymous referees, Nelly Oudshoorn, Barend van der Meulen, Sampsa Hyysalo, Haico te Kulve, Clare Shelley-Egan and Marieke Groenewegen for their helpful comments. I would also like to thank the company's researchers for their time and effort and for allowing me to observe the tests. This chapter is part of a research project which is funded entirely by the University of Twente.

Notes

1   The concept of user representation shares an emphasis on imagining users with 'configuring the user' (Woolgar 1991). However, unlike configuring the user, user representation focuses solely on imagined users and thus allows analytical separation of imagining users and 'scripting' these images into technologies. In addition, Woolgar's concept has been criticised for treating designers as active, and users as passive in design processes, whereas the conceptualisation with 'script' and 'user representations' allows a conceptualisation of 'both designers and users as active agents in the development of technology' (Oudshoorn and Pinch 2008: 551).

2   The name iRo is fictitious. A brief check was conducted and no robot named iRo was found. Any reference to a robot actually called iRo is therefore accidental.

3   See respectively: http://web.mit.edu/agelab/index.shtml, http://psychology.gatech.edu/hfa/, http://www.aal-europe.eu/, http://ieeexplore.ieee.org/Xplore/login.jsp?url=/iel5/4352184/4352185/04352666.pdf?temp=x, http://www.reuters.com/article/inDepthNews/idUST29547120070920?feedType=RSS& feedName=inDepthNews&rpc=22&sp=true, http://www.telegraph.co.uk/news/worldnews/asia/japan/1421359/Robot-nurse-will-care-for-Japans-lonely-old-people.html, http://www.mhi.co.jp/kobe/wakamaru/english/know/index.html, http://paro.jp/english/index.html, (all accessed March 4th 2009).

4   http://www.ai.mit.edu/projects/humanoid-robotics-group/kismet/ (accessed March 4th 2009).

5   Access was obtained partly because the researchers were interested in an outside view on their user-centred methodologies.

6   The researchers did not disclose what kind of experts these were.

7   One man was aged 62, but as he was retired and lived alone the researchers decided to include him in the tests.

8   While finalising this chapter, I learned that the company had, along with several other projects, cancelled the iRo project. However, iRo is still being used for researching and developing robotics elsewhere.

References

Akrich, M. (1992) The de-scription of technical objects. In Bijker, W. and Law, J. (eds), *Shaping Technology/Building Society: Studies in Sociotechnical Change*. Cambridge, MA: MIT Press.

Akrich, M. (1995) User representations: practices, methods and sociology. In Rip, A., Misa, T. and Schot, J. (eds) *Managing Technology in Society; the Approach of Constructive Technology Assessment*. London: Pinter Publishers.

Calasanti, T. and King, N. (2005) Firming the floppy penis: age, class, and gender relations in the lives of old men, *Men and Masculinities*, 8, 1.

Calasanti, T. and Slevin, K. (2006) Introduction: Age Matters. In Calansanti, T. and Slevin, K. (eds) *Age Matters; Realigning Feminist Thinking*. New York, London: Taylor and Francis Group; Routledge.

Epstein, S. (1995) The construction of lay expertise: AIDS activism and the forging of credibility in the reform of clinical trials, *Science Technology and Human Values*, 20, 4, 408–37.

Epstein, S. (1996) *Impure Science, AIDS, Activism and the Politics of Knowledge*. Berkeley: University of California Press.

Feenberg, A. (1995) *Alternative Modernity, the Technical Turn in Philosophy and Social Theory*. Berkeley CA: University of California Press.

Hyysalo, S. (2006) Representations of use and practice-bound imaginaries in automating safety of the elderly, *Social Studies of Science*, 36, 4, 599–626.

Joyce, K. and Mamo, L. (2006) Graying the cyborg; new directions in feminist analyses of aging, science, and technology. in Calasanti, T. and Slevin, K. (eds) *Age Matters; Realigning Feminist Thinking*. New York, London: Taylor and Francis Group; Routledge.

Latour, B. (1992) Where are the missing masses? The sociology of a few mundane artifacts. In Bijker, W. and Law, J. (eds) *Shaping Technology/Building Society: Studies in Sociotechnical Change.* Cambridge, MA: MIT Press.

Laws, G. (1995) Understanding ageism: lessons from feminism and postmodernism, *The Gerontologist,* 35, 1, 112–18.

Mackay, H., Carne, C., Beynon-Davies, P. and Tudhope, D. (2000) Reconfiguring the user: using rapid application development, *Social Studies of Science,* 30, 5, 737–57.

Minichiello, V., Browne, J. and Kendig, H. (2000) Perceptions and consequences of ageism: views of older people, *Ageing and Society,* 20, 253–78.

Oudshoorn, N. (2003) *The Male Pill, a Biography of a Technology in the Making.* Durham NC, London: Duke University Press.

Oudshoorn, N. and Pinch, T. (2008) User-technology relationships: some recent developments. In Hackett, E.J., Amsterdamska, O., Lynch, M. and Wajcman, J. (eds) *The Handbook of Science and Technology Studies.* 3rd Edition. Cambridge, MA: MIT Press.

Reeves, B. and Nass, C. (1996) *The Media Equation: How People Treat Computers, Television, and New Media like Real People and Places.* Stanford, CA: CSLI Publications.

Sparrow, R. and Sparrow, L. (2006) In the hands of machines? The future of aged care, *Mind and Machines,* 16, 2, 141–61.

Star, S.L. and Strauss, A. (1999) Layers of silence, arenas of voice: the ecology of visible and invisible work, *Computer Supported Cooperative Work (CSCW),* 8, 1–2, 9–30.

Weber, J. (2008) Human-robot interaction. In Kelsey, S. and St. Amant, K. (eds) *Handbook of Research on Computer Mediated Communication.* Hershey, PA: Information Science Reference.

Woolgar, S. (1991) Configuring the user: the case of usability trials. In Law, J. (ed.) *A Sociology of Monsters.* London: Routledge.

Wyatt, S. (2003) Non-users also matter: the construction of users and non-users of the internet. In Oudshoorn, N. and Pinch, T. (eds) *How Users Matter: the Co-construction of Users and Technologies.* Cambridge, MA: London: MIT Press.

Index